THE COACH'S COMPANION
WINNING
BASEBALL

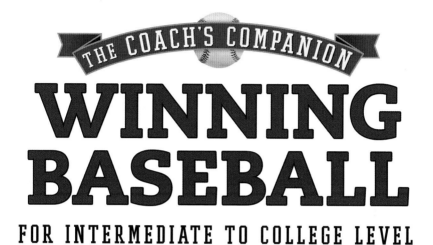

THE COACH'S COMPANION

WINNING BASEBALL

FOR INTERMEDIATE TO COLLEGE LEVEL

Trent Mongero

STERLING
New York

STERLING
New York

An Imprint of Sterling Publishing
387 Park Avenue South
New York, NY 10016

ISBN 978-1-4027-5809-6

Distributed in Canada by Sterling Publishing
c/o Canadian Manda Group, 165 Dufferin Street
Toronto, Ontario, Canada M6K 3H6
Distributed in the United Kingdom by GMC Distribution Services
Castle Place, 166 High Street, Lewes, East Sussex, England BN7 1XU
Distributed in Australia by Capricorn Link (Australia) Pty. Ltd.
P.O. Box 704, Windsor, NSW 2756, Australia

For information about custom editions, special sales, and premium and
corporate purchases, please contact Sterling Special Sales at 800-805-5489
or specialsales@sterlingpublishing.com.

Manufactured in China

2 4 6 8 10 9 7 5 3 1

www.sterlingpublishing.com

Produced by LightSpeed Publishing, Inc. and X-Height Studio

DEDICATION

I would like to dedicate this book to my family. My mother and father encouraged me to dream big, set goals, and persevere when times got tough. Dad spent countless hours teaching me the game of baseball; practicing with me anywhere we could find an open space. He laid the foundation for my future success on the diamond and off. We had numerous father-and-son talks in which he encouraged me to make good choices in my life. Mom stood by me as my biggest fan, driving me hours on end to the next game or practice, and she always loved me unconditionally. My sister, who is not quite two years younger than I am, was often dragged around to ballparks at my expense. She gave up much of her personal time being a supportive sibling.

In addition, I would like to dedicate this series of baseball books to my Uncle John. My father often used my uncle's athletic career to demonstrate the personal traits of sacrifice and commitment that it would take to reach my goals. Witnessing John's induction into the Roanoke College Athletic Hall of Fame in the early 1980s served as an additional inspiration to make a difference for the teams I would play for.

Thanks, mom, dad, sis, and John; without each of you, none of this would be possible.

Lastly, I would like to dedicate this series of books to my former baseball coaches. They each played a role in shaping me as a person and as a ballplayer. In particular, I would like to recognize Ray McDonough, Bob Sorrow, Chris Brunnelle, Clay Gooch, Bobby Guthrie, Mark Scalf, and Randy Ingle. These men inspired me and provided the mental and physical tools needed to succeed on my adventure through each level of baseball.

Contents

FOREWORD

I FIRST CROSSED paths with Trent Mongero when I watched him in pre-game as the UNC-Wilmington Seahawks were about to play my N.C. State Wolfpack in the spring of 1989. I knew immediately we would have our hands full as I watched him prepare for the game. Trent possessed outstanding talent, but his intensity, precision, and hustle set him apart from the other players on the field. My immediate thought was that I would be an outstanding coach and a winner if I had twenty-five Trent Mongeros!

Coach Mongero's playing days gave me a lasting impression of him as a person. When I learned years ago that he was coaching in high school, I knew that he would be very successful winning games and developing young players. But, most importantly, I knew that he would be a great influence in helping young people grow, mature, and become productive members of society. I am honored that Coach Mongero takes the time to visit the University of South Carolina and teach in our baseball camps. On the field and off the field, Trent knows and teaches all the "right stuff!"

I am greatly impressed but not surprised that Coach Mongero has put together the *Coach's Companion* instructional series. These three books are the very best baseball skills and drills manuals that I have ever seen. I have been part of the college game for nearly thirty years. I have learned a lot about the game from a number of people, but I would have had a faster start in the coaching profession if Coach Mongero's books were printed three decades ago.

A lot of coaches are passionate about the game of baseball and volunteer their time for the youth of America. In many cases, they do the best they can when it comes to coaching, but they may not be knowledgeable enough to teach the mechanics of the game. If I were a recreation director, administrator of amateur baseball, or a high school coach, I would make all three of these books required reading. They are perfect teaching guides for anyone wanting to develop fundamentally sound baseball players.

There are numerous teaching tools available on the market. For a fee, you can get almost anything. But I can assure you that you will not find another series of books as good and as reasonably priced as the *Coach's Companion* series. The quality of his books is second to none, and the sweat and integrity that went into this series is unsurpassed.

Readers are going to elevate their baseball experience as a result of soaking in all this important information. In a sport where a ball sailing over the fence gets more attention than great base running, spectacular defense, or even a pitching gem, Trent Mongero has truly "got all of it and hit a home run."

Coach Ray Tanner
Head Baseball Coach
University of South Carolina

A few of Coach Tanner's many accomplishments include:

- 2010 and 2011 NCAA National Champions—University of South Carolina
- Three-time National Coach of the Year
- Three consecutive appearances in the College World Series
- Head Coach of the USA Baseball Collegiate National Team
- Assistant Coach with the U.S. Olympic Baseball Team
- Over 1,000 victories at the collegiate level
- Set NCAA records, winning 16 straight NCAA tournament games and 11 straight College World Series games

ACKNOWLEDGMENTS

I WOULD LIKE to thank the most significant person in my life, my gorgeous wife, for being the true love of my life, and setting such a wonderful example for our children. She patiently allowed me to author *The Coach's Companion* instructional series because we know God has called me into coaching, and we felt it could make a difference for coaches, families, and players who want to reach their full potential on the ball field. She is a source of inspiration and someone I can trust for an honest answer. Her eyes were the very first to scan each and every page in the editing process.

I want to thank my son, Taber, and my daughter, Maris, who had to make the sacrifice of looking for Daddy at the computer, editing video and typing hours and hours on end. This three-book series has taken over seven years from its innocent conception in Richmond County, North Carolina, to its detailed completion in Gainesville, Georgia. It was written and rewritten three distinct times while balancing teaching, coaching, and spending valuable time with my family.

In addition, I was able to call on many friends and business associates to help with details associated with one or all three books in this series. I would like to recognize the following: my current and former players; Sterling Publishing; Robert Astle; Melanie Madden; Scott Calamar; Cecile Kaufman; Candi Clark; Tim Hyers; Scott "Emo" Emerson; UNCW; North Hall High School; Dr. Will Schofield; Gary Brown; Joe Gheesling; Harold Daniels; David Bishop; Richmond Senior High School; Mark Scalf; Randy Hood; Carl Lafferty; Mike Byers; John Mendel; Kelly Aherns; Beau DeHass; JH Photography; Rick Catlin; Davey Waggett; Jay Denham; Kenneth Robinette; Hal Shuler; and Jwink hats.

INTRODUCTION

THANK YOU FOR purchasing *The Coach's Companion: Winning Baseball for Interme-diate to College Level*. This in-depth guide provides coaches, parents, and players with a wealth of vital information to be successful in the game of baseball. This book contains the tools and resources you need to successfully teach and play the game, and to become a winner at the highest levels of amateur baseball.

HOW TO GET THE MOST FROM THIS RESOURCE

Using 21st-century technology, *The Coach's Companion* offers the most com-prehensive way to learn and teach a skill correctly. It utilizes the learning sequence of read, comprehend, apply, evaluate, adjust, and re-evaluate. This will create a solid foundation of knowledge that you can build upon for years to come.

Time, or the lack of time, can rob us from being 100 percent effective as coaches, players, or parents as we try to teach or learn the game of baseball. If you are like the millions who love to coach or play, but you do not have time to read, *The Coach's Companion* is your answer. Because the book and the accom-panying DVD are divided into small parts, you can review specific sections or watch segments of the DVD for practice, games, meetings, or on an as-needed basis. For the coach, parent, or player who can make time to read all three books and watch all the accompanying DVDs in the series, this resource will provide a wealth of information that will help you comprehend the game of baseball as you never have before. Therefore, this entire instructional series is a "must have" in your baseball library.

PART ONE

Advanced Skills for Middle and High School Baseball

Text and skill photos can be very helpful, but they are not the most effective ways to demonstrate motion, team play, techniques, and all the other skills required to be a good baseball player. Follow the photos in this book to understand the key movement parts, but then watch the exercises and demonstrations on the included DVD. The video on the DVD will be your best guide to teaching and learning.

HOW DOES SKILL EXPECTATION WORK?

For a player to reach his full potential, it is critical that he progresses through a baseball system that emphasizes teaching developmentally appropriate physical and mental skills. Book one of *The Coach's Companion* series takes the baseball coach, parent, and player from T-ball (ages 4–6) through player-pitch (ages 9–10). This book

will continue the journey through middle school (ages 11–14) and high school (ages 15–college).

Middle School Baseball (Ages 11–14)

A significant factor impacting performance at this age group is the speed at which the game is played. Players begin to throw the ball harder, run faster, and hit the ball further at this age. They also develop superior mental skills and learn to handle adversity with increasing confidence and success.

Due to the onset of puberty in middle school, a player's body, physical skill, mental capacity, and emotional capacity are continually changing and maturing. It is not uncommon to see some players who physically look like they are ready for high school baseball and others who look as though they belong back at the nine- and ten-year-old level. This inconsistency in physical size and strength presents a big challenge for players and their coaches.

Another obstacle that must be overcome by middle school players and coaches revolves around the field dimensions that can vary for each league, governing association, or tournament. For example, the base paths, the distance from the pitcher's mound to home plate, and the distance from the plate to the outfield fences can vary. However, by the time a player graduates from middle school, he should be ready to advance to regulation baseball distances: base paths of 90 feet and 60 feet, 6 inches from the pitcher's rubber to home plate.

It is critical that coaches and players avoid the temptation to encourage or force a player to specialize in one specific defensive position, for instance, declaring him just a pitcher or shortstop. As a player physically and mentally evolves through middle school and the early years of high school, his preferred position may change. Not to mention, high school freshmen, junior varsity, and varsity teams have various needs from year to year. The more experience a player has with different positions, the more value he offers to his coach and team.

Ideally, once a player reaches middle school, he is ready to learn the physical skills and mechanics of baseball at the highest level. In the Advanced Skill chapters, if a skill set is too advanced for players in the 11- to 14-year age group, it will have a high school symbol 🎓 next to it. This indicates that this particular skill and drill should be implemented by high school players only, and not younger students.

High School Baseball (Ages 15–19)

High school baseball is defined as any baseball team from the ninth through the twelfth grade. This includes freshmen teams, junior varsity teams, and varsity teams. These players usually range from 15 to 19 years old. Most varsity teams are comprised of the best physically and mentally skilled players from all four grades. This means becoming a player in "the starting nine" can become a significant challenge.

The refining of skill mechanics is the main difference between the physical skills needed for high school baseball and those needed for middle school baseball. For instance, the physical process of swinging the bat is the same in high school as in middle school; however, the focus is now on simplifying the key movement within the swing phases to be more efficient and consistent. In addition, certain skill sets such as double play feeds and pivots (for infielders) have many variations, and some are not appropriate for middle-school aged players. High school players should posses the necessary strength, body control, and skill foundation to learn and execute these more difficult plays.

In addition to physical skills, high school players should continue to learn and implement mental skills. There is so much more to the game of baseball than just stepping to the plate and swinging a bat, hoping to get a hit, or stepping onto the pitcher's mound and trying to throw the ball past a hitter. Chapter eight deals specifically with gaining the mental edge as a player.

ADVANCED DEFENSIVE AND OFFENSIVE SKILL CHAPTERS

The first six advanced skill chapters cover infield play, outfield play, pitching, and catcher play. The last skills chapter covers hitting and the specific offensive execution skill of sacrifice bunting. Skills in each chapter are further broken down to introduce appropriate mechanics, drills, and practice ideas. In addition, most skills are followed with discussion about common execution flaws, secrets to help players reach their full potential, and skill progression photos. It is recommended that you continually reference the accompanying DVD to visually reinforce the concepts you are reading about.

CHAPTER 1

ADVANCED INFIELD GROUND BALL MECHANICS

Myth #1: THE BEST INFIELDERS AT THE MIDDLE SCHOOL LEVEL BECOME THE BEST HIGH SCHOOL INFIELDERS AT THE VARSITY LEVEL.

Secret: *Just because players are successful infielders in middle school does not ensure that they will remain among the better infielders as they progress to the high school varsity level. Factors such as genetics and physical maturation can cause some infielders to become better outfielders, catchers, or pitchers.*

Myth #2: A STUDENT MUST POSSESS A STRONG ARM TO PLAY IN THE INFIELD AT THE HIGH SCHOOL LEVEL.

Secret: *While it helps a high school infielder to have a strong arm, also possessing quick feet, "soft hands" (to handle difficult hops cleanly and securely), and the ability to quickly release the ball can often make up for a lack of pure arm strength.*

Myth #3: THE AVERAGE MIDDLE SCHOOL OR HIGH SCHOOL BASEBALL SEASON IS LONG ENOUGH TO PREPARE PLAYERS TO BECOME GREAT INFIELDERS.

Secret: *Most middle school baseball seasons are very short and include a limited number of games. High school seasons are also relatively short. Therefore, after the season has concluded, it may be necessary to play on another team, such as a travel ball team or summer showcase team, to gain the necessary experience to reach full potential as a fielder. The addition of training for agility, speed (the ability to run a certain distance at a fast pace), quickness (the ability to get off to a fast start), eye-hand-coordination, and fielding technique can also turn an average player into an advanced infielder over time.*

INFIELD DEVELOPMENT

Infielding is a general term that represents the various fundamental plays needed to become an advanced infielder. It is helpful if players possess specific physical attributes to increase their odds for success at the higher levels of baseball. For instance, middle infielders are right-handed throwers who possess soft hands, quick feet, and superior hand-eye coordination. Third basemen are also right-handed throwers who are typically big and strong, and they also have quick reflexes and powerful arms. First basemen who throw with either their right or left hands are typically tall to provide a large target for fellow infielders, and they are efficient at picking errant throws out of the dirt.

As players progress through the middle school and high school ranks, their footwork, body control, arm strength, and range should significantly improve. This means they can now successfully cover more territory and make difficult plays, which makes it harder for the offense to get base hits. Thus players should be continually challenged to execute their fielding mechanics at game speed in order to create good muscle memory and increase consistency.

At the high school level and above, hitters generally run to first base in just over four seconds. Therefore, infielders should eventually be able to execute proper fielding fundamentals (from the time the ball is hit until their throw reaches first base) in less than four seconds **(Figure 1.1)**. Players who can consistently field a routine ground ball, make a backhand play, execute a slow roller (a slow ground ball fielded on the run), or turn a double play in less than four seconds will be better prepared to handle pressure situations in the game. For instance, these players know they don't have to emphasize one play over another so they successfully execute each play at game speed, just like they do in practice.

ROUTINE GROUND BALL MECHANICS

Technically there is no such thing as a "routine" ground ball. All plays, whether a four-hopper hit right at the fielder, a ball hit to his backhand side or glove side, a double play feed, or a slow roller are challenging to execute. However, for classification purposes, "routine" is a word used by many in the game of baseball to represent a play that should be made by the defense. Unsuccessfully executing the play would be classified as an "error" by the official scorer. The most common routine play that must be made in the infield is a ball hit on the ground directly at a player or hit slightly to his glove or throwing side.

Middle infielders have the luxury of knowing which pitch is going to be thrown because they can see the catcher's signs to the pitcher. They should use this valuable information to their advantage by deceptively adjusting their positioning as they "creep" (take small steps forward) into their ready position.

They should adjust slightly to their left or to their right based on whether the pitch will be a fastball or an off-speed pitch. For example, if the catcher calls for a curveball to a right-handed batter, the shortstop anticipates the batter will pull this pitch. Therefore, he should attempt to cut down his distance to the third base side by creeping into a ready position in a right/left pattern where he takes a step with his right foot laterally instead of straight towards the plate. This will effectively cut down his distance to the third base side and increase his chances of making a play to that side **(Figure 1.2)**.

Note: The footwork and glove positioning for a left-handed first baseman is opposite that of a right-handed fielder when executing routine ground ball mechanics.

Note: All infielders should wear a protective cup for safety purposes. This will also give them the added confidence to field the ball aggressively and correctly.

 Refer to "Advanced: Infield Skills and Drills" on the DVD. Then select the submenu "Ground Ball Mechanics" for detailed interactive instruction.

1.1

The various angles that a shortstop will use to field the ball and throw to first base in four seconds or less. In essence, this is his "range."

1.2

The shortstop is relaying the pitch signal given by the catcher to his outfielders. In this instance, his open hand tells the outfielders an off-speed pitch will be delivered to the batter.

The following is the advanced skill progression needed for middle school and high school players to field a routine ground ball hit directly at them or slightly to their right.

Phase 1: Ready Position

Before each pitch, the infielder should feel relaxed and think about the potential game situations that could arise if the batter hits the ball. This will allow the fielder to make the correct decision about where the ball should be thrown if it is hit to him. In addition, middle infielders should use the catcher's signal to the pitcher to anticipate where the batter will likely hit the next pitch **(Figure 1.3)**.

When the pitcher is about to release the ball to the hitter, the infielder should begin to creep forward and get his body into a position where he is ready to quickly react to a batted ball. He does this by taking small steps (left then right, or right then left) towards the plate. The infielder's body should end up in an athletic position—with his feet spread apart slightly wider than his shoulders, knees slightly bent, hips slightly flexed, weight slightly forward, glove out in front of his body with the pocket facing the batter, and eyes on the "strike zone" of the hitter. It is critical that both of the player's feet are on the ground before the ball is hit in order to maximize his ability to cover the greatest distance in the shortest amount of time. A player does not want to get too much forward momentum because he will have difficulty reacting side to side **(Figure 1.4)**.

Secret: The middle infielders can share their knowledge of the catcher's signal for the pitch with their outfielders. For example, the shortstop places his throwing hand behind his back as he looks in at the catcher's signal to determine the next pitch. Then the fielder makes a quick fist to indicate a fastball is being thrown, or opens his hand wide to indicate an off-speed pitch is being delivered. Because the signal is given behind the infielder's back, only the outfielders can see it.

Secret: As soon as the pitcher is about to release the ball to the plate, all infielders should focus their eyes on the imaginary strike zone of the hitter instead of watching the ball travel to the plate. This gives players an advantage of knowing where the ball will be hit before it

1.3

The infielder should be relaxed between pitches. He must think about the game situation and relay the pitch sign to the outfielders.

1.4

The infielder should creep into his ready position so he can react quickly to all batted balls on the ground and in the air.

makes contact with the bat. For example, when looking at the imaginary strike zone of a right-handed batter, the shortstop notices the hitter's bat head arrives before the ball (which enters the imaginary strike zone through the fielder's peripheral vision). This hint lets the shortstop know a fraction of a second before contact is made that the ball is going to be pulled. As a result, the shortstop can start to move in that direction before the ball is hit. Successfully implementing this skill will increase his distance to the left and the right.

Phase 2: Approach the Ball

Once the routine ground ball is hit and is bouncing directly towards the fielder, teach players how to use their feet to quickly "round off" or "V-Cut" as they approach the ball. This is achieved by moving the body slightly to the right of the ground ball as the player prepares to field it. This vantage point makes it easier for him to judge the speed of the ball, pick out the correct hop, and eventually create momentum to first base. The player should then move his body to the left in order to put himself in the correct position to receive the ball.

As they round off the ground ball, fielders should speed up or slow down in order to field the hop of their choosing. Ideally, players first look to field a "big-hop" (long hop) when the bounce has passed its peak and the ball is on the way back down. Their second choice is to catch the ball off the "short-hop," where the ball has just struck the ground and is beginning to move back up towards the peak.

As a player begins to move back to the center to put himself in a good position to field the ball, he should stay under control, gradually lowering his body, widening his feet to create a good base (athletic position), and moving his glove

1.5

Infielders should round off the routine ball hit to them in order to create proper angles, momentum, and direction to first base.

1.6

As an infielder nears his fielding position, he should pick out the hop he wants to receive while gradually lowering his body and glove to the ball.

forward in front of his body. The player's last two steps into his fielding position are right and then left **(Figures 1.5, 1.6)**.

Flaw: When an infielder fails to cut down his distance to a routine ground ball, he may be forced to rush his throws to first base.

Flaw: When an infielder chooses the incorrect hop to play, he may be forced to catch the dreaded "up-hop." This is when the bounce of the ball is in between the fielder's desired short hop or long hop. Regularly attempting to catch the up-hop or "in between hop" will cause a fielder to be inconsistent and make unnecessary errors.

Secret: When the ball is hit very hard at the fielder, to his left, or to his back-hand side, there is no need for him to round it off. The player's only concern should be getting into a good fielding position to stay in front of the ball and make a clean catch. Because of the speed of the ball, the player will have the time to create the momentum needed to throw to first base.

Secret: Moving off to the side of the ball allows a player to more accurately judge the speed of the ball and helps him choose the hop he wants to field. Middle infielders tend to round off routine ground balls more often than corner infielders because they are positioned further from home plate and have more time to implement desired footwork.

Secret: Whenever possible, good fielders move their glove to a point lower than the ball to be ready to field it. It's easier and faster to adjust the glove upwards to a ball rather than trying to lower the glove to field a ball that did not bounce as high as the player expected.

Secret: The harder the ball is hit, the quicker the fielder must get his body on center to the ball or he will not be in a good position to correctly field it.

Phase 3: Fielding Position

In order to field a ground ball cleanly, a player should be able to consistently get his body into a good fielding position just before the ball is caught. When a player is in a correct fielding position, his legs should be spread wider than his shoulders, his weight should be on the balls of his feet, and his feet should be slightly staggered with his left foot slightly in front of the right. This allows the player's rear end to be lower to the ground and for him to move his glove further out in front of his body. The fielder should position the fingertips of his glove lower than the ball, and move the glove to a position at the peak of an imaginary triangle created by the top of

1.7

Infielders should bring their bodies into a perfect fielding position to receive a ground ball.

1.8

Notice the placement of feet and hands in this side view of an optimal fielding position.

both feet and his glove. He should position his glove just left of the centerline of his body and keep it open to receive the baseball. His throwing hand should be above or to the side of the glove, ready to secure the ball once it enters the pocket and quickly remove it while his body transitions into a good throwing position **(Figures 1.7, 1.8)**.

Flaw: Narrow feet (legs close together) will cause a player to stand too straight or tall when fielding the ball. This position puts the glove under the body and creates a blind spot for the fielder. This also creates an undesirable situation in which the fielder's feet and glove are "boxed in" (between his knees) while moving into a position to throw. This causes the player to waste time taking extra steps to release the ball.

Flaw: The fielder should not create unnecessary movement with his glove while approaching the ground ball. This includes turning the glove from side to side, presenting the back of the glove to the ball, flipping the glove, or raising the glove up and to the side of the body and then bringing it back down to a fielding position. All of these actions increase margin for error, thus decreasing consistency.

Flaw: If the fielder wears his glove so tightly on his hand that it causes the leather to rest against the skin of his palm, it will create "hard hands," and the ball will tend to rebound out of the glove if it is not secured cleanly on the catch. To reduce this effect, the player should wear his glove semi-loose on his hand, with his wrist relaxed.

Secret: The fielder should square his body to the ball and home plate when creating a fielding triangle. In the event the ball takes a bad hop, the player's body will be in the correct position to knock the ball down to the ground right in front of him. He can then quickly retrieve the ball with his throwing hand and still have a chance to successfully complete the play.

Secret: An advanced infielder often uses his glove to deflect the ball into his throwing hand without closing the leather to secure the catch. This action increases the speed of the transition and allows the player to make his throw to the intended target in the shortest possible time.

Phase 4: Power Position

Teach players how to efficiently link energy from their fielding position to their power (throwing) position to maintain momentum towards the throwing target. Once the ball is fielded, a player should quickly take it out of his glove while simultaneously moving his feet to turn his body perpendicular to his target.

There are two primary ways a fielder can go from a fielding position to a throwing position. If the ground ball was hit firmly, and the hitter does not possess great speed, the fielder can quickly cross his right foot in front of his left foot. This exaggerated movement creates more momentum towards the target, and provides a little extra time for a good transition of the ball to the throwing hand. The second method is to replace the feet or "click the heels." Here the fielder tries to be more efficient with his feet by simply bringing his right foot to his left foot while the left foot moves in line with the target. This method is typically used the most by advanced players. Regardless of which footwork a fielder uses, he must stay low and move through the ball. This will allow him

1.9

Infielders should use quick feet, lower body strength, and upper body mechanics to transition into a power position to throw the ball.

1.10

This infielder is in his power position as he gets ready to throw the ball to first base. Notice his body posture and the position of his throwing arm.

to use power in his legs to take stress off his arm and continue momentum in the direction of his throw.

A player should field and throw in a continuous fluid motion. In order to make a throw, the ball will first be positioned where it is pointed away from the target with a relaxed, four-seam grip. The back elbow will be approximately shoulder high. In addition, the front shoulder, elbow, hip, and toe should all be pointed at the target for a fraction of a second as the fielder throws the ball to first base **(Figures 1.9, 1.10)**.

Flaw: It is preferred that right-handed fielders don't step with their right foot behind their left foot while transitioning into a power position. This action incorrectly redirects the player's momentum by moving it away from the intended target.

Secret: When there is adequate time, fielders should instinctively adjust the ball in their throwing hand to create a four-seam grip. This will help the ball fly straight to the target, improving accuracy.

Secret: Fielders must learn to make a quick and consistent transition of the ball from the glove to the throwing hand so they will not be forced to take unnecessary steps towards the target before throwing the ball. That wastes time and gives the batter a better chance of beating the play.

Secret: To save wear and tear on their arm, most advanced infielders choose not to throw the ball with maximum effort to first base on routine plays. However, if the play is difficult or the fielder drops or bobbles the ball during his transition, he may have to throw it with more velocity to ensure he gets the batter out at first base.

Secret: When taking ground balls in practice but not making throws to bases, all infielders should complete the fielding phases through their power position. This creates correct muscle memory that will improve a player's chances of executing good footwork and a clean transition in the game when it counts. On the contrary, simply fielding ground balls and immediately turning to throw the ball to a coach does not create game-speed footwork.

Secret: It is acceptable after fielding a sharply hit ground ball for the player to take an additional shuffle before releasing the ball to first base. This allows the fielder extra time to ensure an accurate transition of the ball from the glove to the throwing hand, establish a four-seam grip, and get his body in a good position to make the throw.

Phase 5: Throw and Extension

This phase happens very quickly to the naked eye. The player should accelerate the baseball from behind his body to a point out in front of the body where it is released towards the target. The two primary throwing fingers (pointer and middle) should stay on top and behind the ball, and the throwing elbow should remain shoulder-high through release. As the player's momentum continues forward through the throw, the glove-arm elbow and the throwing-arm elbow move closer together. This action reduces the player's chance of working across the body, which would result in an inconsistent release point. The bottom half of the fielder's body simultaneously adds energy into the throw by driving off the ground with the back leg and accelerating the hips into rotation. Upon releasing the ball, the fielder should extend his throwing arm towards the target and snap his wrist, which creates backwards (or twelve-o'clock to six-o'clock) rotation. A fluid arm action and release of the ball, along with created momentum, will add distance and accuracy to his throw **(Figures 1.11, 1.12)**.

Phase 6: Follow Through

Once the player releases the ball towards the target, he should complete the throw by allowing his arm to decelerate naturally and finish just outside his stride-foot hip. The back foot will simultaneously release off the ground and continue to move towards first base **(Figures 1.13, 1.14)**.

Flaw: Players should not stop moving after they throw. This destroys the fluid nature of the play and puts more stress on the arm. In addition, it will reduce the carry of the ball towards the target.

Secret: A fielder should imagine that he is in a narrow hallway going to first base. His goal is to avoid banging any of his body parts into the walls as he throws the ball and maintains his momentum to first base. This will improve throwing accuracy.

1.11

The fielder begins the throw to first base by keeping the throwing elbow shoulder-high.

1.12

The fielder gets good extension to first base while maintaining proper direction with his glove side.

1.13

The infielder should allow his throwing arm to finish naturally outside his glove-side knee while keeping his head up and eyes on the target.

1.14

Once the ball has been released to first base, the infielder should maintain his momentum in the direction of his throw for a couple steps.

Work through the following fielding drills and practice ideas to reinforce good fielding mechanics.

Specific Fielding Drills

 Refer to "Advanced: Infield Skills and Drills," "Infield Drills" on the DVD for the following drills:

Short hop—Improves a fielder's mechanics and confidence when fielding short hops **(Figure 1.15)**.

Short hop to power—Improves a fielder's ability to efficiently transition his body from fielding a short hop into a good power position **(Figures 1.16, 1.17)**.

Ozzie—Improves a fielder's ability to trust his instincts when fielding a difficult short hop **(Figure 1.18)**.

Three step/five step—Improves a fielder's ability to take a good crossover step, read the angle and speed of ground ball, and get into a good fielding position **(Figure 1.19)**.

Fly ball—Improves a fielder's ability to react correctly to fly balls hit to the infield **(Figure 1.20)**.

1.15
See "Short hop drill" on the DVD.

1.16
See "Short hop to power" on the DVD. This photo shows the drill starting position.

1.17
This photo shows the drill ending position.

1.18
See "Ozzie drill" on the DVD.

1.19
See "Three step/five step drill" on the DVD.

1.20
See "Fly ball drill" on the DVD.

Additional Fielding Practice

A. Cap in mouth—Each infielder removes his hat, puts the bill of the cap in his mouth, and holds it in place upside down with his teeth. This small trick reinforces a good fundamental fielding position. Players can execute all fielding drills in this manner to force them to catch the ground ball out in front of their body where they can see it. If they let the ball get too far underneath their torso, they will lose sight of the ball, making a clean catch difficult.

B. Perfect fielding position throws—While they are warming up, each infielder can spend time getting into a perfect fielding position with the ball in his glove prior to making a throw. Each fielder then moves his body into a power position and finishes with a quick throw to emphasize good fielding and throwing mechanics.

C. Wall ball—Players can throw a tennis ball into a wall and move their bodies to field the ball in a perfect fielding position (with or without a glove); then they should quickly transfer to a good throwing position in the direction of their imaginary first baseman. Fielders can simulate routine ground balls, and, with some creativity, can work on double play feeds and pivots. This drill can also be executed with a partner who makes a throw to the wall from behind the fielder, who must successfully react to the speed, angle, and bounce of the ball to make the pre-determined play.

D. Live repetitions—First, the coaches roll ground balls to fielders, then they hit them to the players, and eventually they progress to game-like repetitions, where players field and throw to a base or turn double plays at game speed. Note: An infielder will benefit more from fewer repetitions performed correctly at full speed than, say, fielding one hundred ground balls with lazy mechanics at three-quarter speed.

E. Cone drills—Use cones in creative ways to force players to execute fielding skills correctly. For example, players can go around a cone to get the feel for rounding off a routine ground ball hit right at them. This can help them visually perceive your teaching cues as well as to assist their actual performance in practice or executing specific drills.

F. Stopwatch grounders—Players field ground balls against the time of a stopwatch to ensure they are fielding at game speed. The watch starts when the ball is hit and stops when the ball is caught at first base. On fields with ninety-foot bases, all plays should be executed in four seconds or less.

G. Get wide to field low drill—Ask fielders who are having trouble getting into a proper fielding position to create exaggerated wide-fielding stances with their feet. This will help them get their body extra low and assist them with extending their hands to catch the ball in front of them. A coach should hit firm fungos (or throw the ball firmly) directly at the fielder from thirty to forty feet away. Once players learn to routinely field the ball cleanly from this stance, they should advance to a standard fielding position to make the catch, and quickly transition to a power position to prepare to make their throw.

H. Bare-handed grounders—Direct advanced infielders to take a portion of practice time to field routinely hit ground balls with their bare hands. The ground balls should be hit softly with a fungo bat or rolled by a coach. This helps create soft hands and forces better footwork to get players into a good fielding position. Be sure not to hit the ball too hard because you could possibly injure the fielder's hands or cause players to fear the ball, which can result in bad habits. If a fielder does not catch the ball cleanly to complete the drill, he should always retrieve the ball with his throwing hand off the ground to reinforce the process of when a ball is bobbled or dropped in the game. A variation of this drill can be executed with fielding paddles, which are tools used by some coaches to reinforce soft hands when catching the ball.

I. Pre-game infield—Players take their infield position (SS, 2B, 3B, or 1B), and one to four coaches hit ground balls at the same time to each position. This increases the number of repetitions infielders can get in a short period of time. *Note:* A throw-down base can be dropped twenty feet past first base to allow more than one player to throw to first base at one time.

J. Quick feet quick release drill—Players stand approximately twenty feet apart and see how many throws and exchanges they can make back and fourth in twenty seconds. They should attempt to quickly move their feet and throw the ball at the height at which they receive it.

K. Close your eyes drill—Once the ball is fielded cleanly, the player should close his eyes to complete his throw to first base or his feed to second base. This forces the fielder to trust his instincts and throwing mechanics to make a successful throw. *Note:* This drill is for highly skilled advanced infielders.

L. Jumping rope—Jumping rope is a great exercise to improve footwork. Players need quick feet to be consistent fielders. They should use a variety of footwork combinations to help master body timing and control.

M. Juggling—Infielders should learn to juggle a minimum of three baseballs with both hands and two baseballs at one time with a single hand. This promotes coordination, peripheral vision, and the ability to trust their instincts. When a player becomes proficient with baseballs, he should vary the size and shapes of the objects he is juggling to add increasing difficulty.

N. Transition practice—Simply throw the ball into the air, spinning it in various directions, before making the catch. Once the ball enters the glove, it should be removed immediately without looking at it. Players must quickly feel for a four-seam grip. The process of instinctively finding the four-seam grip is critical for all infielders who want their throws to travel straight in flight to the intended destination.

BACKHAND MECHANICS

As with all types of ground balls, backhand plays offer a unique set of challenges that players must overcome. Initially, the fielder's footwork is exactly the same as preparing for any batted ball. For example, the player will creep into a ready position. However, once the ground ball is hit to the fielder's right (backhand play will be made to the right of a right-handed thrower), he must make critical adjustments to efficiently get to the ball, field it cleanly on the backhand side, and accurately throw to first base **(Figure 1.21)**.

 Refer to "Advanced: Infield Skills and Drills" on the DVD. Then go to the submenu "Backhand Mechanics" for detailed interactive instruction.

The following is the advanced skill progression needed for middle school and high school players to field a ground ball hit to their backhand side.

Crossover Step

Once the ball is hit, the fielder must react by taking a crossover step with his left foot to his backhand side. As he is stepping across his body, the fielder must

1.21 Shown in chalk marks: the different angles that a shortstop can use to field the ball to his backhand side.

stay low to the ground and simultaneously determine the distance and speed of the batted ball. This will impact when and where he will put down his left foot to help him take the best angle to the ball. For instance, if the fielder determines that the only way to catch this ground ball is to intersect it deep on the infield, he should create a deeper angle to the ball by putting his left foot down where he can make a straight line to the ball's path. When a player mistakenly takes the first step with his right foot to make a backhand catch, he has made a "false step." Very little ground is gained on this preliminary movement, and it can cause the fielder to be late and miss the ball **(Figures 1.22, 1.23)**.

Flaw: When a fielder misjudges the speed and distance of a ground ball, he must continually adjust his route in an attempt to make up for the incorrect read. This wastes critical time and creates unwanted momentum heading even farther away from his throw to first base.

When to Use Backhand Mechanics

When a player takes a good crossover step and establishes a good angle to a ball on his backhand side, he may realize that he can actually get in front of the ball to field it. Typically this is beneficial. However, if the player feels like he will have to sacrifice good fielding mechanics in order to "fight" to get his body in front of the ball, he should simply play the ball to his backhand side **(Figure 1.24)**.

Flaw: When a player approaches the ball with lazy feet, it forces him to field the ball to his backhand side when he should have played the ball in front of his body.

Type 1 Backhand: Do or Die

A do-or-die backhand play is one in which the player does not have a choice about how the ball is fielded. He will either catch the ball with backhand mechanics or dive after the ball. As the fielder attacks the ball, quickly moving his feet, he must simultaneously lower his body to bring his nose down to the ball just before making the catch. There is no time to choose which foot will be out in front when the ball enters the glove. The player should take a split second to make sure the ball is secured in the glove. If the left foot happens to be in front, the fielder should quickly shift his feet into a power position using his lower body strength to fight inertia and channel energy into the long throw to first base. If the right foot happens to be in front when the ball is caught, the player will have to take one extra step with his left foot before he can shift his feet to get his body into a power position to throw **(Figures 1.25, 1.26)**.

Flaw: The fielder should not move to the ball with an extended glove arm because this will significantly slow him down in his attempt to make the play.

1.22

Infielders should use proper footwork to their backhand side by implementing a good crossover step.

1.23

This player incorrectly takes a "false step" in attempt to make this backhand play. This critical error in his footwork may cause him to miss the ball.

1.24

This fielder should have used backhand mechanics to play the ground ball because he had to sacrifice fundamental fielding techniques to attempt to get in front it.

1.25

When the ball is hit very hard to the fielder's backhand side, he should get to the ball with either foot in front, crouch low, and watch the ball enter his glove.

1.26

Once the ball is caught, the fielder should quickly transition his feet to get his body into a power position for the throw to first base.

Type 2 Backhand: Round Off

This is an advanced play made by an infielder. Because of the skill required to execute this play consistently, middle-school-aged players should generally avoid attempting the round-off backhand in a game, and focus on getting in front of the ball to make the play to first base. When the ball is hit to the fielder's backhand side, the player takes a crossover step and creates a good angle to the play. As he gets closer to the ground ball, he realizes that he has more time than originally anticipated. As a result, he adjusts his route by cutting down the distance and angle to the ball, which creates momentum towards first base. The fielder will still field the ball to his backhand side by getting low to the ball, cutting off the hop, making a clean exchange of the ball to his throwing hand, and releasing an accurate throw to first base. If possible, he should attempt to follow his throw by continuing his momentum towards the target **(Figures 1.27, 1.28, 1.29)**.

Specific Fielding Drills for Backhand Practice

 Refer to "Advanced: Infield Skills and Drills" and then "Infield Drills" on the DVD for detailed interactive instruction.

Most of the specific fielding drills that were mentioned in the "Routine Ground Ball" skills set above are demonstrated and executed to the backhand side to help refine this specific skill.

SLOW ROLLER MECHANICS

When a ground ball is hit with very little speed at an infielder, a specific skill set is required to execute this fairly difficult play, called a "slow roller." Each infielder has a unique challenge when making this play. Third base is the most difficult position to execute a slow roller because of the distance the fielder must cover, the angle of the throw, and the arm strength and coordination needed to complete the throw. A second baseman also has a very tough angle and often needs a soft touch to his throw due to his close proximity to the first baseman **(Figure 1.30)**.

Refer to "Advanced: Infield Skills and Drills" on the DVD, then go to the submenu "Slow Roller Mechanics" for detailed interactive instruction.

The following is the advanced skill progression needed for middle school and high school players to field a slow-roller ground ball hit directly at them or slightly to their right.

1.27

When this fielder is attacking the ball to his backhand side, he realizes he would have to fight to get in front of the ball, so he decides to round off the play.

1.28

The fielder gets low to the ball and sees it into his glove while gaining momentum in the direction of his throw.

1.29

Once the ball is caught, the player quickly shifts his feet to bring his body into a power position to throw to first base.

1.30

These chalk marks demonstrate two angles that a shortstop can possibly take to a slow roller play.

Approach

Once the ball is hit, the fielder must quickly react by running full speed to the slow-rolling baseball. When he gets close to the ball, he must lower his upper body and position his glove slightly lower than the ball because it is easier to rise up than adjust the body and glove down at the last moment. In addition, the fielder must adjust his feet by chopping down his steps (taking small steps to quickly slow down and improve body control), so he will be in a position to catch the ball in front of or just to the outside part of his left foot (right foot for a left-handed player) **(Figure 1.31)**.

1.31

When the fielder realizes the ground ball is hit softly, he must compensate by running full speed to cut down the distance to the ball.

Flaw: This play will not work if a fielder fails to aggressively attack the slow-moving ground ball. Remember, a player needs to execute the play in less than four seconds to ensure he gets the forced out at first base.

Field and Transition

The fielder must bring his throwing hand down to his glove so he will be in a position to quickly make an exchange from the glove. The ball should be secured while the player's left foot is in contact with the ground, and thrown when the right foot lands. This does not leave time for flawed movements. However, if the fielder senses he has time (for instance, a slow base runner), he can take a few extra steps before making the throw to ensure he has made a good transition and has his body under control. On the other hand, if there is not enough time, the player must field and throw in one step. When this is the case, the player will not have the time to stand up and throw overhand. He will be forced to release the ball from a side-arm angle **(Figures 1.32, 1.33)**.

Secret: The fielder should try to field the ball on the big hop if at all possible. This increases the odds of fielding the ball cleanly and reduces the chances that the fielder will have to throw from an awkward position.

Flaw: A player should not field a slow roller with his throwing hand to try to save time. The general rule of thumb at the high school level and below is to use the glove when the ball is moving. When the ball is one rotation from stopping or has come to a stop, the fielder can pick it up with his bare hand.

1.32

The fielder should lower his body to field the ball in front of his left foot.

1.33

The fielder should quickly transition the ball to his throwing hand and position himself to make his throw when his right foot lands.

1.34

The fielder should account for his body speed and angle to first base by adjusting his throw accordingly.

Flaw: If an infielder's throwing hand is not close enough to his glove when the ball enters, this slows his transition process. It often forces him to take extra steps before throwing the ball to first base.

Throw and Follow

The fielder must be able to account for his body speed and direction when throwing to first base. He should compensate by throwing the ball the appropriate distance up the first base line so it can have the time to angle back to the first baseman for the catch. The ball will naturally follow the direction that the fielder is traveling **(Figures 1.34, 1.35)**.

1.35

The fielder should continue his momentum for a few steps after the ball is released.

Additional Slow Roller Practice

A. Stationary throws—Fielders get into a position with their body low, the ball in their glove in front of their left foot, and their throwing hand close to the glove. On the coach's command, the fielders transition the ball into their throwing hand and throw the ball as their right foot plants into the ground.

B. Running slow roller drill—Fielders start with the ball in their glove and run full speed towards home plate. They must reach into their glove and throw the ball to first base while keeping their momentum going to the plate. During the first phase of the drill, the fielder does not bend over as if he is fielding a slow rolling ball hugging the ground. In the second phase of the drill, the player should lower his body a little to simulate making the catch on a bouncing slow roller. The last phase of the drill is to place a tennis ball stationary on the ground to simulate where the ball would have been caught if it were actually rolling on the infield. The fielder must aggressively run to the tennis ball; quickly chop down his steps as he lowers his body and glove to the ball; simulate making the catch in front of his left foot; continue moving through the play, exchanging the actual ball from his glove; and complete the throw to first base on the run. Emphasize the concept of fielding the ball near the player's left foot and throwing when his right foot lands. This teaches players how to make the quickest transition and release possible when fielding a slow roller with a glove.

C. Thrown slow rollers—A coach gets halfway from the plate to the infield position he is drilling. He should roll the ball towards the fielders who must implement slow roller mechanics to make the throw to first base.

D. Fungo slow rollers—A coach at the plate hits slow rollers at various speeds and with various sized hops to allow fielders to adjust to the ball and execute the play, implementing correct mechanics.

CHAPTER 2

ADVANCED MIDDLE INFIELD
DOUBLE PLAY FEEDS AND PIVOTS

Myth #1: IT'S NOT IMPORTANT TO TEACH ADVANCED DOUBLE PLAY FEEDS AND PIVOTS TO MIDDLE INFIELDERS BECAUSE ADVANCED ATHLETES WILL FIGURE OUT A WAY TO QUICKLY THROW THE BALL TO SECOND BASE (FEED), OR CATCH THE BALL AT SECOND BASE AND THROW IT TO FIRST BASE (PIVOT) IN ORDER TO SUCCESSFULLY TURN A DOUBLE PLAY.

Secret: *Successfully turning a double play or not executing the play is often the difference of a mere fraction of a second. Implementing the correct fielding technique, efficiently releasing the feed to second base, using proper footwork at second base, and making an accurate throw to first base are all needed to consistently "turn two."*

Myth #2: AS LONG AS THE SHORTSTOP AND SECOND BASEMEN LEARN ONE TYPE OF FEED AND PIVOT, THEY WILL BE PREPARED TO EXECUTE ALL DOUBLE PLAY SCENARIOS IN A GAME.

Secret: *Teaching one type of double play feed and pivot for middle infielders will usually suffice for youth baseball. However, once a player enters middle school, he should be taught various double play feeds and pivots in order to "turn two" regardless of where the ball is fielded in relation to second base. Not being armed with the various feeds and pivots can ultimately cost a team the game; it can also mean the difference between whether a player wins or loses the starting shortstop or second base position.*

Myth #3: MIDDLE INFIELDERS SHOULD NOT ADJUST THEIR STANDARD POSITION WHEN BASE RUNNERS ARE ON FIRST AND/OR FIRST AND SECOND BASE BECAUSE IT OPENS A BIG HOLE FOR THE BATTER TO HIT THROUGH ON EACH SIDE OF THE INFIELD.

Secret: *When there are fewer than two outs and base runners are on first base and/or first and second base, middle infielders should adjust their positioning to double play depth by moving closer to the plate and to second base. This position affords them the opportunity to execute a double play feed and corresponding pivot without becoming rushed or out of control.*

DOUBLE PLAY FEEDS AND PIVOTS

A double play is a defensive maneuver that infielders should master for the specific defensive position they play. This chapter focuses on the different double play feeds and pivots executed by advanced middle infielders (short-stop and second basemen). A standard double play usually consists of a feed, a pivot, and then one final catch to record two forced outs on one batted ground ball. The particular style of feed executed by the fielder will depend largely on where and how hard the ball was hit, and the speed of the base runners, along with where the defender is positioned at the time of the play. The same is true of the pivot that middle infielders choose to implement at second base. Where the feed (throw) will be received has much to do with the pivot that is implemented. It is critical that middle infielders are taught and given a chance to practice a variety of feeds and pivots. This allows them to correctly react when a double play is attempted in an actual game.

When there are base runners on first base, or first and second bases, and less than two outs, the middle infielders should move a few steps closer to the plate and second base to create double play depth. In this position, they can get to second base with enough time to execute the correct pivot. A 6-4-3 double play consists of a feed made by the shortstop (6), a pivot executed by the second baseman (4), and a catch of a thrown ball by the first baseman (3). A 4-6-3 double play consists of a feed made by the second baseman (4), a pivot executed by the shortstop (6), and a catch of a thrown ball by the first baseman (3). A 5-4-3 double play consists of a feed made by the third baseman (5), a pivot executed by the second baseman (4), and a catch of a thrown ball by the first baseman (3). A 3-6-1 double play consists of a feed made by the first baseman (3), a pivot executed by the shortstop (6), and a catch of a thrown ball by the pitcher (1) covering first base.

 Refer to "Advanced: Infield Skills and Drills," then "Double Play Feeds and Pivots," and then "Double Play Depth" on the DVD for detailed interactive instruction on how to create fundamentally sound double play depth.

As players grow in strength, skill, and experience, the types of double play feeds and pivots used by middle infielders will become more varied and com-plex. Remember, at the high school level and below, base runners must slide directly into the base. This protects middle infielders; it also reduces the need to significantly clear distance from the base before making the throw to first base as needed at the highest levels of the game to avoid being "taken out" by the base runner's slide. In addition, all middle infielders should treat potential double plays with the mentality that "one (out) is a must, and two (outs) are a plus." Therefore, it is counterproductive to try to be so quick turning a double play that the middle infielder making the pivot misses the sure out at second base, or even worse, both base runners end up safe. Also, it is not necessary to complete the second phase of a double play with a throw to first base when there is no realistic chance of making the out. Unnecessary throws only lead to possible mistakes.

SHORTSTOP FEEDS

A feed from shortstop consists of fielding a ground ball to any part of the left side of the infield, and delivering an underhand or overhand throw to the second baseman in attempt to turn a double play. There are five specific short-stop feeds that are covered in this chapter. Three of these feeds are appropriate for players ages 11 and up, and two are appropriate for ages 15 and up **(Figure 2.1)**.

 Refer to Advanced: "Infield Skills and Drills," then "Double Play Feeds and Pivots," and then "Shortstop Feeds" on the DVD for detailed interactive instruction on the five types of shortstop feeds.

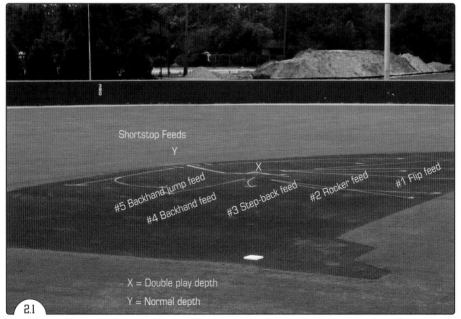

2.1

This photo shows the five possible double play feeds a high school shortstop would be responsible for executing.

The following is the advanced skill progression needed for middle school and high school infielders to execute double play feeds from shortstop.

Shortstop Feed 1: Flip

This is a basic double play feed made by a shortstop to a second baseman when the ground ball is hit directly to or to the left of his position. Because the momentum of the play takes the shortstop towards second base, the shortstop should deliver this feed underhand to make it easier for the second baseman to handle.

If there is time, the shortstop should cut down the distance to the ground ball and get into a good fielding position. This also helps create momentum that will be used to make the flip feed. If the ball is hit directly at the fielder and he chooses to use a flip feed, he should slightly round off the ball to create momentum to second base. The player should communicate "flip, flip, flip" to let the second baseman know the ball will be delivered underhand (**Figures 2.2, 2.3**).

Flaw: The shortstop should not wait for the routine ground ball to come to him before making the flip feed. If he does, this wastes valuable time and allows base runners more opportunity to beat the throw to second and the pivot to first base.

2.2

To execute a flip feed, shortstops should cut down the distance to the ground ball and create momentum towards second base.

SEPARATION

Teach the shortstop how to correctly field the ball with both hands working together to quickly separate the ball from the glove. Once the ball is in the bare hand, the fielder should create space between the glove and the ball so the second baseman can easily see the feed (**Figure 2.4**).

Flaw: The shortstop should not move both hands towards the second baseman; this makes it difficult for the second baseman to quickly find the ball and determine the appropriate pivot to implement.

2.3

The fielder should lower his body to the ball and get into a perfect fielding position.

DELIVERY

To avoid wasting time, the shortstop should stay low to the ground, gradually raising his body through the feed (delivery of the ball to his second baseman). When holding the ball, the fielder's wrist should lock to decrease the ball's rotation through the air. Simultaneously, he should pull the glove into his chest to clearly expose the ball to the second baseman. The fielder should use his leg strength to continue momentum towards second base, and release a firm feed in the direction of the front corner of the base (the corner closest to the pitcher's mound). A good flip feed should be received by the second baseman somewhere from belt- to chest-height **(Figure 2.5)**.

Flaw: If the shortstop stands up to make the flip feed, he wastes time and interferes with momentum. Or worse, he stands up and throws the ball overhand to the second baseman from this short distance, which puts his teammate in a defensive mode to receive the feed.

Flaw: The shortstop should not remove the ball from his glove and bring it outside his right leg to feed it in a "bowling" manner to the second baseman. This wastes time and can impact the accuracy of the flip feed.

Flaw: The shortstop should not use a snap action of his wrist to get the feed to the second baseman. This often results in a high feed or a low feed, and it is difficult for the second baseman to make a quick pivot.

2.4

The shortstop should quickly separate the ball from the glove to make the flip feed to the second baseman.

FOLLOW

Once the feed has been released to the second baseman, the shortstop should maintain his momentum by continuing past second base **(Figure 2.6)**.

Flaw: If the shortstop halts as soon as he lets go of the underhand feed, it will slow the ball and can change the direction of the feed.

2.5

The shortstop's legs should generate momentum to flip the ball underhand to the second baseman.

Shortstop Feed 2: Rocker

This is a basic double play feed made by a shortstop to a second baseman when the ground ball is hit routinely towards or slightly to the right of the shortstop. Because the momentum of the play takes the shortstop away from second base, he should make the feed overhand.

2.6

After the feed is made, the shortstop should continue moving to a point beyond second base to maintain his momentum through the delivery of the ball.

Teach your shortstop to move to the right and cut down the distance to the ground ball if there is time. The key is for him to get into a good fielding position to receive the ball. The only slight adjustment in footwork is that the shortstop will slightly set his left foot back (left toe to right heel) before the ball is caught; this puts his hips in a position where they can freely rotate to make the feed **(Figures 2.7, 2.8)**.

Flaw: If the shortstop gets his feet set too early and has to wait for the ball to come to him, he may be in danger of receiving a bad hop while sacrificing time needed to turn the double play.

Flaw: If the shortstop fields the ball underneath him, his glove may get trapped with his throwing hand inside his knees, making it difficult for a quick exchange of the ball.

Flaw: If the shortstop fields the ball with his left foot in front of his right foot, this locks the hips and forces him to move his left foot to make a good feed; this wastes valuable time.

SEPARATION

Teach the shortstop how to correctly field the ball with both hands working together in front of his body to quickly separate the ball from the glove. The fielder should remain at the level at which he fielded the ball to save time. Once the ball is in his bare hand, the fielder should clear his glove to make the ball visible to the second baseman **(Figure 2.9)**.

Flaw: The shortstop should not rise up or lower down before making the feed to second base.

2.7

To execute a rocker feed, the shortstop should cut down the distance to the ball while working to get in front of it.

2.8

The player should get into a good fielding position with his left foot set slightly back in order to free his hips to start the feed to second base.

Flaw: The shortstop should not take extra steps after catching the ball to get into position for the feed.

Flaw: The fielder should be careful not to allow his accumulated momentum to continue through the fielding process; this would eventually force him to lose balance towards third base while making the feed.

DELIVERY

To avoid wasting time needed for the play, the shortstop should quickly snap his wrist to release the feed to the front corner of second base. At the same time, he should bring his glove to his glove-side ribs to help create torque for his throw. The second baseman should receive the

2.9
The shortstop should quickly separate the ball from his glove, while maintaining his posture, to make the rocker feed to his second baseman.

ball somewhere between belt- to chest-high, preferably over the corner of the base closest to the pitcher's mound **(Figures 2.10, 2.11)**.

Flaw: The shortstop should avoid winding up to deliver a hard throw to the second baseman. This wastes time and can end up disturbing the footwork and transition of the pivot at second base.

2.10
The shortstop should quickly and accurately snap his feed to the second baseman.

2.11
The shortstop should complete the rocker feed by allowing his throwing hand to finish outside his glove-side elbow or knee.

Because of the speed of the ground ball, the shortstop does not have time to set his left foot slightly behind him as he would with the rocker feed.

The fielder must work hard to get into a perfect fielding position before concerning himself with the feed to second base.

Shortstop Feed 3: Step-Back

This is a basic double play feed made by a shortstop. It is a slight variation of the rocker feed but modified due to the speed at which the ball is hit or the distance that the fielder must cover. The best time to implement the step-back feed is when a very hard ground ball is hit at or to the right of the shortstop. Because the momentum of the play takes the shortstop away from second base, he should make the feed overhand. The fielder cannot allow the ball to get past him, so teach the shortstop to get in front of the ball. He should attempt to field the ball using perfect fielding mechanics without pre-setting his feet to speed up the feed, unlike the rocker feed. The key is to get into a good fielding position to make sure the shortstop catches the ball **(Figures 2.12, 2.13)**.

SEPARATION

Teach the shortstop how to correctly field the ball with both hands working together in front of his body to quickly separate the ball from the glove. At the same time, he will quickly take a drop step with his left foot to clear the hips to make the feed to second base. To save time, the fielder should remain at the level he fielded. Once the ball is in his bare hand, the fielder should clear his glove to make the ball visible to the second baseman **(Figure 2.14)**.

Flaw: The shortstop should not rise up or lower down before making the feed to second base.

Flaw: The shortstop should avoid taking extra steps to position himself for the throw to second.

Secret: In extreme cases—if the ball was received in an awkward fielding position—the fielder may need to shift both feet at the same time to clear the hips.

Once the ball is caught, the shortstop should quickly take a drop step with his left foot to clear his hips.

The shortstop should quickly and accurately snap his feed to the front corner of second base.

Secret: Because of the speed of the batted ball, the shortstop may be off-balance to some degree as he fields the ball. Therefore, he must use his lower body strength to fight inertia to get his feet and upper body under control to make the feed.

DELIVERY

To avoid wasting time needed for the play, the shortstop should quickly snap his wrist to release the feed to the front corner of second base. At the same time, he should bring his glove to his (glove-side) ribs to help create torque for his throw. The second baseman should receive the

The shortstop should complete the step-back feed by allowing his throwing hand to finish outside his glove-side elbow.

ball somewhere between belt- to chest-high, preferably over the corner of the base closest to the pitcher's mound (Figures 2.15, 2.16).

Flaw: If the shortstop winds up to deliver a hard throw to the second baseman, he wastes time, and this can end up disturbing the footwork and transition of the pivot at second base.

Flaw: The shortstop should avoid taking extra steps towards second base before throwing the ball. This is unnecessary and wastes valuable time.

Shortstop Feed 4: Backhand Catch 🎓

This is an advanced feed made by a shortstop. Because of the difficulty of this play, middle-school-aged players should generally avoid attempting this feed in a game and focus on making the play to first base.

When the ball is hit very hard to the right of the shortstop, he must implement an effective crossover step and take a good angle to the ball. Because the ball will be fielded in a backhand position, he will not have time to pre-set his feet for a feed to second base. The first priority is to make sure the shortstop gets his body low to the ball and secures the ball in his glove.

Because the momentum of the play takes the shortstop away from second base, he should make the feed overhand **(Figures 2.17, 2.18)**.

SEPARATION

After the shortstop makes the catch, he should quickly bring both of his hands together to move the ball from his glove into his throwing hand. Simultaneously, he must adjust his feet and upper body into a position where he can make the feed to second base. If the ball is fielded with the left foot in front, he can quickly adjust both feet perpendicular to second base to square his hips and shoulders to make a snap throw. If the ball is fielded with his right foot in front, he has two options. He can plant his right foot and immediately turn the shoulders to second base to throw. Or he can take one more step with the left foot, and quickly adjust both feet to a position perpendicular to second base, and then square his hips and shoulders to make a snap throw **(Figure 2.19)**.

2.17

The shortstop should take a crossover step to create a good angle to a ground ball hit hard to his backhand side.

2.18

The player should get low to the ball to ensure that he catches it before he concerns himself with the proper footwork to make his feed.

2.19

The shortstop should quickly adjust his feet to a position perpendicular to second base while separating the ball from the glove.

2.20

The shortstop should attempt to maintain a good posture position to quickly throw to the second baseman.

DELIVERY

The shortstop should quickly snap his wrist to release the feed to the front corner of second base. At the same time, he should bring his glove to his (glove-side) ribs to help create torque for his throw. The second baseman should ideally receive the ball somewhere between belt- to chest-high, preferably over the corner of the base closest to the pitcher's mound (**Figures 2.20, 2.21**).

2.21

The player should snap his throw to the second baseman and complete his mechanics by allowing his throwing hand to finish outside his glove-side elbow.

Shortstop Feed 5: Backhand Jump 🎓

This feed is an advanced variation of the backhand feed made by the shortstop. Because of the difficulty of this play and the athleticism and the arm strength required to successfully execute it, middle-school-aged players should generally avoid attempting this feed in a game, and focus on making the play to first base.

2.22

The shortstop should take a crossover step to create a good angle to a ground ball hit hard to his backhand side.

2.23

The player should get low to the ball to ensure that he catches it before he concerns himself with the proper footwork to make his feed.

When the ball is hit very hard to the right of the shortstop, he must implement a good crossover step and take a good angle to the ball. Because the ball will be fielded on the move in a backhand fashion, the player will not have time to pre-set his feet for a feed. The first priority is to make sure he gets his body low to the ball and secures it in his glove **(Figures 2.22, 2.23)**.

SEPARATION
Teach the shortstop to quickly bring both hands together after making the catch to separate the ball from the glove into the throwing hand. Simultaneously, once the ball is caught, the fielder will push hard off of his left leg to lift himself up in the air. The fielder must use superior body control to turn his shoulders while in flight to create a good throwing position **(Figure 2.24)**.

DELIVERY
As in similar deliveries, the shortstop should quickly snap his wrist to release the feed to the corner of second base closest to left field. At the same time, he should bring his glove to his (glove-side) ribs to help create torque for the throw. The second baseman should ideally receive the ball with his right foot on the base, stretching to receive the ball in a way similar to a first baseman stretching for a throw. The goal is to get one out on the play unless the feed to second is perfect, and the runner to first base is moving slowly **(Figure 2.25)**.

Secret: It is very important the middle infielders at least get the first out at second base on the double play attempt. This keeps the batter at first base, which allows a future double play if there are less than two outs.

2.24

The shortstop should quickly push off the ground with his left leg to get airborne. Simultaneously, the player must turn his body perpendicular to second base while separating the ball from the glove to make the feed to the second baseman.

2.25

The shortstop should quickly snap his wrist while in the air to make his feed to the second baseman.

SECOND BASEMAN PIVOTS

A pivot from a second baseman consists of receiving a feed from the shortstop or third baseman for a force out at second base, and quickly making a relay throw to first base for the second force out needed to turn a double play. We'll cover four specific second baseman pivots: one of them is appropriate for all players ages 11 and up; three are appropriate for players ages 15 and up **(Figure 2.26)**.

 Refer to "Advanced: Infield Skills and Drills," choose "Double Play Feeds and Pivots," and then "Second Baseman Pivots" on the DVD for detailed interactive instruction on the four types of pivots made by second basemen.

The following is the advanced skill progression needed for middle school and high school infielders to execute double play pivots from the second base position.

Second Baseman Pivot 1: Left On/Left Off

This is the most fundamental double play pivot used by a second baseman when the ball is hit on the ground to the left side of the infield (to the shortstop or third baseman). Once the ball is hit, the second baseman should hustle to his base to be ready for a possible double play feed. His goal is to be there early so he can stay under control and handle all feeds.

Four Second Baseman Pivots

Second baseman's route to second base to start his double play pivot footwork

3   4

2   1

Point where the second baseman starts to get himself under control

Base path

2.26

This photo shows the four possible double play pivots a high school second baseman is responsible for executing.

2.27

The second baseman should quickly move from double play depth to the bag.

As the second baseman approaches the base, he should widen his legs to slow down and bring his body under control. Simultaneously, he should raise up his hands while bringing his elbow close to his side. His glove should be open with the throwing hand close by, as if his thumbs were tied together with a short string, giving the fielder a good target to feed the ball. Ideally, his right foot should be positioned on the clay next to the back corner of the base (the corner closest to center field), and his left foot should be on the base or ready to step onto the base once the feed is made. His body should be squared to the shortstop (or third baseman, whoever is making the feed) with his knees and hips flexed in a good athletic position (**Figures 2.27, 2.28, 2.29**).

POWER POSITION AND THROW

Once the second baseman sees the ball in the air, he simply lets it come to him. He receives the ball with his left foot on the base, hands together, and elbows relaxed. Then he quickly removes his left foot from the base, plants it on the clay while simultaneously creating a good power position, and uses good throwing mechanics to efficiently release the ball to first base (**Figures 2.30, 2.31, 2.32**).

Flaw: A player should not take unnecessary steps before throwing the ball to first base. This is a waste of time.

Flaw: The fielder should avoid pushing his body up in the air or too far from the base while stepping off with the left foot. This takes momentum away from first base and wastes valuable time. The throw can't be made until the left foot hits the ground.

2.28

The player should widen his feet to get into position with his right foot near the back corner of the base. He should square his shoulders to the teammate making the feed, and keep his glove up to give his teammate a target.

2.29

The second baseman should react to the feed by placing his left foot on the base with his knees flexed and let the ball travel to his glove.

2.30

The second baseman should quickly remove his left foot from the base and use his feet to create a power position towards first base.

2.31

The player should throw the ball from the same level that he receives the feed.

2.32

Once the ball is released, the second baseman should remove his cleats from the ground by pushing off of his left foot.

Flaw: A player should avoid stepping with his left foot into the base path of the oncoming base runner.

Secret: When receiving good feeds, advanced second basemen use the glove to deflect the ball into their throwing hand, which is quicker than catching the feed, reaching in the glove, taking out the ball, and then throwing.

Secret: The second baseman should keep his knees flexed when he steps on and off the base. This will help him quickly put his left foot on the ground to throw. Keep in mind the player cannot throw the ball until his left foot plants.

Secret: When the second baseman senses that he does not have much time, he will simply throw the ball to first base from the same height he receives the feed. This is quicker than raising his hands above the shoulders to throw.

Secret: Once the ball is fed to first base, the second baseman can release his cleats from the clay by pushing his left leg off the ground, just in case the base runner decides to slide out of the base line into the player.

Second Baseman Pivot 2: Across the Bag

This is an advanced pivot made by a second baseman. Because of the difficulty of this play, middle-school-aged players should generally avoid attempting this pivot in a game. Once the ball is hit, the second baseman should hustle to his base to be ready for a possible double play feed. His goal is to be there early so he can stay under control and handle all feeds.

As the second baseman approaches the base, he should widen his legs to slow down and bring his body under control. Simultaneously, he should raise his hands up while bringing his elbow close to his side. His glove should be open, with the throwing hand close by, as if his thumbs were tied together with a short string, giving the fielder a good target to feed the ball. Ideally, the second baseman's right foot should be positioned on the clay next to the back corner of the base (the corner closest to center field), and his left foot should be on the base or ready to step onto the base once the feed is made. His body should be squared to the shortstop (or third baseman, if that's who is making the feed) with his knees and hips flexed in a good athletic position (**Figures 2.33, 2.34**).

2.33

The second baseman should quickly move from double play depth to the bag.

POWER POSITION AND THROW
Once the second baseman sees the ball heading in the air to the middle or front corner of the base, he simply places his left foot on the front quadrant of the base and moves his right foot and body to the ball. The feed is received with hands together, elbows relaxed, and the player's

2.34
The player should widen his feet to get into an athletic position with his right foot near the back corner of the base.

2.35
The second baseman should place his left foot on the base with his knees flexed.

2.36
The player lets his right foot travel over the base and plant into the clay in line with home plate.

2.37
The player quickly releases a snap to his first baseman.

2.38
Once the ball is on the way to first base, the second baseman should push off of his left leg to clear his cleats from the ground. This prevents the base runner from taking him out on his slide.

left foot on the base to record the out. As the ball is transitioned to the throwing hand, the player's right foot lands across the base and the left foot follows, creating a good power position to first base. The second baseman uses good throwing mechanics to efficiently release the ball to first base **(Figures 2.35, 2.36, 2.37, 2.38)**.

Flaw: When a second baseman is in a hurry, he sets himself up for problems. If he incorrectly anticipates a good feed and starts across the base, a poor feed can tie up his hands and feet. This can cause the pivot to fail or to be performed significantly slower.

Secret: When possible, the second baseman wants to take his right foot across the base, moving it closer to first base. However, an advanced player can step straight to the ball with his right foot and make up for the loss of momentum with pure arm strength.

Second Baseman Pivot 3: Back Side Variations

This is an advanced pivot made by a second baseman. Because of the difficulty of this play and the arm strength needed to execute it effectively, players should generally avoid attempting this pivot in a game until they are in high school. Once the ball is hit, the second baseman should hustle to his base to be ready for a possible double play feed. His goal is to be there early so he can stay under control and handle all feeds.

As the second baseman approaches the base, he should widen his legs to slow down and bring his body under control. Simultaneously, he should raise his hands up while bringing his elbow close to his side. His glove should be open, with the throwing hand close by as if his thumbs were tied together with a short string, giving the fielder a good target to feed the ball. Ideally, the second baseman's right foot should be positioned on the clay next to the back corner of the base (the corner closest to center field), and his left foot should be ready to step onto the base once the feed is made. His body should be squared to the shortstop (or third baseman, if he's making the feed) with his knees and hips flexed in a good athletic position **(Figures 2.39, 2.40)**.

2.39

The second baseman should quickly move from double play depth to the bag.

2.40

The player should widen his feet to get into position with his right foot near the back corner of the base, square his shoulders to the fielder making the feed, and keep his glove up to give his teammate a target.

POWER POSITION AND THROW

Once the second baseman sees the ball heading in the air towards the back corner of the base, or away from the base to the left-field side, he should place his left foot on quadrant three of the base (see "Quadrants of second base" on the DVD) and position his right shoulder behind the arriving feed. If the ball enters the glove while the player's left foot is on the base, there is no need to tag the base again, and the second baseman can simply push off his planted right foot to make his throw. However, if the throw pulls the pivot off second base before the ball is caught, the second baseman must touch the base again with his left foot as he makes his throw to first base **(Figures 2.41, 2.42, 2.43, 2.44, 2.45)**.

2.41

The second baseman should react to a feed to the back side of the base by shifting his feet, placing his left foot on the rear of the base, and stepping with his right foot in the direction of the ball to make the catch.

Flaw: A second baseman should not worry about avoiding the base runner with his throw to first base. It is the base runner's responsibility to slide or avoid getting hit with the throw.

Secret: After he releases the ball to first base, the second baseman can stay behind the base; this will protect him from the sliding base runner.

2.42

The player should quickly take the ball out of his glove while bringing his body into a power position towards first base.

2.43

If the second baseman catches the ball while his left foot is in contact with the base, he can throw to first base without touching the base again.

2.44 The fielder should throw the ball directly to first base. It is the base runner's responsibility to slide, to avoid being stuck by the ball.

2.45 Once the ball is on the way to first base, the fielder should use the base to create a barrier between him and the base runner sliding into the bag.

Second Baseman Pivot 4: Reverse

This is an advanced pivot made by a second baseman. Because of the difficulty of this play and the footwork and arm strength required, middle-school-aged players should generally avoid attempting this pivot in a game. Once the ball is hit, the second baseman should hustle to his base to be ready for a possible double play feed. His goal is to be there early so he can stay under control and handle all feeds.

As the second baseman approaches the base, he should widen his legs to slow down and bring his body under control. Simultaneously, he should raise

2.46 The second baseman should quickly move from double play depth to the bag.

his hands up while bringing his elbow close to his side. His glove should be open, with the throwing hand close by as if his thumbs were tied together with a short string, giving the fielder a good target to feed the ball. Ideally, his right foot should be positioned on the clay next to the back corner of the base (the corner closest to center field), and his left foot should be on the base or ready to step onto the base once the feed is delivered. His body should be squared to the shortstop (or third baseman, whichever player is making the feed) with his knees and hips flexed in a good athletic position **(Figures 2.46, 2.47)**.

2.47

The player should widen his feet to get into position with his right foot near the back corner of the base. He should square his shoulders to the shortstop, and keep his glove up to give his teammate a target.

POWER POSITION AND THROW

Once the second baseman sees that the ground ball is headed up the middle of the field behind second base (slightly to the shortstop side), he must adjust his footwork to receive a difficult feed from his teammate. He moves his right foot to touch the base, and simultaneously squares his shoulders to follow the path of his shortstop. The second baseman will end up with his back facing first base and the oncoming base runner. If the feed from the shortstop is off line or slow, the second baseman acts as a first baseman and stretches for the ball with his left foot to record the forced out. Once the feed is received, the fielder should use the base as a natural barrier to avoid the cleats of the base runner sliding into second base.

An advanced variation of the play can be attempted if the feed from the shortstop is strong and accurate, and the base runner heading to first base is slow. The second baseman can choose to quickly switch his feet in order to receive the ball, with his left foot in contact with the base for the forced out. This will enable him to efficiently adjust his body into a power position to make his pivot throw to first base. Some advanced players prefer to keep their right foot on the base to make this play, and quickly adjust their footwork after securing the forced out. Either way, the player must quickly and accurately release the ball to complete the double play **(Figures 2.48, 2.49, 2.50, 2.51)**.

2.48

If the second baseman realizes there is no chance to turn the double play, he should adjust his footwork to place his right foot on the back of the base.

2.49

If the second basemen feels that he still has a chance to turn a double play, he adjusts his footwork to place his left foot on the base to create a better throwing position.

2.50

The player receives the feed to assure one out on the play at second base, then spins his body to throw to first base in attempt to turn two.

2.51

Once the player releases the throw, he should attempt to use the base to protect him from the base runner sliding into second base.

SECOND BASEMAN FEEDS

A feed from a second baseman consists of fielding a ground ball to any part of the right side of the infield, and delivering an underhand or overhand throw to the shortstop in an attempt to turn a double play. We will cover five specific second baseman feeds, two of which are appropriate for all players ages 11 and up (Figure 2.52).

 Refer to Advanced: "Infield Skills and Drills," choose "Double Play Feeds and Pivots," and then "Second Baseman Feeds" on the DVD for detailed interactive instruction on the five types of feeds made by the second baseman.

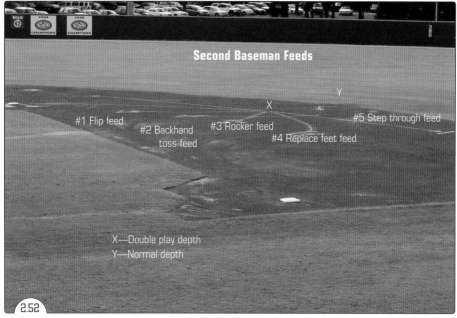

This photo demonstrates the five double play feeds a high school second baseman would be responsible for executing.

The following is the advanced skill progression needed for middle school and high school infielders to execute double play feeds from the second base position.

Second Baseman Feed 1: Flip

This is a basic double play feed made by a second baseman to a shortstop when the ground ball is hit at or to the right of the second baseman. Because the momentum of the play takes the second baseman towards his base, he ideally should make the feeds underhand.

If there is time, the player should charge the ground ball and get into a good fielding position. This creates momentum that will be used to make the flip feed. If the ball is hit right at him and he chooses to use a flip feed, he can slightly round off the ball to create momentum towards second base. The fielder should shout "flip, flip, flip" to let the shortstop know the ball will be delivered underhand (Figures 2.53, 2.54).

Flaw: The second baseman should not wait for the ground ball to come to him before making the flip feed. This would allow base runners more time to beat the throw to second and the subsequent pivot to first base.

Secret: When the ground ball is fielded very close to the base, the second baseman should turn the double play unassisted. This means he lets his

2.53

The second baseman should close the distance to the ground ball to his right side while creating momentum towards the flip feed to the shortstop.

2.54

Whenever possible, the fielder should create a good position to consistently receive the ball in front of his body.

shortstop know he is taking the play himself. After catching the ball, he simply steps on the base, throws to first base, and gets out of the way of the oncoming base runner.

Secret: When the ground ball is close to second base but too far for the second baseman to turn the double play unassisted, he should put a soft touch on his feed by giving it an arc right over the base. This allows the shortstop to handle the flip feed from the second baseman with ease. As a result, the shortstop can accelerate the ball through the air and quickly transition to throw to first base to complete the double play.

SEPARATION
Teach the second baseman how to correctly field the ball with both hands working together so he can quickly separate the ball from the glove. Once the ball is in his bare hand, the fielder should create space between the glove and ball in order for the shortstop to easily see the feed (**Figure 2.55**).

DELIVERY
To avoid wasting time, the second baseman should stay low to the ground, gradually raising his body through the delivery of the flip feed. When the ball is in hand, the fielder's wrist should lock in order to decrease the ball's rotation as he simultaneously pulls his glove into his chest to expose the ball to the shortstop. The fielder should use his leg strength to continue momentum towards second base and release a firm feed in the direction of the back corner of the base (the corner closest to the right field). A good flip feed should be received by the shortstop somewhere from belt- to chest-high (**Figure 2.56**).

2.55

The second baseman should quickly separate the ball from the glove to make the flip feed to the shortstop.

2.56

The second baseman's legs should generate momentum as he flips the ball underhand with a locked wrist to his shortstop.

2.57

After the feed is made, the second baseman should continue his momentum created in the play.

FOLLOW

Once the feed has been released to the shortstop, the second baseman should maintain his momentum by continuing past second base **(Figure 2.57)**.

Second Baseman Feed 2: Backhand Toss

This is an advanced feed made by a second baseman to a shortstop when the second baseman has positioned himself in double play depth closer to first base, and the ground ball is hit at or to his right. Because the momentum of the play takes the second baseman in the direction of his base, he ideally should make a backhand toss feed, instead of a flip feed, to compensate for the greater distance the feed has to travel.

When approaching the ground ball, he should gradually lower his body and keep his throwing hand nearby to make a quick transition from the glove. Teach your second baseman to charge the ground ball, if there is time, and to get into a good fielding position. This creates momentum that will be used to make the backhand toss feed. If the ball is hit directly to the second baseman, and he chooses to use a backhand toss feed, he can slightly round off the ball to create momentum to second base. The fielder should shout "toss, toss, toss" to let the shortstop know the ball will be delivered with a backhand toss **(Figures 2.58, 2.59, 2.60)**.

2.58

The second baseman should close the distance to the ball and create momentum to execute the backhand toss feed.

Flaw: The second baseman should not wait for a routine ground ball to come to him before making the backhand toss feed. This gives base runners more time to beat the throw to second and the subsequent pivot to first base. It also makes it much tougher to create the speed the released ball needs to reach the shortstop.

Secret: The backhand toss feed should be delivered very firmly to the shortstop. The extra pace on the ball will make it easier for the shortstop to handle it when a base runner is bearing down on him.

2.59

The player should gradually lower down and present his open glove to the ball. His throwing hand should start to move closer to the glove to be ready for the transition.

2.60

Whenever possible, the second baseman should create a good field position and receive the ground ball out in front of his body.

2.61

The second baseman should point his throwing elbow where he wants to deliver his backhand toss feed to the shortstop.

2.62

The second baseman should use his momentum to generate explosiveness to feed the ball over the bag to start a double play.

SEPARATION

Teach the second baseman how to correctly field the ball with both hands working together to quickly separate the ball from the glove. Once the ball is in his bare hand, the fielder should point his throwing elbow at his target **(Figure 2.61)**.

DELIVERY

To save time, the second baseman should stay low to the ground, gradually raising his body through the delivery of the backhand toss feed. He must also use his leg strength to generate increased momentum on the feed. He must then accelerate the ball to the shortstop while simultaneously pulling his glove back from the feed and into his rib cage **(Figure 2.62)**.

Flaw: If a player incorrectly uses a backhand toss feed when he is very close to the shortstop, it can put the shortstop on the defensive as he attempts to execute his pivot.

Secret: Some second basemen prefer to execute this style of feed on any ground ball coming at them or to their right side. To effectively use this type of feed at a close distance, the fielder must develop a soft touch so he can lay the ball up in front of the shortstop, who can accelerate his body through the ball when executing his pivot.

FOLLOW

Once the feed has been released to the shortstop, the second baseman should maintain his momentum by continuing past second base **(Figure 2.63)**.

Flaw: When the second baseman stops while releasing the feed to his shortstop, the momentum needed to enhance his accuracy is destroyed.

2.63

After the backhand toss feed is made, the player should continue his momentum by moving to a point past second base.

Second Baseman Feed 3: Rocker

This is an advanced feed made by a second baseman to a shortstop when the ball is hit at or to the left of the second baseman, and he has time to set his feet before making the throw to the shortstop. Because the momentum of the play takes the second baseman away from his base, he should make the feed overhand. Teach your second baseman to move to the left and cut down the distance to the ground ball if there is time. The key is to get into a good fielding position to receive the ball. The second baseman will slightly drop his right foot back (right toe to left heel) before the ball is caught to position his hips where they can freely rotate to make the feed to second base **(Figures 2.64, 2.65)**.

Flaw: If the second baseman sets his feet too early and has to wait for the routine ground ball to come to him, it puts him in danger of receiving a bad hop while sacrificing the time needed to turn the double play.

Flaw: If the second baseman fields the ball underneath him (which boxes his glove and throwing hand inside his knees), it will be difficult to make a quick exchange of the ball.

Flaw: When the second baseman fields the ball with his right foot in front of his left foot, his hips will lock, which forces him to move his right foot or both feet to make a good feed. This wastes time.

Flaw: The second baseman should avoid rushing and make sure to field the ball cleanly before attempting to make the rocker feed to his shortstop.

2.64

The second baseman's goal is to pre-set his feet with his right foot slightly back from his left foot to avoid wasting time when implementing the rocker feed.

2.65

The player should create a proper fielding position and catch the ball out in front of his body.

SEPARATION

Teach the second baseman how to correctly field the ball with both hands working together in front of his body to quickly separate the ball from the glove. The fielder should remain at the same level he fielded the ball to save time. Once the ball is in his bare hand, the fielder should clear his glove to make the ball visible to the shortstop **(Figure 2.66)**.

Flaw: The second baseman should not raise or lower his body before making the feed to second base. This wastes time and can alter the accuracy of the feed.

2.66

The second baseman should separate the ball from his glove while maintaining his body height so that he is in a position to make an accurate rocker feed to shortstop.

Flaw: The second baseman should not take extra steps, after catching the ball, to get into position to make the feed. This also wastes time.

Flaw: If the fielder allows the momentum that was created getting to the ground ball to incorrectly continue through the fielding process, he may be put off balance while making the feed to second base.

DELIVERY

The second baseman should quickly snap his wrist to throw to the corner of second base closest to right field. At the same time, he should bring his glove to his (glove-side) ribs, which helps create torque for his throw. The shortstop should receive the ball somewhere between belt- to chest-high **(Figure 2.67)**.

2.67

The second baseman should quickly and accurately snap his feed to his shortstop.

2.68

The second baseman should take a good crossover step to gain ground to his left.

Flaw: If the second baseman winds up to deliver a hard throw to the shortstop, he will waste time, and may end up disturbing the footwork and transition of the pivot at second base.

Second Baseman Feed 4: Replace Feet

This is a basic double play feed made by a second baseman. It is a slight variation of the rocker feed but modified due to the speed at which the ground ball is hit or the distance that the fielder must cover to get to the play. The best time to implement the replace feet feed is when a very hard ground ball or a one-hopper (a ball that bounces once) is hit to the left of the second baseman. Because the momentum of the play takes the second baseman away from his base, he should make the feed overhand. The fielder cannot allow the ball to get past him, so teach your fielder to get in front of the ball at all costs. The player should attempt to field the ball with perfect mechanics without presetting his feet to speed up the feed, as executed with the rocker feed. The key is to get into a good fielding position to make sure the second baseman catches the ball before concerning himself with the footwork needed to complete his feed (**Figures 2.68, 2.69, 2.70**).

SEPARATION

As with previous feeds, teach the second baseman how to correctly field the ball with both hands working together in front of the body to quickly separate the ball from the glove. At the same time, he will quickly move both feet simultaneously to a position perpendicular to second base in order to clear his hips to make the feed to that base. The fielder should remain at the same level at which he fielded the ball to save time. Once the ball is in his bare hand,

2.69

The fielder should lower his body to the ball as he starts to present his open glove to make the catch.

2.70

The second baseman should create a perfect fielding position, focusing first on catching the ball cleanly.

the fielder should clear his glove to make the ball visible to the shortstop **(Figure 2.71)**.

Flaw: The second baseman should not rise up or lower down before making the feed to his shortstop.

Flaw: The second baseman should not take extra steps to get into position for the feed to second base.

Secret: Because of the speed of the batted ball, the second baseman may be a little bit off-balance as he fields the ball. Therefore, he must use his lower body strength to fight inertia to get his feet and upper body under control to make the feed.

2.71

Once the ball has been fielded, the second baseman should quickly separate the ball from his glove while simultaneously shifting both feet to square his body with second base.

DELIVERY

The second baseman should quickly snap his wrist to release the feed to the corner of second base closest to left field. At the same time, he should bring his glove to his (glove-side) ribs to help create torque for his throw. The shortstop should receive the ball somewhere between belt- to chest-high **(Figures 2.72, 2.73)**.

2.72

The second baseman should use his lower body strength to stop momentum and rotation while preparing to use his upper body to throw the ball.

2.73

The player should attempt to maintain close to the same height as he fielded the ball when he makes his feed to the shortstop.

Second Baseman Feed 5: Step Through 🎓

This is an advanced feed made by a second baseman. Due to the difficulty of this play, middle-school-aged players should generally avoid attempting this feed in a game and focus on making the easier play to first base. When the ball is hit very hard to the left of the second baseman, he must implement a good crossover step and take a good angle to the ball. Because the player must field the ball when extended to his glove side, he will not have time to set his feet for a feed. The first priority is to make sure he lowers his body to the ball and secures the ball in his glove.

Since the momentum of the play takes the fielder away from second base, he should make the feed overhand to his shortstop **(Figures 2.74, 2.75)**.

2.74

The second baseman should take a good crossover step and establish an appropriate angle to the ball to get into a good glove-side fielding position.

2.75

The player must lower his body to the ground and follow the ball into his glove to ensure that he makes the catch before he can concern himself with a possible feed to second base.

Flaw: If a fielder is in a rush to throw to second base to start the double play, he will not field the ball cleanly and both base runners may end up safe.

Secret: When a player does not field the ball cleanly, he must abort any thought of turning a double play and focus on getting the out at first base.

SEPARATION

After making the catch, the second baseman should quickly bring both of his hands together to move the ball from the glove into his throwing hand while turning his back to the infield. Simultaneously, he must adjust his feet and upper body to a position where he can make the feed. If he fields the ball with his left foot in front, he can quickly adjust both feet to a position perpendicular to second base to square his hips and shoulders to make a snap throw. If he fields the ball with his right foot in front, he has two options. The first is to plant his right foot and immediately turn his shoulders to second base to throw. The second option is to take one more step with the left foot, and then quickly adjust both feet to a position perpendicular to second base to square his hips and shoulders to make a snap throw **(Figure 2.76)**.

2.76

The second baseman should quickly turn his back to the infield and adjust his feet to a position perpendicular to second base while separating the ball from the glove.

DELIVERY

The second baseman should quickly snap his wrist to release the feed directly over second base. At the same time, he should bring his glove to his (glove-side) ribs to help create torque for his throw. The shortstop should assess the probability of completing the double play. His first priority is getting the out; therefore, he may act in a manner similar to the first baseman and stretch for the forced out. If he feels he has a chance to make the turn, he will complete the pivot **(Figures 2.77, 2.78)**.

SHORTSTOP PIVOTS

A pivot from a shortstop consists of receiving a feed from the second baseman or first baseman for a forced out at second base, and quickly making a relay throw to first base for the second forced out needed to turn a double play. We explain three specific shortstop pivots, two of which are appropriate for players ages 11 and up, and one that is appropriate for players ages 15 and up **(Figure 2.79)**.

2.77

The second baseman should use his lower body strength to stop momentum and rotation while he prepares his upper body to throw the ball.

2.78

When the player makes his feed to the shortstop, he should try to stay close to the same height as he fielded the ball.

2.79

This photo demonstrates the path that the shortstop takes to second base to be in the position to execute one of his three possible double play pivots.

 Refer to "Advanced: Infield Skills and Drills," then choose "Double Play Feeds and Pivots," and then "Shortstop Pivots" on the DVD for detailed interactive instruction on the three types of pivots made by shortstops.

The following is the advanced skill progression needed for middle school and high school infielders to execute double play pivots from the shortstop position.

Shortstop Pivot 1: Back Foot Drag

This is the most fundamental double play pivot used by a shortstop when the ball is hit on the ground to the right side of the infield (to the second baseman or first baseman). Once the ball is hit, the shortstop should hustle to second base to be ready for a possible double play feed. His goal is to be there early, so he can stay under control and handle all feeds. As the shortstop approaches the base, he should widen his legs to slow down and lower his center of gravity to bring his body under control. Simultaneously, he should raise his hands while bringing his elbow close to his side. His glove should be open with the throwing hand close by, as if his thumbs were tied together with a short string, giving the fielder a good target to feed the ball. Ideally, the shortstop's right foot should be positioned on the clay behind the base (the side facing left-center field), and his left foot should fall just outside the corner of the base facing center field, ready to step towards the throw. His body should be squared to the player making the feed, with his knees and hips flexed in a good athletic position (**Figures 2.80, 2.81**).

2.80
The shortstop should be positioned in double play depth and react quickly to second base when the ball is hit to the pitcher, first baseman, or second baseman.

2.81
As the fielder nears second base, he should get under control and give his teammate a target by raising his hands to where he would like to receive the feed.

2.82

The shortstop should simultaneously step to the feed with his left foot while receiving the ball, making sure to keep his throwing hand close to the glove for a quick transition.

BAG SWIPE

When the shortstop recognizes the feed is on target, he should step to the ball with his left foot while reaching out to receive the ball with his glove, being careful not to lock his arms. Simultaneously, his right foot should drag or swipe across the back of the base to record the first out of the double play **(Figure 2.82)**.

Flaw: If the shortstop allows momentum to take him towards right field, he will wind up in an awkward position to make his throw to first base.

Flaw: If the shortstop reaches for a feed with his glove, and his throwing hand is nowhere near the glove, he will waste time moving the ball from the glove to his throwing hand.

Flaw: If the player receives the feed with one or both of his arms locked straight in front of his body, the transfer of the ball from the glove to the throwing hand will take longer, thus requiring extra steps before he throws the ball to first base.

Secret: The shortstop should track the feed, judge its accuracy, and let it travel to the base before accelerating his body through the pivot to complete the double play.

Secret: Most advanced shortstops don't actually catch the ball when making a pivot. They simply re-direct it from the leather of the inside of the glove (without closing the glove) to the throwing hand to make the quick throw.

POWER POSITION

As the shortstop drags his right foot across the back of the base, he should use his lower body strength to counteract inertia or momentum. This allows him to redirect his body into a good power position to first base, and make a quick, accurate throw **(Figures 2.83, 2.84, 2.85)**.

Flaw: When throwing to first base, the shortstop should not worry about avoiding the base runner. It is the runner's job to slide and get out of the way of the throw.

Secret: A quick, firm release is better than a muscled-up hard throw. It is not the force of the throw to first base that matters; it is how quickly the shortstop can get the ball out of his possession and on its way to first base.

Shortstop Pivot 2: Left Foot On 🎓

This is an advanced pivot made by a shortstop to handle some feeds made by the first baseman, and, in special instances, the second baseman or pitcher. Because of the difficulty of this play, including the

2.83

The shortstop should use his right foot to swipe the back of second base and redirect his body into a good power position.

footwork and arm strength needed, middle-school-aged players should generally avoid attempting this pivot in a game. Once the ball is hit on the ground to the right side of the infield, and the shortstop recognizes the play will be made in front of the base path between first and second base, the shortstop

2.84

The player's momentum should clear him from the path of the oncoming base runner as he makes his throw to first base.

2.85

Once the throw has been released, the shortstop should remove his cleats from the ground by pushing off his left foot to lift his body into the air.

2.86

The shortstop should quickly move from his double play depth position to the bag.

2.87

The player should widen his feet to bring his body under control. He should move to the inside of second base (mound side), place his left foot near or on the bag, bring his glove up with throwing hand close by, and square his shoulders to the first baseman.

should hustle to second base for a possible double play feed. His goal is to be there early so he can stay under control and handle all feeds. As the short-stop approaches the base, he should widen his legs to slow down and bring his body under control to the infield grass side of second base. Simultaneously, he should raise his hands while bringing his elbow close to his side. His glove should be open with the throwing hand close by, giving the fielder a good target to feed the ball. Ideally, his right foot should be positioned on the clay next to the front side of the base (the side closest to third base), and his left foot should be ready to step on to the base once the feed is made. His body should be squared to the player making the feed. His knees and his hips should be flexed, and his body should be in a good athletic position **(Figures 2.86, 2.87)**.

Flaw: If the shortstop commits to the right-field side of second base, as with the back foot drag pivot, he will wind up in an awkward position to turn the double play, and the first baseman will be forced to throw the ball across the path of the base runner.

Flaw: The shortstop should never throw the ball to first base in an attempt to complete the double play if no one is covering the bag. The shortstop has the field of play in his view so he should be able to recognize whether someone is covering first base before he releases the ball.

2.88

Once the shortstop has received the feed, he should quickly step off the base with his left foot to create his power position.

2.89

The player should accurately throw to first base to complete the double play.

Secret: The shortstop should make sure he gets the first out at second base before concerning himself with a throw to first base.

Secret: An advanced shortstop will recognize who is covering first base (the first baseman or the pitcher), sense if he is not at the bag yet, and throw the ball with a softer pace to give his teammate time to set up and make the catch for the second out of the double play.

POWER POSITION AND THROW

Once the shortstop sees the ball heading in the air to the middle or front corner of the base, he simply places his left foot on quadrant four (as taught on the DVD) of the base and raises his hands to the ball. The

2.90

Once the ball has been thrown, the shortstop should release his cleats from the ground by pushing up off of his left foot.

feed is received with hands together, elbows relaxed; the player's left foot stays on the base to record the out. As the ball is transitioned to the throwing hand, the player's left foot drops beside the base (out of the way of the oncoming base runner), creating a good power position to first base. The shortstop uses good throwing mechanics to quickly make the relay throw to first base to record the second out on the play **(Figures 2.88, 2.89, 2.90)**.

Flaw: The shortstop can get in trouble if he rushes by anticipating a good feed to the infield side and commits his footwork too early in that direction. If the feed ends up being poor, the player will have to change his position; this will likely cause the pivot to be performed significantly slower.

Secret: When possible, the shortstop can release his cleats from the clay after his throw by pushing off of his left leg. This will help to protect his knees in the event the base runner slides out of the baseline and into him.

Shortstop Pivot 3: Take It Yourself

This is an advanced pivot made by a shortstop. This play avoids an unnecessary feed to the second baseman on a double play ball fielded near second base. Because of the difficulty of this play, including the timing, lower body control, footwork, and arm strength needed, middle-school-aged players should generally avoid attempting this pivot in a game (unless they just happen to catch the ball a step or two from second base). When the shortstop recognizes the ball is hit up the middle, he must execute a crossover step and create a good angle to intersect the ball. He must lower his body to make the catch cleanly, and then redirect his momentum in order to touch second base

2.91

The shortstop should take a crossover step to create a good angle to the ground ball.

2.92

The player must make sure he catches the ball by watching it enter his glove. He must then use his lower body strength to redirect his momentum towards second base.

2.93

The shortstop should verbally communicate with his second baseman by yelling, "mine, mine, mine" and touch the bag for the first out.

to start the double play. The shortstop must verbally communicate with his second baseman, "mine, mine, mine," so the second baseman will stay out of the way. **(Figures 2.91, 2.92, 2.93)**.

POWER POSITION AND THROW

Once the shortstop fields the ball, he generally has two choices about the footwork to implement for the pivot. His first choice is to continue the momentum and direction used to catch the ball across the back of the base for the unassisted pivot. He should establish lower body control to swipe his right foot across the back side of the base; this puts him into a power position to quickly start the double play relay to first base.

The other option is to transfer the momentum and direction the shortstop used to get to the ball to continue to second base for the unassisted pivot. He should gain lower body control and throw the ball to first just before arriving at second base. The shortstop's left foot should land on the back side of second base as he throws to record the first out, and then he should push off the base once the ball is released so he can create distance between the base and the oncoming base runner. He can also jump into the air by pushing off with his left foot to release his cleats; this protects his knees in the event the base runner slides past the base, creating contact **(Figures 2.94, 2.95)**.

2.94

The player should accurately throw to first base to complete the double play.

2.95

Once the ball has been thrown, the shortstop should release his cleats from the ground by pushing up off of his left foot.

Work through the following double play drills and practice ideas to reinforce good feed and pivot mechanics.

Specific Double Play Drills

Box feed—Improves the mechanics of various feeds made by the shortstop and second basemen by employing many repetitions in a short period of time. The coach creates a square, placing cones 15 to 30 feet apart (or a big triangle if there are only three players). Flip feeds are made at a shorter distance between cones. Rocker feeds, backhand feeds, and step-through feeds are made with greater distances between cones. One fielder goes to each cone to use it as his station or starting point for each feed. The coach should have players work on one particular feed at a time. The ball starts in the glove of one player, who creates a perfect fielding position at his cone. When ready, the fielder makes the desired feed using the appropriate mechanics. He should deliver the ball to his left to simulate a feed made by a shortstop, and to his right to simulate a feed made by a second baseman. When the partner at the next cone (station) catches the ball, that player continues the pattern of the drill by getting into a fielding position and making the same feed to the subsequent player. The process continues around the square until the coach stops it. Start with feeds made by the shortstop and then progress to feeds made by the second baseman.

Box pivots— Improves the mechanics of various pivots made by the shortstop and second baseman by employing many repetitions in a short period of time. The coach creates a square, placing throw-down bases or cones 30 to 40 feet apart (create a big triangle if there are only three players). One fielder goes to each base; he will use the base for practicing the correct footwork for each pivot. The coach should instruct players to work on one particular pivot at a time. One player starts the rotation by throwing a simulated feed to his partner, who executes the proper mechanics of a pivot. However, after making the pivot, the partner should simulate the throw to first base instead of actually throwing the ball. This way, the most recent player to execute a pivot can start the drill again by making a simulated feed to the next base. The ball will eventually work its way around to the square and back to the starting point. For example, the player to the left positions his feet for a "left foot on—left foot off" pivot of a second baseman. The player with the ball throws it overhand to his teammate, who then executes that pivot and finishes with a simulated throw to first base. Once the simulated throw is complete, it is that player's turn to start the drill again. He throws the ball to the player to his left, who executes the same pivot and simulates his throw to first base. The most recent player to execute the pivot and simulated throw becomes the next person to start the drill over, and the ball eventually makes its way around the square, back to the starting point.

Additional Double Play Practice

A. Dry feeds—The coach or parent chooses the particular shortstop or second baseman feed to work on. He starts the player in a perfect fielding position, as if he has already moved to the ball and fielded it. The player begins with a ball resting in his glove to remove the element of a moving ball. On command, the middle infielder uses proper mechanics to execute the desired feed. This allows the player to concentrate on the actions of his lower and upper body to successfully complete the play.

B. Dry pivots—The coach or parent starts the shortstop or second baseman at double play depth with the ball in the player's glove. On command, the middle infielder quickly approaches second base and simulates receiving a feed from his teammate. This allows the fielder to concentrate on the footwork of the pivot without worrying about receiving the actual feed. The player finishes the executed pivot by making a throw to first base.

C. Rolled feeds—The coach chooses the particular shortstop or second baseman feed to work on. He starts the middle infielder at double play depth. The player moves his feet to field the rolled ball, and executes the mechanics of the desired feed.

D. Controlled pivots—The coach or parent starts the shortstop or second baseman in double play depth. On command, the middle infielder breaks to second base, ready to make the pivot. When the player nears the base, the adult makes a throw (simulated feed) for the shortstop or second baseman to execute a pivot. The fielder can finish the pivot by simulating a throw to first base, making an actual throw to a first baseman, or throwing to a screen at first base.

E. Modified double plays—All shortstops form a line, one behind another, at the shortstop double play depth position. All second basemen form a line, one behind another, at the second base double play depth position. A coach chooses one particular feed to work on at a time. He repeatedly rolls the ball to the desired location, and the fielder executes the feed while a teammate performs the correct pivot at second base. Once fielders show proficiency with their feed and pivot mechanics, the coach can back up and repeat the process with a fungo bat at home plate.

F. Stopwatch double plays—All infielders start at their double play depth position. One coach hits various double play balls to random infield positions. Another coach starts a stopwatch when the ball hits the bat to start the ground ball. The watch is stopped when the ball is caught by the first baseman. All double plays should be executed in less than four seconds on a regulation ball diamond.

CHAPTER 3

ADVANCED PLAY FOR FIRST AND THIRD BASES

Myth #1: ON ANY TEAM, FIRST BASEMEN AND THIRD BASEMEN ARE INTERCHANGEABLE BECAUSE THESE TWO POSITIONS REQUIRE VERY SIMILAR SKILL SETS.

Secret: *This is partially true. Most third basemen can play first base, however, the opposite is not usually true. Third base requires a strong arm, quick reflexes, and the ability to throw on the run. First basemen can be less mobile and typically don't require the arm strength of their corner infield counterpart.*

Myth #2: GENERAL INFIELD DRILLS (USED BY ALL INFIELDERS) ARE ENOUGH TO PREPARE CORNER INFIELDERS FOR THE SPECIFIC HIGH-LEVEL EXECUTION OF THIRD BASE AND FIRST BASE PLAY.

Secret: *All infielders should execute a series of "general" fielding drills to improve their overall mechanics and instincts. However, in addition, corner infielders should execute a separate series of drills that are specific to the skills needed to play either first base or third base.*

Myth #3: FIRST BASE IS THE EASIEST OF THE FOUR INFIELD POSITIONS TO PLAY. THEREFORE, AS LONG AS THE PROSPECT CAN CATCH THE BALL EFFICIENTLY, HE POSSESSES THE SKILL SET NEEDED TO BECOME AN ADVANCED FIRST BASEMAN.

Secret: *The position of first base is critical at any level. This is especially true at the highest levels of the baseball. When the other infielders know they just need to get the ball close to first base and it will be caught, it allows them to play with added confidence.*

FIRST AND THIRD BASE DEVELOPMENT

Once a player reaches the middle school level, high school level, or above, his skill set, based on his position, must become more specific and precise. Games are won and lost based on individual performance at first and third base. It takes much more than hitting ground balls every day to prepare corner infielders for what they are expected to execute under game pressure to help their team win close games. The old adage, "baseball is a game of inches," is especially true when it comes to corner infield execution. For example, a first baseman who pulls his foot off the base when receiving a throw—or a third baseman who is incorrectly positioned—may open the door for the offense to drop a drag bunt down the third base line. This chapter will focus on the specific skills and related drills needed to be an advanced corner infielder. Keep in mind that all the infield skills taught in chapter one are critical to first and third base play.

FIRST BASE

At the middle and high school levels, the first baseman becomes a critical position in the infield. A superior first baseman will usually make the difference between winning and losing close ball games for his team. When the third baseman, shortstop, and second baseman trust the abilities of their first baseman, they, too, perform better because of the confidence he inspires. For instance, if the other fielders know they can make a bad throw and the ball will still be caught, it allows them to play loose. On the contrary, when fielders think their first baseman needs a good throw or the play won't be made, they play tight because anything less than perfect throws will cost the team an error.

It is critical that coaches spend practice time with their first basemen. As with all other defensive positions, first basemen must practice their specific skills. These include basic footwork around the base, stretching for the ball, picking up balls thrown in the dirt, making tags on errant throws that take the fielder into the path of the base runner, starting double plays, making feeds to pitchers covering the first base bag, and catching fly balls in foul territory, just to name a few.

 Refer to "Advanced: Infield Skills and Drills" and then "First Base Play" on the DVD for detailed interactive instruction.

The following is the advanced skill progression needed for middle school and high school fielders to play the position of first base.

Footwork at First Base

Teach the first baseman to move quickly to the base when the ball is hit to the infield. The player should place his throwing-side heel up on the front side of first base (the side parallel to the foul line) to create a safe distance from the base runner, who will pass behind him in attempt to beat the play. In addition, the first baseman should widen his stance so his heels are near each corner of the base (or his throwing-side foot can be in the middle of the base), square his body to face the person making the throw, remain relaxed, and be ready to stretch for a good throw or react to a bad throw **(Figure 3.1)**.

Flaw: If the first baseman places his heels against the side of first base, his throwing-side foot will no longer touch the base when he stretches to make the catch, and the base runner will be safe.

Secret: It is easier to rise up than it is to lower down to make a low catch. Therefore, the first baseman should keep his body in an athletic position, consciously carrying himself with a low center of gravity.

Receiving Throws

The first baseman should wait to see if the throw is on target before stretching to catch the ball. When the thrown baseball is close to first base, the player must stride towards the ball with his glove-side foot, and reach with the glove to meet and receive the baseball at the farthest possible distance from first base. The first baseman's throwing-side foot must stay on the side of the base for the forced out.

3.1

The first baseman should quickly get to the base, place his throwing-side heel on the outside front corner of the base, and square his body to the person throwing the ball.

When receiving throws off the baseline, first basemen should be taught how to adjust their feet on the base to increase their reach in the direction of the throw. To receive a throw to the right-field side of the base, the first baseman should shift both heels to the far side (outfield side) of the base before stretching to catch the ball. To receive a throw to the home-plate side of the base, the first baseman should shift both heels to the infield side of the base before stretching to catch the ball. Again, it is critical that a first baseman keeps his throwing-side foot on the base to record a possible forced out. If the throw requires him to vacate the base, he should come off the base, make the catch, and if there is time, attempt to tag the base runner. Whenever a first baseman tags a runner, he should spin with the base runner's momentum to disseminate some of the energy of a possible collision, to decrease the odds of a potential injury, and to reduce the chance of the ball coming out of his glove **(Figures 3.2, 3.3, 3.4)**.

3.2

The first baseman should wait for the ball to get close to the base before stretching to receive the throw.

3.3

Teach first basemen how to adjust their footwork to the outfield side in order to catch a ball thrown off-target.

Flaw: Some first basemen stretch for the ball but actually catch the ball close to their body, which defeats the purpose of stretching while wasting valuable time.

Flaw: Some first basemen stretch violently for the ball, which pulls their throwing-side foot off the base before the catch and jeopardizes the forced out.

Flaw: Some first basemen prematurely stretch for the throw, and then realize it's not accurate. They com-

3.4

First basemen can also adjust their footwork to the infield side to catch a ball thrown to the home plate side of the base.

pound the problem by incorrectly attempting to adjust to the ball by reaching out to the side with their glove, but this doesn't always work. The result is often an errant throw, or the base runner is safe.

Picking Balls in the Dirt

Picking or digging an errant throw out of the dirt is the most difficult catch to teach first basemen. Some throws will bounce somewhere before the base. First basemen must be taught the fundamentals of how to execute a pick,

3.5

The first baseman should get to the base and square himself up to the infielder making the throw.

3.6

When the player senses that the throw will bounce in the dirt, he should lower his center of gravity to prepare to stretch and make the pick.

3.7

The player should keep his glove palm towards the ground as long as possible when picking the ball out of the dirt.

and they must work related drills to gain the instincts and confidence to accomplish this tough play. As with any ground ball, the first baseman should get to the base and use proper footwork to square himself up to the player making the throw. Once a first baseman determines that he cannot stretch to catch the ball in the air, he must bend his knees to lower his body and glove to the ground. Once the ball is close to the base, he should start the glove low to the clay and stretch to the ball, moving the glove through the hop. A short hop or a long hop by the ball is the best to field, but often the first baseman does not have a choice as to which hop he will have to handle **(Figures 3.5, 3.6, 3.7, 3.8)**.

3.8

The first baseman should extend his glove through the hop while keeping his throwing-side foot on the base for the forced out.

Flaw: If the first baseman flips his glove fingers up in the air in a scooping action, he exposes the glove wrist and forearm, and reduces the odds for a clean pick of a ball from the dirt.

3.9
The first baseman should hold base runners by creating an athletic position with both feet in fair territory, providing a good target for the pitcher.

3.10
Once the ball is caught on a pick-off attempt, the player should make a quick tag in front of first base to intercept the runner when he returns to the bag.

Secret: The baseman should attempt to "kill the hop" by keeping his glove palm parallel to the ground for as long as possible. This helps ensure that he will make the difficult pick.

Holding Base Runners

There is a specific technique for correctly holding base runners on first base and making an effective tag when the pitcher attempts a pick-off. The first baseman should give his pitcher a big throwing target by holding his glove open belt-high near the corner of first base closest to the mound. The fielder should create an athletic position with his left foot inside the foul line (in fair territory). He must remain ready to react to an errant pick-off attempt. The first baseman's highest priority is to keep any throws from getting past him. However, if the throw from the pitcher is accurate, he can put a quick tag on the base runner. To make an effective tag, the first baseman should let the throw travel to his glove, instead of reaching forward to catch the ball. This saves time and increases the chances for an out. Once the ball is secured, the first baseman should quickly tag the front of the base to allow the base runner to slide into the glove. Then the first baseman should quickly pull the glove away from the tag to show the umpire his glove with the ball. When an errant pick-off attempt pulls the first baseman off the base and into the direction of the base runner, he should quickly react out and up to avoid a collision and still make the catch (**Figures 3.9, 3.10**).

Flaw: If a base runner is obviously safe, and the first baseman snaps the tag on the runner and shows the umpire his glove with the ball, the umpire will

3.11

Once the pitcher commits his delivery to the plate, the first baseman should accelerate off the base and square himself to the plate.

3.12

The player must be ready to field his position if the ball is hit to him or to his side.

lose trust in the player. This may remove the possibility that the player can sell an out on a close pick-off attempt later in the game.

Vacating First Base

There is a specific technique to correctly hold base runners on first base, which will allow the first baseman the freedom to field his position once the ball is delivered to the plate. As the pitcher begins his delivery to the plate, the fielder will take a big step with his left foot and then rotate his right foot around to square his hips and shoulders to the batter. If there is time, the first baseman can take one or two shuffles towards second base to cover more territory in the hole that is created between him and the second baseman, while holding the runner on first **(Figures 3.11, 3.12)**.

Flaw: If the first baseman keeps moving towards second base, and never sets his feet and body to be ready to field the ball, he will have problems for his recovery and for fielding an easy ground ball hit down the line in fair territory.

Underhand Feed to Pitcher

When a ground ball is hit to the first baseman, he will usually carry the ball to the base for an unassisted "put-out," or make an underhand feed to the pitcher covering first base for the forced out. The first priority on any ground ball is to get into a good fielding position. Once the ball is secured, the first baseman should stay low, separate the ball from the glove, and use his lower

3.13

The first baseman must be in a ready position to react to the ground ball hit in his direction.

3.14

When ground balls are hit directly to the fielder, or slightly to his right or left, he must make sure he gets into a perfect fielding position.

3.15

The first baseman should keep his body low as he separates the ball from his glove to be ready to feed the pitcher covering first base.

3.16

The first baseman should use his legs to generate momentum in the direction of the feed. He should get extension and throw underhand, chest-high, to the pitcher to help him easily catch the ball and touch the base for the forced out.

body strength to create momentum for his feed. After momentum is established, the fielder should clear his glove from the ball and lock his wrist and forearm to deliver a firm toss feed (belt- to chest-high) that the pitcher can easily catch, while touching the base with his foot for the out. It is important that the first baseman maintain his momentum to first even after the feed is released. This keeps the ball moving in the intended direction **(Figures 3.13, 3.14. 3.15, 3.16)**.

Flaw: The first baseman should use his glove side to create torque needed to make a longer underhand feed to the pitcher. If he does not, and the glove-side hand does not work beside the ribs, he will lose power and direction on his feed.

3.17

The first baseman should creep into his ready position to prepare to react to a play in his direction.

3.18

The fielder should take a crossover step to initiate a good angle to the ground ball.

Secret: The first baseman should stay low to make the catch and gradually rise up as he prepares to deliver his underhand feed to the pitcher.

Overhand Feed to Pitcher

When a ground ball takes the first baseman hard to his right and moves him away from first base, his priority is to successfully field the ball. Once he secures the ball, he can turn back to the infield side, square his shoulders to the pitcher, and make an overhand feed to his moving target covering the base. The other option is for a left-handed player to spin to the outfield side, turn his back to the infield, square his shoulders to the pitcher, and make an overhand feed to his moving target covering first base. The first baseman should make his throw chest-high and then follow through his throw a few steps to help create the proper direction of the feed (**Figure 3.17, 3.18, 3.19, 3.20, 3.21**).

3.19

The first baseman should attempt to get in front of the ground ball. If that is not possible, he should either backhand (right-handed) or field it on his glove side (left-handed).

Flaw: If the first baseman throws the ball too hard, too low, or behind the pitcher, it will be very difficult for the pitcher to catch the ball and touch the base at approximately the same time.

Secret: If there is time, the first baseman should lead the pitcher with the feed in order to get him the ball before he gets to first base. This gives the pitcher

3.20

If the first baseman has time, he should get his body into a power position before making an overhand throw to his pitcher.

3.21

The fielder should lead his pitcher with a firm, chest-high overhand throw that the pitcher can catch on the way to touching first base for the forced out.

extra time to concentrate on first making the catch and then stepping on the base for the out. When a pitcher has to catch the ball, touch the base, and avoid the base runner at the same time, it can cause him to either miss the ball, the base, or both.

Secret: The first baseman should do everything to keep a ground ball from getting by him. This includes knocking down the ball any way possible. Because he is so close to first base, he should have time to pick up the ball and make a feed to the pitcher covering the bag for the out.

Starting a Double Play

This is an advanced play made by a first baseman. Because of the difficulty of this play, middle-school-aged fielders should generally avoid attempting to start a double play from first base and simply focus on getting the forced out at first base.

When there are runners on first base with less than two outs, and the ball is hit hard to the first baseman, he can start a double play in one of two ways. First, if the ground ball takes the fielder towards second base, he should field the ball cleanly, separate the ball from the glove, clear the path of the base runner advancing to second, get into a power position, and make a chest-high throw to the shortstop who is covering second base. If the first baseman has not traveled a great distance away from his base, he should attempt to retreat to first base after his throw to receive the relay there from the shortstop. However, if the play pulls the first baseman a good distance from his base, he should forfeit the bag to the pitcher, who will attempt to receive the relay

3.22

The first baseman should use good footwork to hold the runner on base.

3.23

When the pitch is delivered to the plate, the fielder should move off first base to be in a position to field a ground ball.

3.24

If possible, the first baseman should create a perfect fielding position to receive the ball in front of his body.

throw back to first base from the shortstop. *Note:* If the first baseman is right-handed, it is acceptable for the fielder to turn his back to the infield when making his throw to second base.

The second option for starting a double play is chosen when the ground ball takes the first baseman back towards first base. In this instance, he should first tag the bag for the forced out before redirecting his feet and body just inside the base line to clear the base runner going to second base. He should quickly get into a good power position to throw while simultaneously yelling, "tag, tag, tag!" He should quickly deliver the ball chest-high to his shortstop at second base for the tag out that will complete the double play **(Figures 3.22, 3.23, 3.24, 3.25, 3.26)**.

Flaw: First basemen should not stand up before starting a double play to second base because this will interfere with their momentum.

3.25 The fielder should quickly transition the ball to his throwing hand while getting his body into a power position to throw to his shortstop at second base.

3.26 The first baseman should finish his throw and continue his momentum in the direction of his throw.

Secret: A first baseman must clear the runner going to second base by moving a couple of steps towards the infield or outfield sides. He does not want to hit the base runner with his throw to the shortstop at second base.

Foul Fly Ball

First basemen are responsible for most fly balls in foul territory headed towards the first base dugout side. It is critical that the fielder keeps his eyes on the fly ball at all times. If he must look away to locate where he is on the field, he must quickly pinpoint the ball in flight. The earlier he can do this, the better. The first

3.27 The first baseman should creep into a good fielding position to be ready for a play in his direction.

baseman must quickly move his feet to the location where he feels the ball will land. This will give him the extra time needed to adjust in case he slightly misjudges the ball. It is best if the first baseman catches the ball as he moves back towards the infield in case he has to make a throw to another base **(Figures 3.27, 3.28, 3.29, 3.30, 3.31)**.

3.28

The fielder should execute a proper drop step to take a good route to the pop-up in foul territory.

3.29

If possible, the fielder should get behind the fly ball and move through the catch so he is in the best position to make a throw if base runners are aboard.

3.30

If the fielder is on the run and nears an obstacle such as a fence, he should slide feet first to attempt to make the catch to protect his body.

3.31

The first baseman should finish the catch by getting his body into a power position.

Flaw: First basemen often drift to the ball to time the catch, which may cause their momentum to pull them towards the outfield. This gives base runners an advantage if they decide to tag-up and advance to the next base.

Secret: A first baseman should check out the field before the game to determine how much foul territory he is responsible for, and look to see if there is a warning track that will alert him if he is getting close to a fence. He must also make note of any obstacles, such as an infield tarp, that he may have to navigate around to make a play. Finally, he should pay attention to the wind and sun to determine whether they will become variables that can impact a fly ball in the game.

Secret: If the fielder is on the full run and is nearing an obstacle, such as a dugout railing, he should slide feet first and attempt to make the catch in order to protect his body from injury.

Work through the following drills and practice ideas to reinforce good first base mechanics.

Specific First Base Drills

 Refer to "Advanced: Infield Skills and Drills" and then "Infield Drills" on the DVD for the following drills:

Note: First basemen should execute all the general fielding drills in chapter one under "Ground Ball Mechanics" before advancing to specific drills for first base.

A. Picks—Improve the confidence of a first baseman stretching to catch the ball in the air or in the dirt thrown from all infield positions. Two players (or more) and a coach stand 20 feet away from first base (with a ball in their glove), forming a semicircle around the base. Each feeder should be in the general direction of an infield position (third base, shortstop, second base). All three feeders alternate throwing the ball to the first baseman, who implements correct footwork at the base and stretches to make the proper catches. The first baseman then throws the ball back to the person who made the feed. Feeders should begin with throws in the air and then progress to throws in the dirt. Finally, alternate the type of throw so the first baseman learns to react to different types of throws.

B. Fungo Picks—A coach rotates around the infield, hitting ground balls at various speeds to the first baseman at the bag. The fielder must correctly position himself on the base and square himself up to the coach. He picks out the hop and makes a pick to his glove side or backhand side.

C. Fly balls—A coach positions himself on the infield grass in the general direction of home plate. He throws the ball at various speeds, heights, and in different directions to give the first baseman an opportunity to make all sorts of plays on fly balls. The fielder should attempt to catch the ball moving in towards the infield if possible. If not, he should quickly make the catch and adjust his feet and attention to the possible advancing base runners.

Additional First Base Practice

A. Errant throws and tag—Improves a first baseman's ability to catch an errant throw up the line towards the base runner and to make a corresponding tag. A coach (or teammate) should give the command for the first baseman to run to the base from his defensive position and quickly set up for a throw, facing the coach. The coach should then make an errant throw up the base line in the air or in the dirt. If the first baseman cannot stay on the base to make the catch, he should abandon the base, make the catch, and then reach back, attempting to tag the invisible base runner. Remind the fielder to spin with the runner to help avoid injury.

B. Feeding the pitcher—The first basemen form a rotation where one player acts as the pitcher covering first, and another player rolls ground balls to the third partner, who fields the ball and uses proper mechanics to make an underhand or overhand feed to the pitcher covering first base.

C. Start double plays—The first baseman starts on the base as if holding on a base runner. When the coach throws the ball into the air to hit, the first baseman should vacate the base and get into a good fielding position. Once the ground ball is hit, the first baseman should react by starting the appropriate double play.

D. Relay practice—First basemen form a rotation where one player acts like the right fielder or center fielder, another player acts like the catcher, and the final player is the actual first baseman performing the relay transition. The outfielder makes (good and bad) throws that must be handled by the first baseman. The first baseman quickly and accurately makes relay throws to the catcher to simulate throwing a runner out at the plate. The players simply rotate so each player gets a turn.

THIRD BASE

At the middle school and high school level, the defensive infield position of third base becomes more important. The skills needed to field a routine ground ball, make a backhand play, and handle a slow roller are similar to other infield positions and have been covered throughout chapter one and on the accompanying DVD. For this reason, they will not be repeated in the remaining pages of this chapter.

Ground Ball Mechanics

Please see fielding mechanics in chapter one. Third basemen use the fielding technique in the same way as all other infield positions. However, they typically don't have as much time as the shortstop or second baseman to react to a batted ball. Therefore, they generally don't round off the ball as often. The goal of a third baseman is to stay low and keep the ball in front of him even if it means playing

3.32

This player uses fundamental fielding mechanics to handle a routine ground ball hit right at him.

3.33

This player is in the process of fielding a ground ball to his backhand side.

the ball off of his body (similar to a goalie). Because middle school and high school third basemen rarely position themselves deep behind third base, but rather play even with or in front of the base, they have the time to gain momentum after the catch to make their throw to first or second base **(Figure 3.32)**.

Backhand Mechanics

Please see the "Backhand Mechanics" section in chapter one. Third basemen use the same general technique to field ground balls to their backhand side. However, they typically don't travel more than a couple of steps before receiving the ball. If the ball is hit to their backhand side, they should do everything in their power to get in front of it. A ball that gets past the third baseman, down the base line, will likely become a double for the batter **(Figure 3.33)**.

3.34

This third baseman is fielding a slow-rolling ground ball.

Slow Roller Mechanics

Please see "Slow Roller Mechanics" in chapter one. Third basemen use slow roller mechanics on a regular basis to field sacrifice bunts, drag bunts, and swinging bunts (when the batter is fooled by the pitch and hits the ball softly off the bat like an actual bunt). It is critical that third basemen use their gloves to catch the slow roller if the ball is still bouncing or rolling. However, if the ball comes to a complete stop, fielders can pick up the ball with their bare hands, which eliminates the need for a transition from the glove to the hand and saves valuable time. In addition, if the play allows, third basemen should set their feet to throw to first base. If they don't have time, they must move hard through the ball and make their throw on the run **(Figure 3.34)**.

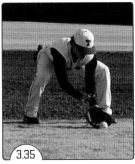

3.35

Whenever possible, the third baseman should get into a proper fielding position before making his double play feed to second base.

3.36

Once the ball is fielded, the third baseman should take a shuffle or two towards second base to get into his power position.

3.37

The third baseman should make a firm, accurate feed to the front corner of second base (closest to the pitcher's mound).

Double Play Feeds

There are only two typical ways a third baseman makes a feed to his second baseman to start a 5-4-3 double play. The first is to field a ball coming directly at him or to his left, and take a shuffle or two with his feet as he transitions to a power position to throw. This gives the second baseman adequate time to get to second base to make a pivot. The slower the ball is hit, the fewer shuffles the third baseman can take before making the feed to second base. The second option is to field the ball to his backhand side. On this play, the third baseman should attempt to create balance before making his feed. This gives the second baseman time to get to second base to make his pivot.

3.38

Once the fielder releases his feed, he should continue his momentum for a few steps.

If the ball is hit extremely hard to the backhand side of the third baseman, he may have to take a shuffle or two towards second base to gain momentum and provide adequate time for his teammate to get to second base. **(Figures 3.35, 3.36, 3.37, 3.38)**.

Fly Balls in Foul Territory

Third basemen are responsible for most fly balls in foul territory headed towards the third base dugout side. It is critical that the fielder keeps his eyes on the fly ball at all times. If he must look away to determine where he is on the field, he must quickly relocate the ball in flight. The player must quickly move his feet to the location where he feels the ball will land. This will give him extra time to

3.39
The third baseman should creep into a good fielding position to be ready for a play in his direction.

3.40
The fielder should execute a proper drop step to take a good route to the pop-up in foul territory.

3.41
If possible, the fielder should get behind the fly ball and move through the catch so he is in the best position to throw if base runners are aboard.

adjust in the event he slightly misjudged the ball. The third baseman is best to catch the ball while moving forward towards the infield in case he has to make a throw to another base **(Figures 3.39, 3.40, 3.41, 3.42, 3.43)**.

Flaw: Third basemen often drift to the ball to time the catch, which may cause their momentum to pull them away from the infield. This gives base runners an advantage if they decide to tag-up and advance to the next base.

Secret: A third baseman should check out the field before the game to determine how much foul territory he is responsible for, and look to see whether there is a warning track that will let him know when he is getting close to a fence. He must also make note of any obstacles, such as an infield tarp, that he may have to navigate around to make a play. Last, he should pay attention to the wind and sun to determine if they will become variables that can impact a fly ball in the game.

General Fielding Drills Used by Third Basemen

Please see "Specific Fielding Drills" in chapter one. Third basemen should execute these drills with all other infielders before working on drills specific to their position **(Figure 3.44)**.

Specific Drills for Third Basemen

A. Picks and tags—Improve the confidence of third basemen catching poor throws and placing a tag on the base runner. Two players (or more) and a coach get 20 feet away from third base (with a ball in each of the players' gloves), forming a semicircle around third base. Each feeder should be in the general direction of an outfield position (left field,

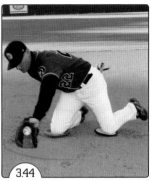

3.42

If the fielder is on the run and nears an obstacle such as a fence, he should attempt to make the catch, protect his body, and still make the play.

3.43

The third baseman should finish the catch by getting his body into a power position.

3.44

Third basemen should execute all fielding drills such as the Ozzie drill shown here.

center field, or right field) or the catcher. All three feeders alternate throwing the ball to the third baseman, who starts by straddling the base and adjusts his feet to the side of the base nearest to the oncoming throw. If the throw is way off line, the player should vacate the bag and do everything in his power to keep the ball from getting by him. The third baseman should then throw the ball back to the person who made the feed. Begin with throws in the air and then progress to throws in the dirt. Finally, alternate the type so the third baseman can react to different types of throws.

B. Fungo picks and tags—A coach rotates around the infield, hitting ground balls at various speeds to the third baseman, who correctly positions himself by straddling the base and squaring up to the coach. The third baseman then catches the ball in the air or on the ground and quickly places a tag on front of the base (the side of the base where the base runner would slide when arriving from second base). The player should keep all plays in front of him and vacate the bag only for balls that could possibly get by him to the fence. If a tag is made, he should practice quickly showing his glove (with the ball in it) to the umpire.

C. Fly balls—A coach or teammate positions himself on the infield grass in the general direction of home plate. He throws the ball at various speeds, heights, and in different directions to give the third baseman an opportunity to make all sorts of plays on fly balls. The fielder should attempt to catch the ball while moving towards the infield if possible. If not, he should quickly make the catch and adjust his feet and attention to the possible advancing base runners.

D. Slow rollers—Players take turns being the feeder somewhere near home plate. They throw various slow rollers that the third baseman charges, fields, and throws to first base. The other option is to simulate a throw to first base and hold on to the ball. This helps create muscle memory of the quick transition of the ball from the glove to the throwing hand, and the subsequent body control and footwork needed to make an actual throw.

E. Double play feeds—The third baseman starts at his defensive position. The goal of the third baseman is to get into a good fielding position and start a double play by making a feed to second base. The other options are to roll the ball (instead of hitting it), as well as to simulate a feed to second base (in place of actually making the throw) to create correct muscle memory.

F. Relay practice—Third basemen create a rotation where one player acts as the left fielder, another acts as the catcher, and the final player is the actual third baseman. The outfielder makes good and poor relay throws that must be handled by the third baseman, and then quickly and accurately relayed to the catcher. The players simply rotate so each player gets a turn making relays.

CHAPTER 4

ADVANCED OUTFIELD PLAY

Myth #1: PLAYING OUTFIELD IS NOTHING MORE THAN CATCHING FLY BALLS AND FIELDING GROUND BALLS. THEREFORE, THIS POSITION DOES NOT REQUIRE AS MUCH EMPHASIS IN PRACTICE AS OTHER POSITIONS.

Secret: *Outfield play requires the development of a specific skill set that is much more comprehensive than catching routine fly balls or fielding ground balls hit past the infielders. Practice time should be devoted to improving these important skills because superior outfield play can win games while average outfield play can lose games.*

Myth #2: AT THE HIGHER LEVELS OF BASEBALL, THE LESS SKILLED PLAYERS ARE MOVED TO THE OUTFIELD AND THE BETTER PLAYERS ARE MOVED TO THE INFIELD.

Secret: *At the higher levels of baseball, all defensive players should be skilled and specifically versed at their positions. There is no place to hide a bad fielder in baseball. Outfielders are just as important to winning games as players at any other defensive position.*

Myth #3: OF ALL THE SKILLS NEEDED TO BE A SUPERIOR OUTFIELDER, SPEED IS THE SINGLE GREATEST ASSET A PLAYER SHOULD POSSESS TO HELP HIS TEAM WIN GAMES.

Secret: *Speed is a sought-after asset for advanced outfielders. However, other skills can make up for or significantly increase a player's efficiency. For example, becoming a smart player by understanding the game situation, making quick and accurate reads of the ball off the bat, taking proper angles to the ball, and quickly releasing the ball to the cutoff man can help someone take outfield play to a higher level.*

OUTFIELD DEVELOPMENT

Outfield play is a general term used to represent all the specific fundamental skill sets needed to play the position correctly. Starting at the lower levels of baseball, outfield play is generally considered the most under-coached and least-drilled aspect of defense. Most coaches assume that allowing their players to roam around catching fly balls during batting practice is all the players need to be ready to compete in the game. This does not even scratch the surface when it comes to developing an advanced outfield prospect.

The fundamental skill sets and related drills taught in this chapter correlate specifically to all three outfield positions: left field, center field, and right field. Outfielders can throw either right-handed or left-handed. However, each outfield position typically requires players to possess specific physical attributes to increase their odds for defensive and offensive success, which together will give their team the best chance to win.

Corner outfielders (left fielders and right fielders) are typically big, strong players with above-average strength. They usually possess average speed, but they use their knowledge, experience, and physical skills to make routine and difficult plays. Offensively, it is common for corner outfielders to swing the bat with above-average power and generally hit in the middle of the lineup.

In comparison, center fielders usually have smaller frames, average arm strength, great body control, and run very quickly. They also have the ability to make difficult catches in the outfield gaps. In addition, they typically have tremendous game instincts, which allow them to take charge of their teammates while roaming the large open space surrounding them. The center fielder is the captain of the outfield; he has fly ball and ground ball priority over corner outfielders and all infielders. Offensively, center fielders typically hit for less power, steal bases, and score many runs for their team. Because of their speed, it is common for center fielders to hit at the top or bottom of their lineup.

Each day an outfielder steps foot on a ball field for a game or practice, he is faced with numerous variables he should immediately make note of that can help him play his best. This is especially true when visiting unfamiliar venues. Note factors such as:

- The location and intensity of the sun, and the direction and intensity of the wind.
- The condition of the playing surface including the moisture content and length of the grass.
- The outfield fence dimensions including the height and composition of the fence.
- The size of the warning track including how many strides a player can take until impacting the fence.
- The composition of foul territory including its size and hazards such as bull pens, light poles, field tarps, or fence gates.

Skills sets for advanced outfield include the specific mechanics needed to efficiently catch fly balls, line drives, and ground balls. Also included are the abilities to make plays at the wall, hit the cutoff man, communicate with other outfielders, and understand fly ball priority.

Fly Ball and Ground Ball Mechanics

Outfielders should be well versed in handling all different types of fly balls and ground balls. In addition, they must be able to navigate balls hit with backspin, topspin, and sidespin; balls hit into the wind, with the wind, and across the wind; fly balls hit on bright sunny days, cloudy days, and in the rain. As you can see, there are many ever-changing variables that must be overcome successfully for advanced outfielders to do their job well and help their team win games. These skills don't appear overnight . . . they are developed with intense training.

Specific skills needed to catch fly balls and ground balls include creating a good ready position; getting quick jumps on the ball (reacting quickly); taking correct angles to the ball (judging the ball); working through the catch to create momentum (when possible); making a good catch; getting a crow hop and quickly releasing the ball to the correct target; and hitting the cutoff man. Therefore, coaches must allot practice time to teach fundamental outfield play, as well as execute relevant drills to provide the repetitions players need to polish these skills. Coaches must also provide outfielders with experience executing specific plays based on the number of outs, game score, and how many runners are on base. These will develop the confidence to react correctly to game situations.

 Refer to "Advanced: Outfield Skills and Drills." Then select one of the following sections from the submenu: "Angles," "Adjustments," "The Catch," "Crow Hop and Throw," and "Cutoff Man" on the DVD for detailed interactive instruction.

The following is the advanced skill progression needed for middle school and high school players to catch a fly ball or field a ground ball hit directly at them, to their right or left, over their shoulders, at the fence, and towards the infield.

Phase 1: Ready Position

When the pitcher is about to release the ball to the hitter, each outfielder should begin to gradually creep forward to get his body into a ready position to quickly react to a batted ball. This is accomplished by taking small steps (left then right or right then left) towards the plate. The outfielder's body should end up squared to the plate in an athletic position—legs spread with feet wider apart than shoulders, knees slightly bent, hips slightly flexed, weight slightly forward, glove out in front of the body with the pocket facing the batter, and eyes on the "strike zone" of the hitter. It is critical that both of the player's feet are on the ground before the ball is hit; this maximizes a player's ability to cover the greatest distance in the shortest amount of time. In addition, in order to ensure the best routes possible to a batted ball, fielders should limit the amount of momentum moving forward towards the plate **(Figures 4.1, 4.2)**.

Flaw: Generally, if an outfielder is not given enough instruction, practice, and drill time, he tends to react incorrectly or hesitate on every ball hit to the outfield. This is usually because he is concerned that a ball will be hit over his head. It will delay the outfielder by creating a bad jump or an improper route to the ball.

Secret: Outfielders should not position themselves too deeply in the outfield in fear of having the ball hit over their head. They should use the outfield fence as a form of "out of bounds" and somewhat challenge hitters to hit the ball over their head. Many more balls will fall short and be difficult to catch than will be batted hit over their heads and remain in fair territory. Of course, in later innings (to protect a lead), outfielders should back up to ensure the ball will not be hit beyond them so they can prevent the extra base hit or a big inning for the opposition.

Secret: Outfielders should be aware of game situations and outs, including all of their team's pick-off plays, bunt defense, and first and third defenses in order to be prepared to quickly move into a backup position. There is a place for outfielders on every single play that happens in a game.

Secret: As soon as the pitcher is about to release the ball to the plate, outfielders should focus their eyes on the imaginary strike zone of the hitter, instead of watching the ball travel to the plate. This gives them the advantage of knowing where the ball will be hit before it contacts the bat. For example, when looking at the imaginary strike zone of a right-handed batter, the center fielder notices the head of the hitter's bat arriving before the ball. This indicates to the fielder, a fraction of a second before contact is made, that the ball is going to be pulled. As a result, the center fielder can begin to move in that direction before the ball is hit. Implementing this skill effectively will increase the fielder's range.

Secret: Because the shortstop and second baseman can see the catcher's signs to the pitcher, they have the luxury of knowing the type of pitch that is going to be thrown. Therefore, outfielders should request for their middle

4.1 Outfielders should relax between pitches as they consider the game situation and pick up the pitch signal from the middle infielders.

4.2 Outfielders should creep into a proper ready position so they can quickly react to a batted ball in any direction.

infielders to relay, in advance of each delivery, which pitch is going to be thrown by giving a quick hand signal behind their back. A closed fist means a fastball and an open hand means an off-speed pitch. Outfielders should use this information by deceptively adjusting their positioning as they creep into their ready position to be closer to where they anticipate the ball will be hit. They should adjust slightly to their left or right based on whether the pitch will be a fastball or an off-speed pitch. This effectively cuts down the distance to the anticipated side and increases their chances to be a few feet closer to a batted ball.

Drop Step versus Crossover Step

When the baseball is hit in the air over the outfielder's shoulder or is hit on a line (in the air or on the ground) into the outfield gaps, or if the outfielder determines the fly ball will eventually land behind him, he should take a drop step to create a good angle to efficiently track down the ball.

A drop step is executed by taking a backwards step with the foot closest to the direction of the ball. This effectively opens the hips and body in the general direction the player needs to travel to make the catch. This also decreases the chance that the outfielder will take a bad route (angle) to the ball. For example, if the baseball is heading over the outfielder's left shoulder, he should take a drop step with his left foot. A ball hit over his right shoulder would require a drop step with the right foot. However, if the ball is hit directly over the outfielder's head, he should take an exaggerated drop step with his glove-side foot. This will open his body so he can run directly off to the side of the ball to make this very difficult catch.

When the baseball is hit in the air or on the ground directly to the outfielder's side, or hit in towards the plate and angled to either side, the player should implement a crossover step. A crossover step will allow the outfielder to take the shortest route to the baseball in the least amount of time by stepping across the body with the opposite foot, such as right foot crossing in front of left. For example, if the baseball were hit to the center fielder's right, slightly in towards the plate, he would implement a crossover step with his left foot as he establishes the best route to make the catch **(Figures 4.3, 4.4)**.

4.3

Baseballs hit behind an outfielder require a drop step to take a good angle to the play.

4.4

Baseballs hit to the outfielders' sides or towards the infield require a crossover step to take a good angle to the play.

Flaw: Outfielders who use improper footwork when tracking down balls in the air or on the ground take poor routes and waste time getting to the play. They also tend to put themselves in a bad throwing position if they are fortunate to make the catch.

Secret: When a ball is hit on a line directly at an outfielder, he should turn his body sideways to the plate with his glove side forward and his glove out in front of him. This allows the player to move forwards or backwards to adjust to the ball once he decides where the ball is headed and where it will land if not caught.

Traveling to Fly Balls

It is critical that outfielders quickly get to the projected destination of a fly ball while keeping their eyes fixed on the white dot in the sky as they run. This means traveling in a straight line or the shortest distance from point A (the starting point) to point B (where the ball will land). This often allows players to make last-second adjustments to get into the best possible position for the catch. Outfielders should run softly on their feet to prevent their heads from jarring up and down, which creates the illusion of the ball bouncing in the sky **(Figure 4.5)**.

NO BASE RUNNERS

When there are no base runners, outfielders just need to be concerned with making the catch. This means they can run directly to the ball and even make the catch moving away from the infield.

4.5

The outfielder should run softly on his feet as he tracks the ball to judge where it will land.

WITH BASE RUNNERS

Outfielders should do everything they can to make the catch while moving directly towards their target in order to prevent runners from advancing extra bases. Advanced outfielders understand the importance of working through a fly ball before making the actual catch in order to gain momentum towards their throwing target. The fielder should quickly move to a spot a short distance behind where the ball will intersect the ground. Once there, he should immediately redirect his momentum by squaring his shoulders towards his throwing target. When the ball is nearing the ground, the outfielder should move forward through the ball to make the catch **(Figure 4.6)**.

Flaw: Outfielders should avoid lazily moving or drifting to fly balls or ground balls by trying to time their arrival to the ball with the actual catch. This can put a player in jeopardy if he happens to misjudge the path of the ball. Also, he will not be in a good position to make a throw to the base.

Flaw: Outfielders should avoid running for a difficult catch with their glove arm extended because this slows them down. They should lift and open the glove to the ball just before the catch.

Flaw: An outfielder should not simply stand still and watch his teammates make a play, even if the play does not involve him. Each outfielder should know where to be in every situation. For example, the left fielder should move close to third base to back up a possible throw from right field.

Secret: If there are base runners aboard and two outfielders can make the catch, the player with the best arm should call it because he will have the best chance to throw out the advancing runner.

4.6

The outfielder should move behind where he thinks the ball will land in order to move through his catch and gain momentum in the direction of his throw.

Secret: If the outfielder significantly misjudges where the catch will be (i.e., because of spin on the ball or the wind) and takes a drop step to the wrong side, he should use the "head snap" technique to correct his route to the ball. This is especially true if the ball is hit hard in the air and there is no time to spare. The player executes a head snap by turning his back to the plate and swinging his chin to where he thinks his body should travel to make the catch. This will cause him to lose sight of the ball for a split second, but it will allow him to make the quickest adjustment possible to recover and make the catch.

Secret: Once the outfielder knows he can make the play, he should call for the ball to ward off his teammates and prevent a possible collision. Commands such as "ball, ball, ball," "I've got it, I've got it, I've got it," or "mine, mine, mine" are all acceptable. Whatever words are used, they should be consistently applied. In addition, the off-fielder (the person not making the play) should also command, "take it, take it, take it" to confirm he is not making the play. It would be a flaw to call for the ball too early or call off another infielder or outfielder who is camped underneath the ball ready to make the catch.

Secret: When a fly ball is hit to a player in the outfield, the next nearest outfielder to the catch should attempt to back up the play. It can never be assumed that a player will make the catch. He may lose the ball in the sun, take a bad route to the ball, or he could pull a muscle or trip on his way to the ball.

Traveling to Field Ground Balls

There are two general ways for outfielders to approach ground balls hit to them. The key difference between the two is the determination of whether there are base runners aboard while the batter is at the plate.

NO BASE RUNNERS

If there are no runners on base when the ground ball is hit to the outfielder, he should attack the ball under control to cut down the distance to it. Once he is ten feet away or so, he should chop down his steps to slow his body and lower himself into a perfect fielding position (like an infielder). His goal is to keep the baseball in front of him and quickly hit the cutoff man. If the ball is dropped, the outfielder should pick it up with his throwing hand **(Figures 4.7, 4.8, 4.9, 4.10)**.

Secret: All three outfielders must react quickly to all ground balls even if the bounces are headed in the direction of an infielder. Once in a while, batted balls will get past the initial line of defense, and if the outfielders are not in backup positions, the runner can take extra bases.

WITH BASE RUNNERS

If the ball is hit on the ground with runners on base, or if there is a chance of the batter taking extra bases, the outfielder should attack the ball under control to cut down the distance. If the ball is off to either side, the fielder should create an angle slightly behind where he will intersect it; this allows him to slow him to a controlled position and gain momentum in the direction of the throw. If the ball is dropped or mishandled, the outfielder should pick it up off the ground with his throwing hand **(Figures 4.11, 4.12, 4.13, 4.14)**.

4.7
When there are no base runners aboard, the outfielder should take a good angle or "route" to the ground ball.

4.8
The fielder should cut down the distance to the baseball to prevent the batter from taking second base.

4.9
The outfielder should get into a perfect fielding position (like an infielder) and make sure he keeps the ball in front of him.

4.10
The fielder should efficiently get into his power position to feed the ball to his cutoff man, who will throw it back to the pitcher.

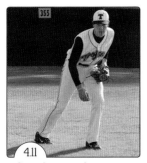

4.11

When there are base runners, the fielder must take a good angle to the ball, work to a point past the ball, and gain momentum in the direction of the eventual throw.

4.12

The fielder should lower himself to the ball and field it next to his glove-side foot. He must watch the ball enter his glove to be sure he does not mishandle the play.

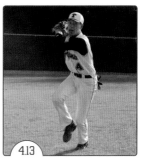

4.13

The outfielder should use a crow hop to gain momentum and add direction into his throw.

4.14

The fielder should release a strong, accurate throw to the glove side of his cutoff man, who will be lined up in the direction of the play.

Secret: If the field is in poor condition, the fielder must be sure the ball does not take a bad hop or hug the ground as he is fielding it. The goal is to make the play on the ball before making any throws.

Secret: When a ground ball is hit to a player in the outfield, the next nearest outfielder to the ball should attempt to back up the play. It can never be assumed that a player will successfully handle the ball. He may take a bad route to the ball, make an error while fielding the ball, or pull a muscle or trip on the way to the ball.

The Fly Ball Catch

Once an outfielder has taken a good route to the ball and is in position, it is important that he tries to catch the ball with two hands above his eyes, if possible. This prevents him from losing sight of the ball and moving his head unnecessarily to make the play. However, due to the vast territory that each outfielder is responsible for covering, players must be versed at making many types of catches. Each type of catch must be taught, practiced, and mastered in order to become an advanced player.

ROUTINE CATCH

On a routine catch of a fly ball, outfielders should set their throwing-side foot behind them, accelerate their body into a crow hop, and quickly gain momentum in the direction of their throw. The player should make the catch above his face, letting the ball travel to his glove. He should avoid stabbing at or jumping to the ball. He should firmly secure the catch by placing his bare

4.15
Whenever possible, the outfielder should catch the fly ball just to the side of his nose on his throwing side. His right foot should be behind him as he makes the catch.

4.16
The fielder should move through the catch in order to add direction and momentum into his crow hop.

4.17
The outfielder should finish his crow hop in a power position, ready to release the ball to his cutoff man.

hand on top of the ball. This allows for a quick transition of the ball into the throwing hand as he moves through the crow hop into his power position **(Figures 4.15, 4.16, 4.17)**.

Flaw: An outfielder should avoid back-pedaling at all costs because he can easily trip or lose his balance as he is making the catch.

BACKHANDED CATCH

When an outfielder is on the run tracking a fly ball or line drive to make a play on the throwing side of his body, he will be forced to attempt a back-hand catch. This is a difficult catch for any age player, and it requires superior hand-eye coordination. Just before the catch, the outfielder should position his glove-side elbow so it is pointed at the ball. This will put the glove in the best position to receive the ball **(Figures 4.18, 4.19)**.

GLOVE-SIDE OR REVERSE-PIVOT CATCH

When an outfielder is on the run tracking a fly ball (or ground ball) to make a play on the glove side of his body, he is forced to make a glove-side catch. This is a difficult catch because of all the elements that are moving, including the player at a high rate of speed, and the ball. Just before the catch, the outfielder should place his glove so the palm of the glove hand is open, which is the best position to receive the ball. If there are runners on base, the outfielder should quickly turn his body away from the infield for a split second to perform a

4.18

When an outfielder is on the run after a ball hit to the opposite side from his glove, he will need to execute a backhand catch.

4.19

As soon as the ball enters the fielder's glove, he should secure it with his throwing hand and make his transition to throw.

reverse pivot, after the catch. This creates the torque and momentum he needs to quickly release the ball, instead of taking the time to stop and turn towards the field to get into a power position to throw the ball **(Figures 4.20, 4.21, 4.22)**.

"FIND THE FENCE" CATCH

When a ball is hit very deep and has the possibility of becoming a home run, the outfielder must sprint to the fence even if it means taking his eyes off the ball for a split second. A player should only drop his eyes from the ball if he knows his chance of catching up to it is very slim. However, if he does, he

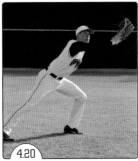

4.20

When a ball is hit hard to the outfielder's glove side, it will likely require the player to make a glove-side catch.

4.21

As soon as the ball enters the fielder's glove, he should allow its momentum to spin his body away from the infield.

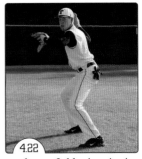

4.22

As the outfielder is spinning to his glove side, he should transition the ball into his throwing hand and bring his body into a power position to make his throw to the cutoff man.

should picture the continued path of the ball in his mind. Once he is near the fence, he should regain sight of the ball and get into position where he thinks the ball will land. By feeling for the fence with his bare hand, he can position himself just far enough away so he can jump vertically without slamming into the wall. Once he makes the catch, he can crow hop or immediately get into his power position to throw to his cutoff man **(Figures 4.23, 4.24, 4.25, 4.26)**.

4.23
On a "find the fence" catch, outfielders should take a steep angle drop step and run at full speed to the wall. If possible, they should keep their eyes on the ball in flight.

4.24
The player should attempt to get to the wall as quickly as possible so he can feel for the fence with his throwing hand or glove to set up for his vertical jump.

4.25
The outfielder should extend his body and glove straight up into the air to avoid colliding with the wall while trying to prevent a home run.

4.26
Once the ball is caught, the outfielder should quickly get into his power position and throw to his cutoff man.

Secret: Players must know how the ball will bounce off the fence before the game starts. They must also know whether the fence is forgiving in case they have to plow into it on a full run to make a catch.

Secret: Outfielders must be the eyes for one another as they attempt to make catches near or up against the outfield fence. They should verbally communicate "got room, got room, got room" if the player still has room to retreat, or "fence, fence, fence" if the player is close to impacting the wall.

DIVING CATCH

A diving catch is one of the most difficult catches an outfielder can make. A diving catch to the backhand side, which is moving away from the infield, is the hardest of all. Players must learn how to dive without regard for their bodies. This actually decreases the chance of injury. The player's goal is to move the glove to where the ball will be traveling, not where it is at that second. The player must also make slight adjustments with his glove, following the ball in flight, until he nabs it. Once an outfielder determines he is going to "lay-out," he should extend his body a foot or two above the turf while running full speed and jumping headfirst for the ball. This reduces the impact and will allow him to slide on the grass as if he were sliding into a base headfirst.

Flaw: An outfielder should never dive for a ball by placing his throwing hand underneath him in an attempt to cushion his impact with the ground. This can cause the player to break a wrist or hyperextend an elbow.

Secret: Center fielders are more likely to dive for fly balls than corner outfielders because their teammates back them up in the event they miss the ball. On the contrary, left and right fielders should be cautious about diving for the ball, especially when the play is down the lines near foul territory. If they miss the ball, there will be no one to back them up to retrieve it, and the base runner may get one or two extra bases on the play.

Crow Hop into a Power Position

When an outfielder catches a fly ball or ground ball with base runners aboard, he must learn how to gain momentum towards his target. Players should learn how to implement a crow hop, which makes it easier to throw the ball with more velocity and distance. The further the player is from his target, the more explosive his crow hop should be. It is critical to quickly execute this action to efficiently get the ball to the target.

As the outfielder catches the ball, he should simultaneously drive his back leg forward towards his target. This creates additional momentum to throw the ball while turning the body into a power position without wasting time. The focus should be on driving forward and not jumping up **(Figure 4.27, 4,28)**.

4.27

This is a front view of an outfielder executing a crow hop. Notice how he drives his back foot from the back to the front to generate strength and momentum into his power position.

4.28

In this side view of an outfielder transitioning through his crow hop, he gains momentum and channels power into his throw to the cutoff man.

Flaw: If an outfielder misjudges a fly ball and moves backwards when making the catch, this takes away momentum from his throw, increases the time the ball is in his possession, and reduces the effectiveness of his crow hop and throw to the cutoff man.

Flaw: When executing a crow hop, the player should avoid stepping behind his front foot with the back foot to get into his throwing position. Although it may seem similar to stepping in front, this action creates less drive and often interferes with the outfielder's momentum and direction to his target.

Secret: Some advanced outfielders with very strong arms may choose to implement a modified crow hop in order to release the ball as quickly as possible to their target in an attempt to throw out an advancing base runner. The movement of a modified crow hop involves the outfielder changing his footwork. As the catch is made, the player's back foot moves quickly towards the front foot, the front foot moves to the target, and the ball is released.

In the power position, the outfielder's hand with the ball should be behind his body, pointed away from the target with a relaxed grip. The back elbow is held approximately shoulder-high. The front shoulder, elbow, side of the hip, and toe should all be pointed at the target **(Figure 4.29)**.

Flaw: When an outfielder senses that base runners will not advance, he may incorrectly throw the ball gently or lob it back into the infield. This looks unprofessional, and it can cause bad habits to develop, along with the possibility that the bad throw will be mishandled, which indirectly could allow base runners to advance.

Flaw: An outfielder who makes an ineffective transition of the ball from his glove to his throwing hand will need to take extra steps or hop on his back foot before throwing the ball. This action wastes time and reduces the effectiveness of a properly executed crow hop.

Throw and Follow

The three phases of throwing, extension, and follow through combine to make one complete movement. This process happens very quickly to the eye. In order for the outfielder to complete his crow hop and release the ball, he should accelerate it from behind his body to the release point in front of his body while maintaining momentum towards the target. The bottom half of the fielder's body simultaneously thrusts energy into the

4.29

Once an outfielder completes his crow hop, he should be in his power position as he prepares to make a strong, accurate throw to his cutoff man.

throw by pushing off the grass with the back leg, accelerating the hips into rotation. The fielder should extend his throwing hand completely towards the target to release the ball. He should stay on top of and behind the ball, and snap the wrist hard to create backwards rotation. His head should be aligned directly above his front knee when the ball leaves his hand. Once the ball is released towards the target, he should finish by allowing his arm to decelerate naturally and come to rest just outside the stride-foot knee. The back foot will release off the ground, heel to the sky, and eventually finish forward in front of the stride foot. This process allows the outfielder's hips to finish rotating; momentum continues forward towards the target even though the ball is gone **(Figures 4.30, 4.31, 4.32)**.

Flaw: Outfielders should avoid unnecessarily throwing a ball to bases to show off their arm when there is no legitimate chance of making a play. This puts the team in jeopardy by possibly allowing base runners to advance on a long or errant throw.

Flaw: An outfielder should not attempt to throw out a base runner at home plate instead of throwing the ball to his cutoff man to keep other base runner(s) from advancing into scoring position.

Secret: Outfielders should always try to throw the ball with a four-seam grip. This will allow the ball to travel in a straighter path to its destination and give a truer bounce when it hits the ground.

4.30

The outfielder should create a four-seam grip, keep his elbow up, and stay on top of the baseball when making his throw.

4.31

The fielder should get good extension to create an accurate throw to the cutoff man's glove side.

4.32

Once the ball is released, the fielder should take a few steps to continue his momentum in the direction of his throw.

Secret: When making a play to his cutoff man, the outfielder should throw the ball chest- to belt-high to the glove side so it's easier for the receiver to make a quick transition and throw the ball to the intended destination.

Secret: Outfielders should attempt to make all throws to bases using a trajectory that will allow the ball to be cut off by an infielder. The throw should also have enough carry to reach the base (if not cut) on a line or only take one long hop. This type of hop will be easier for the infielder to catch and allow him to place the tag on the base runner.

Work through the following fielding drills and practice ideas to reinforce proper outfield mechanics.

Specific Outfield Drills

 Refer to "Advanced: Outfield Skills and Drills" and then "Outfield Drills" on the DVD for the following drills:

A. Tree—Improves an outfielder's drop step or crossover step, route to the ball, approach, crow hop footwork, and ability to work through fly balls and ground balls **(Figure 4.33).**

B. Fly ball patterns—Improve outfielders' abilities to run down a fly ball to their glove side or backhand side, run softly on their feet, adjust their positioning to a ball in flight, and set their feet to crow hop once the ball is caught **(Figure 4.34)**.

C. Head snap—Improves an outfielder's ability to adjust his incorrect read and change his route to a ball in flight to make a catch to his backhand side or glove side **(Figure 4.35)**.

D. "Find the fence"—Improves an outfielder's technique and confidence when making a play up against the fence or attempting to rob a batter of a home run **(Figure 4.36)**.

4.33

See "Tree drill" on the DVD.

4.34

See "Fly ball patterns" on the DVD.

4.35

See "Head snap drill" on the DVD.

4.36

See "Find the fence drill" on the DVD.

Additional Outfield Practice

A. Crow hop drill—Teach outfielders to practice crow hops by placing a ball in their glove and asking them to get into a fly ball or ground ball receiving position with their throwing-side foot behind them. Instruct them to place their caps on the ground just ahead of their front or glove-side foot. On the coach's command, they should execute a crow hop by driving the back foot up and over the cap while transitioning the ball from the glove to the throwing hand. The body should finish in a correct power position, or they can continue with an actual throw to their cutoff man. Progress to removing their hats from the ground; their partners can slowly roll the ball or they can toss it directly to each other as they perform a correct crow hop. Lastly, the coach can line them up and hit fungos in the air and on the ground where they perform their crow hops.

B. Ground ball drill—The outfielders set up in a line about 50 yards from the fungo hitter (coach) as he hits ground balls at various speeds and angles, one at a time to each player. The outfielders treat the first five rounds of ground balls as they would in a game with no base runners aboard. They should use proper footwork and take proper angles to each batted ball, and cut down the distance to the play to get in front of the ball in a perfect fielding position, and transition to throw to their cutoff man. The second five rounds should be treated as do-or-die ground balls in a game with runners on base; the outfielder attacks the ball, fields it, crow hops, and throws to the cutoff man.

C. Fly ball communication and priority—The coach tells outfielders to form two lines about 25 yards apart. One player from each line starts the drill. The coach determines which line represents the center field position (CF has priority over LF and RF), and hits a fly ball or ground ball between the two players. The pair must use their communication skills and rules for fly ball priority to take charge of the ball and make the play. Once the ball is caught, the receiver should quickly transition into his crow hop and throw the ball to the cutoff man.

D. Hit the cutoff man drill—The coach forms a line of outfielders and rotates through different players who simulate being the cutoff man for one rotation. The coach tosses a fly ball to the fielder, who quickly crow hops and throws a strike to his teammate (the cutoff). The cutoff man should vary his distances to make throwing to him more challenging.

E. Play the wall drill—The coach forms a line or two of outfielders and asks them to start closer to the outfield fence than usual (for the sake of proper execution of the drill). The coach hits various fungos in the air and on the ground to the wall. The players must use proper footwork to play the ball off the fence and immediately make an accurate throw to the cutoff man. If the ball is stationary or resting against the fence, one player should lower his upper body over the ball while picking it up with his bare hand. Once the ball is secured, that player should quickly throw the ball to his cutoff man.

F. Play the sun drill—The coach should line up the players so they have to battle the sun to catch the ball in the air. He either throws fly balls or hits pop-ups with a fungo bat. The outfielders must learn to use their bare hands, gloves, and/or sunglasses to find the ball, shade the sun, and still make the catch. A cutoff man can be added in order for the fielders to complete the play.

G. Diving drill—The coach can form a line of players on the outfield grass. He should instruct the fielder to start running to his left or to his right, and the coach should throw the ball ahead of the player, leading him to a point where he must dive to make the catch. *Caution:* This drill has the potential to cause injury if players are not confident about their outfield diving skills.

H. Square drill—The coach should form a large square, placing cones approximately 15 to 20 yards apart. Players form lines at each cone. The coach stands off at a distance and attempts to throw baseballs into the center of the square at different speeds and heights. Players take turns as one player at a time faces home plate and uses the proper footwork and angles to attempt to make the catch, even if the player has to dive. If it is an easy catch, he should use verbal signals to call the ball. Once the catch is made, he should get up and hit (make an accurate throw) the assigned cutoff man.

I. Fungo blocking drill—The coach should form a line of outfielders. The coach hits a very hard ground ball to the player who is up, and each player must find a way to keep the ball in front of him by getting low and blocking the ball with his glove and body. Once the ball has been stopped, it should be retrieved with the player's bare hand and quickly thrown to the cutoff man. The goal is not to hurt the player, but to give him confidence making a play and stopping a hard-hit ball from getting past him to the fence. Coaches should not perform this drill on fields that are not well manicured because the ball can take erratic or bad hops that can cause injury.

J. Long hop throws—The coach forms lines of outfielders in left field, center field, and right field. He rotates throwing or hitting fly balls and ground balls to each line as the players attempt to throw an accurate long hop to another assigned player (or extra infielder) at second base, third base, or home plate.

K. Fungo fly balls and ground balls—The players form lines at their preferred or assigned outfield positions. The coach stands at the plate (preferred), on the infield grass, or behind second base and hits ground balls and fly balls of all speeds, heights, and distances. The fielder must react with the proper footwork, routes (angles), and communication to make the play and come up and hit the cutoff man. One variation is to position the catchers at second base, pretending it is home plate. The cutoff man will make good and bad throws to second base, where the catchers receive the ball and place a tag on an imaginary base runner sliding into home plate.

L. Play it live (batting practice)—All outfielders should go to their preferred or assigned positions. They should play every batted ball with game reaction and speed. As one player takes off from a position to field a ball, the next outfielder at that position steps up and gets ready to make the next play on any ball hit in his general direction. To add variation, teammates in the outfield can play a game of 21. Outfielders receive two points for every ball they catch in the air during batting practice and one point for every ground ball they field. This usually increases their intensity and focus, and makes shagging fly balls (catching baseballs during batting practice) more meaningful. The first outfielder who reaches a score of 21 wins—the winner must finish with an exact score of 21. If a player goes over by catching a ball in the air when he only needs one point, he must revert to a score of 15 and pick up his points from there. Players are not allowed to physically battle for the fly ball. Note: The ball must bounce at least one time to be considered a ground ball.

M. Waterfall drill—Outfielders form a line right behind second base or at any other open space on the field. The coach instructs the first player in line to drop step in a pre-determined direction. As soon as the coach raises the ball to throw, the player executes an open step (outfield footwork) and reads the speed, height, and direction of his throw. The player takes off after the fly ball and makes the catch using proper technique. He should then set his feet, crow hop, and throw the ball back to the coach, who acts as the cutoff man. The routine of the drill continues until the coach changes the general direction of his throw. For example, he changes from the player's glove side to the player's throwing side. He should also take time to help players work on making catches directly over their heads. Because of the short distance between the outfielders and the coach in the drill, players can get many good repetitions in a short period of time. They also get adequate rest as other players take their turn practicing the drill.

CHAPTER 5

ADVANCED PITCHING

Myth #1: A PITCHER MUST IMPLEMENT HIS WINDUP DELIVERY MECHANICS WHEN THERE ARE NO RUNNERS ON BASE.

Secret: *Most pitchers choose to throw from the windup when there are no base runners aboard, but it is not mandatory. Examples of pitchers who often choose not to throw from the windup are middle-relief pitchers and closers.*

Myth #2: THE CIRCLE OR "O.K." GRIP IS THE ONLY EFFECTIVE WAY FOR PITCHERS TO THROW A CONSISTENT AND DECEPTIVE CHANGEUP.

Secret: *The circle changeup or O.K. changeup grip is one way to throw this effective off-speed pitch. However, there are various other grips that can be implemented to create the desired effect of deceiving a batter.*

Myth #3: THE MORE TYPES OF PITCHES IN A PLAYER'S ARSENAL, THE MORE EFFECTIVE HE WILL BE IN THE GAME BECAUSE HE CAN USE THEM ALL TO DECEIVE HITTERS AND KEEP THEM OFF BALANCE.

Secret: *A pitcher is better off mastering two pitches he can command for a strike in any pitch count than knowing five different types of pitches but being unable to throw them effectively on a consistent basis. The first pitch that all pitchers should attempt to master is a fastball. The second most important pitch for a player to command is a well-thrown and located changeup.*

PITCHER DEVELOPMENT

There are few coaches, players, or parents in the game of baseball (at any level) who would argue against the importance of dominant pitching in winning games. Therefore, most middle school, travel ball, summer ball, or high school coaches strive to identify players in their program, or recruit athletes, who can pitch effectively. They spend time building on their strengths and eliminating their weaknesses in order to increase the odds of defeating hitters.

Most coaches desire pitchers who have strong arms. However, this is not necessary for players to be effective on the mound. In fact, players who can repeat their delivery mechanics (in the windup and stretch), throw strikes with their fastball, manipulate the ball to move, and command an off-speed pitch often have greater success than a player who just throws forcefully. However, when a coach finds a player who has above-average velocity, is mentally tough, and fits the above criteria, he has a special pitcher in his midst. If he is fortunate enough to have many pitchers who are above average, the team has a greater chance for an extraordinary season.

Pitchers come in all different shapes and sizes, including tall, short, heavy, thin, right-handed, and left-handed. What makes a player effective on the mound is his ability to consistently synchronize his body parts to create a powerful kinetic chain to effectively transfer energy from his feet, up through his core, and into the release of the pitch. This process is the essence of pitching mechanics. Because so many body parts must precisely sync up to throw a baseball, it does not take much for things to go wrong. In fact, if any body part is working too soon or too late in a pitcher's delivery, the body will attempt to compensate to achieve the desired result. This often places an inordinate amount of stress on the fragile joints and surrounding connective tissue of the throwing shoulder and elbow, which often results in soreness, pain, longer recovery periods, and possible short- or long-term injury.

Therefore, it is beneficial to recognize that the best pitchers at the highest levels tend to get their body parts to certain places at specific times within their mechanics in order to create an efficient, repeatable, and deceptive delivery. In fact, the best pitching coaches recognize throwing uniqueness as an "asset," as long as the player possesses these common components within the five phases of their pitching mechanics.

At the middle school and high school level, players should be able to apply effective pitching mechanics from both the windup and the stretch delivery. However, pitchers at this age usually face additional challenges because they tend to pitch in addition to playing another primary defensive position. For example, they may pitch and play shortstop or right field. This means they have to pay even greater attention to their arms to be sure they are getting adequate rest and recovery time to avoid overuse and possible injury. In addition, they may throw the ball from a different arm slot than their defensive position. This means possibly having to make adjustments to their release point when they step on the mound to pitch, such as in the last inning when they are called on to close out the game.

Chapter six in the first volume of *The Coach's Companion* series addresses the twelve most common pitching flaws and provides appropriate drills to fix them for players ages ten and under. This is a good resource if players above the age of ten are still exhibiting these common flaws in their delivery.

WINDUP DELIVERY

Typically, most pitchers will work from their windup when there are no base runners aboard or there is only a runner on third base. This allows the pitcher to create a comfortable tempo. It is common for good pitchers to work fast. This means they don't take a lot of time between each pitch. They stay on the mound clay, receive the ball back from the catcher, toe the rubber, get their sign for the pitch, and go at the batter again. However, the pitcher's pace should not impede a comfortable delivery. When a pitcher effectively works fast, he keeps the batter on his toes by not giving him much time to adjust between pitches. It is critical that a pitcher does nothing during this initial process to tip the next pitch to the batter. Every movement must be calculated and performed consistently from pitch to pitch. Most right-handed pitchers throw from the right side of the pitcher's rubber, and most left-handed pitchers throw from the left side of the pitcher's rubber to create more deception with the pitch angle to the plate. However, a pitcher's first concern is comfort over his placement on the rubber, and he should make an adjustment in his placement if it improves his ability to throw strikes.

 Refer to "Advanced: Pitching Skills and Drills" on the DVD. Then choose the submenu "Windup Delivery" for detailed interactive instruction.

The following is the advanced skill progression needed for middle school and high school pitchers to deliver a pitch from the windup.

Phase 1: Drop Step and Pivot

Before the delivery can begin, a pitcher should stand with his feet approximately shoulder width apart, with both feet in contact with the pitcher's rubber. His glove and throwing hand should be positioned together somewhere between his belt and chest-high. He should receive the pitch signal from the catcher in this position. His body should be squared to the plate or turned slightly to his throwing side. For example, a right-handed pitcher may slightly face third base. He begins his windup by implementing a short drop step directly back or at a forty-five degree angle. This movement creates rhythm while

5.1

The pitcher should get into a relaxed position while engaged on the rubber to receive the sign from the catcher.

5.2

A side view of a pitcher looking in for his sign.

5.3

Pitchers take a drop step to allow them to transfer their weight and keep their head steady over their pivot foot.

5.4

A side view of a pitcher implementing a drop step.

5.5

The pitcher should turn his pivot foot parallel to the pitcher's rubber to create a foundation for good balance and future direction to the plate.

5.6

A side view of a pitcher creating a good foundation for balance with proper foot placement parallel to the rubber.

allowing the pitcher's weight to lightly transfer to his glove-side foot. Simultaneously, he should turn his throwing-side foot parallel and against the pitcher's rubber. This position allows the player to create good balance and direction to the plate while keeping his head motionless over his pivot foot (**Figures 5.1, 5.2, 5.3, 5.4, 5.5, 5.6**).

Flaw: If a pitcher rocks his entire body by pulling his head and body off the centerline from the rubber to the plate as he takes a drop step and pivot, this will likely impede his balance and direction later in the delivery.

Flaw: If something goes wrong at the beginning of the windup, it is common for this error to throw off the pitcher's rhythm, tempo, and mechanics throughout the remainder of his delivery.

Secret: Some pitchers choose to modify their drop step by taking it directly to their side or even slightly in front of their pivot foot. This is acceptable as long as the player's head stays still over his pivot foot, and he can create consistent low and high dynamic balance with his knee lift.

Phase 2: Dynamic Balance

Once the pitcher has planted his pivot foot firmly parallel to the rubber, he should raise his glove-side knee and thigh to a comfortable height, all the while keeping his head over his back foot. In addition, he should slightly flex his back knee as he turns his front knee in towards the centerline of his body to load his hips. It is critical that he maintains his balance through the lowest and highest levels of the thigh lift (**Figures 5.7, 5.8**).

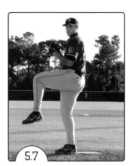

5.7

Pitchers should create dynamic balance and hip load throughout lifting their front knee and thigh.

5.8

A side view of a pitcher creating dynamic balance and effectively loading his hips in the delivery.

Flaw: If a pitcher's front foot is extended away from his body, creating distance between the foot and his back knee, he tends to swing the front foot around to the plate instead of going directly to the plate.

Secret: A pitcher should allow his front foot to relax so his toe is pointed slightly towards the ground. This helps him maintain his balance.

Secret: The pitcher's hands and front knee should be in sync to help the player maintain rhythm and tempo in his delivery. For instance, if he chooses to start his hands high in his setup, they should remain there until the knee has reached its highest point. Once the knee drops to start the lateral direction to the plate, his hands should follow. The other scenario consists of a pitcher who starts his hands low in his setup. This player should raise his hands with his front knee as if they were attached with a string. Then the knee and hands will continue to mirror each other on the way down.

Phase 3: Direction

A pitcher's goal is to create a controlled lateral movement to the plate by leading with his front side and driving with his back side. As his hands follow his front knee down, they should separate near his navel. This initiates an equal and opposite movement of the arms and hands. As the thumb of the gloved hand works down, forward, and up, finishing where the throwing elbow is pointed at the catcher, the thumb of the throwing hand works down, back, and up, finishing with the back elbow shoulder-high, with the ball pointed away from the target. Simultaneously, the lower body creates direction by striding directly to the plate and leading with the outside of the front heel in order to keep the pitcher's hips closed and loaded as long as possible. The stride foot will eventually rotate so the toes are pointed at the plate just before

5.9

Pitchers should create good direction by keeping their hips closed and leading the controlled lateral movement to the plate with the outside of the stride foot.

the foot lands on the clay. The player's eyes should be focused on the catcher's mitt. The pitcher is now in the power position **(Figure 5.9)**.

Flaw: A pitcher should not land open or closed to the plate to deliver his pitch. Either landing creates poor direction and will force the pitcher's body to compensate for this error, which can cause an inconsistent release point.

Flaw: A pitcher should not allow his foot to land on either the heel or toe. Ideally, the player's stride foot should land as flat as possible on the clay, which will give him a firm base to throw into and around.

Secret: A pitcher who attempts to take his chin to the catcher's glove typically improves his direction to the plate.

Secret: When a pitcher keeps his upper body and hips closed as long as possible, it creates tremendous torque or hip rotation, which equates to greater arm speed, hand speed, and ball speed.

Secret: The pitcher's body should stay closed up to 70 to 80 percent of his stride length to the plate. This keeps him from leaking open and losing hip explosiveness.

Phase 4: Power Position

The fourth and fifth phase of a pitcher's delivery happen in a fraction of a second. However, it is important to be able to visualize what a power position looks like. As soon as the player's stride foot impacts the earth to create a power position, the body quickly places a large workload on the throwing shoulder and elbow. The shoulders will be slightly tilted with the lead shoulder above the rear shoulder. This assists the arm to accelerate from zero miles per hour up to maximum velocity and back down to zero to throw the ball. Therefore, it is beneficial for the pitcher's body to remain in an athletic stance throughout the landing and pitching delivery. When a photo is taken of a pitcher in his power position, his stride foot should be planted flat on the clay and almost pointed directly to the plate (slightly closed). There will be flexion in his knees and hips, and the player's head will be centered with his feet, his chin resting near his front shoulder, and his eyes peering in at the catcher's target. The pitcher's throwing elbow will create a backwards "L" with shoulders tilted and the ball facing away from the target. A right-handed pitcher will hold the ball near a ten o'clock position with his throwing palm facing the short-stop. A left-handed pitcher will hold the ball near a two o'clock position with his throwing palm facing the second baseman. The player's front elbow and shoulder should be pointed directly at the target **(Figures 5.10, 5.11)**.

Flaw: A pitcher should use his body efficiently and not over-stride or understride into his power position. Ideally the player should have a stride length somewhere close to five and one-half times his own foot length.

Flaw: If a pitcher attempts to "muscle up" in order to create more ball velocity, he creates unwanted tension, and tight muscles are slow muscles. Ideally, 90 percent effort equals 100 percent velocity.

5.10

Pitchers should get into a good power position by creating correct body alignment with their front and back side.

5.11

A side view of a fundamental power position.

Secret: When a pitcher is in his power position, his glove should be slightly lower than the front elbow to help generate more torque in his delivery.

Secret: The pitcher should push off of the pitcher's rubber with the inside of his back toe to create more torque with the hips and add momentum into his delivery.

Phase 5: Release and Finish

When the pitcher's stride foot lands (foot plant), his front knee should be in a firm but flexed position in order to give the body a firm foundation to work around. The pitcher can then deliver the pitch to the plate by accelerating the baseball from behind his body to the release point out in front of his body. During this process, the throwing elbow will naturally transition from flexion to extension as the player's chin moves forward directly towards the target. During the throw, the pitcher's glove-side elbow should naturally transition from pointing at the target to a position beside the hip. The pitcher's lower body will contribute energy into the pitch by pushing off the rubber with the back leg, which creates momentum and accelerates the hips to help complete their rotation. The pitcher should release the ball by snapping his wrist hard to create backwards rotation (a fastball). A pitcher should visualize that he is throwing through a narrow hallway to the catcher's glove so neither his body parts nor the ball hit the imaginary walls. Once the ball is released, the pitcher should finish his mechanics by allowing his throwing hand to pronate (the hand does this naturally) and come to rest just outside his stride-foot knee. Simultaneously, the glove-arm elbow should naturally transition from beside his glove-side hip to somewhere behind the hip so the throwing shoulder can finish pointed at the target. During the release of the ball, the player's back foot will drag the clay for a short distance and then release off the ground, heel to the sky, and eventually finish in front of or beside the stride foot. This process allows the hips to finish rotating and to return to a position to field the ball **(Figures 5.12, 5.13, 5.14, 5.15, 5.16, 5.17)**.

5.12

Pitchers should allow their body to naturally move forward towards their glove as they work down "the hallway" to deliver the pitch.

5.13

Side view of the same stage, the pitcher's glove-side elbow will eventually release behind the player's front hip as his throwing hand gets near extension.

5.14

Pitchers should achieve extension of their throwing hand to the target while maintaining good posture with their glove-side leg.

5.15

Through extension and finish, the player's chin will move over and past his front knee, which acts to flatten out his back as he completes the pitch.

5.16

To correctly finish the delivery of a pitch, the player's throwing hand should naturally come to a stop just outside his stride-foot knee.

5.17

Side view of the finishing position.

Flaw: If a pitcher attempts to create extra ball speed by "pulling" or jerking his head and front shoulder off line to the plate, this will create an inconsistent release point and place extra strain on the shoulder and elbow.

Secret: A pitcher should attempt to create a consistent release point for every pitch in his arsenal. This will effectively create deception, as a batter will have more difficulty determining the actual pitch in flight.

Secret: To create better direction to the plate, the pitcher's back knee should also stay on line to the target as long as possible while the back toe drags the clay.

Secret: The pitcher should try to take his nose in the direction of the catcher's mitt to help keep his body in line and allow the body to be in the best position to assist decelerating the arm.

See Figures 5.18 through 5.25 for a full recap of the windup from start to finish in side-view.

5.18
Get sign

5.19
Drop step

5.20
Pivot

5.21
Dynamic balance

5.22
Power position

5.23
Throw

5.24
Extension

5.25
Finish

Stretch Delivery

At the middle school and high school levels, pitchers will encounter base runners who will attempt to steal bases. Therefore, a pitcher should learn how to implement stretch mechanics. Because many players attempt to simplify the pitching process when they first begin pitching at younger ages, this is not usually a difficult adjustment. However, learning how to effectively hold base runners is another problem that must be addressed successfully. Contrary to popular belief, base runners actually steal off the pitcher rather than the catcher. Therefore, a pitcher must learn to give his catcher a chance to throw out base stealing attempts by varying his looks and moves to a base and working quickly to the plate. Most pitchers choose to implement some type of low balance stretch delivery to still benefit from their hip load without sacrificing the time needed to use a high balance delivery.

 Refer to "Advanced: Pitching Skills and Drills" on the DVD. Then choose the submenu "Stretch Delivery" for detailed interactive instruction.

The following is the advanced skill progression needed for middle school and high school pitchers to deliver a pitch from the stretch.

Phase 1: Set Position

The pitcher initially creates a good athletic position by placing his back foot parallel to and against the pitcher's rubber on his preferred side. The player's front foot should be slightly farther than shoulder-width from his back foot and his front shoulder; the side of his front knee and front foot should be aligned directly to the point of home plate. From this initial position, the player's hands can be relaxed at his side, with the ball preferably in his throwing hand, or the player can lean slightly forward, resting the glove against his front thigh. He should alternately glance at the catcher giving signs and the base runner establishing his lead **(Figure 5.26)**.

In order to transition into his "set position," the pitcher simply adjusts his front foot closer to his back foot while simultaneously bringing both hands together to intersect somewhere between his chin and his waist. He should pause in this position for a split second while continuing to look at the catcher's target and the runner on base until deciding to start his delivery **(Figure 5.27)**.

Flaw: When a pitcher does not have an exact routine that he implements on each and every pitch, he may tip his pitches to the batter. The only things that should change are the looks and moves he makes to first base, and the time he spends in his set position so the runner will have a more difficult time getting a quick break or jump when stealing a base.

Secret: Some pitchers prefer to create an initial open stance (with their front foot closer to first base) before they establish their set position. This enables them to see the actual leads that base runners are able to achieve at first base.

5.26

Pitchers should set up against the rubber before looking for their sign from the catcher.

Phase 2: Low Balance Load

To create a balance point from his stretch position, the pitcher should raise his front knee to a comfortable position somewhere around the middle of his thigh. As with the windup delivery, the player's front knee should turn in slightly towards the center of his body. This simple action closes and loads his hips, providing additional torque and power. To sync the tempo between his lower body and upper body, the pitcher's hands should mirror the action of the front knee either during the knee lift and/or the descent. For example, if the pitcher's hands start low in their set position, they should come up as the knee rises and go down when the knee descends. Conversely, if the pitcher prefers his hands high in his set position, he should keep them still on the knee lift and then drop them when the knee falls. During the lift and descent of the front knee, the ankle should remain relaxed and close to the back knee. The pitcher's head should be aligned with his navel. The pitcher is now in a loaded position, balanced over his back foot **(Figure 5.28)**.

5.27

Pitchers should create a fundamental set position with their throwing and glove hands held somewhere between their chin and waist.

Flaw: Many pitchers attempt to combat an opponent's running game by implementing a slide-step delivery. This type of delivery, in which a pitcher simply lifts his front foot and takes it straight to the plate, does save time. However, it places additional stress on the player's throwing shoulder and elbow. It may also make it more difficult for pitchers to consistently sync their upper body actions with their lower body because of how quickly the lower half works.

Secret: A pitcher should have different moves that he can use to help keep base runners in check. These moves must be practiced and perfected with an emphasis placed on quick feet and quick release.

5.28

To give their catchers a chance to throw out base runners, pitchers should raise their front knee slightly while loading their hips to create a "low balance load" before delivering a pitch to the plate.

Note: Because the following phases of the "Stretch Delivery" are identical to the "Windup Delivery," please refer to the previous section for detailed information on Phase 3: Direction, Phase 4: Power Position, and Phase 5: Release and Finish **(Figures 5.29, 5.30, 5.31, 5.32)**.

5.29

Pitchers should get into a good power position by creating correct body alignment (direction) to the plate with their front and back side.

5.30

A pitcher should accelerate his throwing hand to the target while maintaining good posture with his glove side.

5.31

Through extension and finish, the player's chin will move over and past his front knee, which acts to flatten out his back as he completes the pitch.

5.32

To correctly finish the delivery of a pitch, the player's throwing arm should naturally come to a stop just outside his stride-foot knee.

Work through the following pitching drills and practice ideas to reinforce good windup and stretch mechanics.

Specific Pitching Drills

 Refer to "Advanced: Pitching Skills and Drills" and then "Pitching Drills" on the DVD for the following drills:

Coach hand-off—Improves a pitcher's ability to create a good balance point and hold it before making the pitch **(Figure 5.33)**.

Coach toss balance—Helps a pitcher reinforce his balance point before he commits to creating direction in his delivery **(Figure 5.34)**.

Towel—Helps a pitcher emphasize the extension and finish elements of the pitch **(Figure 5.35)**.

Ball toss (Phases I and II)—Phase one of the drill emphasizes the correct back and front arm action. Phase two of the drill uses two baseballs to emphasize correct upper body positioning **(Figure 5.36)**.

Mechanics or pump drill (Phases I through IV).

Phase I: Emphasizes the correct drop step, pivot, and dynamic balance in the pitcher's delivery.

Phase II: Emphasizes correct separation and tempo.

Phase III: Emphasizes correct hip load, release, and throw.

Phase IV: This phase of the drill ties the first three phases of the mechanics drill together **(Figure 5.37)**.

Shuffle—Helps a pitcher emphasize correct direction and momentum in his delivery while landing on a flexed but firm front leg. This drill is great for players who lock their front knee when delivering a pitch **(Figure 5.38)**.

Bucket—Helps a pitcher emphasize correct balance and hip load in his delivery **(Figure 5.39)**.

🎓 Hop-hop—This is an advanced drill due to the body control and balance that it takes to execute properly. This drill emphasizes direction and momentum into a pitch while keeping the pitcher's weight over the back foot for as long as possible **(Figure 5.40)**.

T-alignment—Helps a pitcher focus on a controlled lateral movement and direction in his delivery **(Figure 5.41)**.

See "Coach hand-off drill" on the DVD.

See "Coach toss balance drill" on the DVD.

See "Towel drill" on the DVD.

See "Ball toss drill" on the DVD.

See "Mechanics (pump) drill" on the DVD.

See "Shuffle drill" on the DVD.

See "Bucket drill" on the DVD.

See "Hop-hop drill" on the DVD.

See "T-alignment drill" on the DVD.

Additional Pitching Practice

A. Dry mechanics—Coaches and/or pitchers should take time to execute their mechanics through the phases of the windup and stretch delivery without a baseball. The focus should be on completing each segment correctly and smoothly. Preferably, this should be executed in front of a mirror.

B. Flat ground work—Pitchers should use the time when they are not on an actual game mound to work on their pitching mechanics. Basically, everything they do on the clay can be done on the grass. Additionally, this forces pitchers to make adjustments with their stride foot or landing foot. Every mound is different because some are tall and others are flat. Therefore, it is critical that pitchers get a feel for their release points in order to command their pitches, regardless of the mound conditions.

C. Long distance bull pens—Instruct catchers to back up 4 to 6 feet from their original catching position behind the plate. This extra distance makes the pitcher create better extension to finish his delivery.

D. Throwing mechanics drills—Each of the six throwing drills that emphasize proper throwing mechanics are taught in detail on the DVD for the first book in the *Coach's Companion* series.

E. Kneeling figure eight—Reinforces rhythm and tempo in the upper body when throwing the ball.

F. Kneeling power position—Reinforces a good power position before the throw to improve accuracy.

G. Standing figure eight—Creates rhythm and tempo with the whole body when throwing the ball.

H. Standing power position—Creates a correct power position with the lower and upper body when throwing the ball.

I. Boxers—Creates rhythm and teaches how to transfer energy from the back side of the body to the front side.

J. Jump-backs—Teaches players how to incorporate their whole body when throwing the ball.

K. Throwing long—Pitchers use this drill for various purposes. Some choose to throw long as a means of improving arm strength. Others choose to throw long to prepare their arm to pitch in a game. Either way, the pitcher should use proper throwing mechanics, emphasizing the explosion of his lower body and hips to create arm speed and good extension to his target. He should also implement his changeup grip every second or third throw to emphasize correct arm speed and the feel of the ball leaving the hand. The pitcher's goal is to keep his fingers on top of and behind the ball at release.

L. Touch throws—A coach can emphasize a pitcher's extension and finish in his delivery by placing a small object (such as a bean bag or tennis ball) on the ground diagonally in front of where the pitcher will complete his pitch with his stride foot. The coach should watch a few repetitions of his natural stride and delivery, and then place the bag 4 to 6 inches diagonally outside his stride foot. The coach should emphasize that the pitcher should try to touch the object on the completion of each pitch.

M. Simulated games—Pitchers should take part in simulated games or modified scrimmages to mentally prepare to throw against hitters in a real game. In addition, this helps pitchers learn that once they throw the ball to the plate, there are other responsibilities, such as fielding their position and backing up bases.

N. Game stress pens—In order to prepare pitchers for actual games, coaches should be creative in the bull pen environment. There are times, especially before actual game outings, that it is beneficial to create as much game stress on the pitcher as possible. For example, if there is an extra person available, make him wear a batter's helmet and stand in the right-handed and left-handed batter's box with a bat. This helps pitchers mentally prepare for a time when a hitter will be standing in the box during a game.

TYPES OF PITCHES

At the middle school level, pitchers should learn to command two types of pitches: a fastball and a changeup. They will be doing themselves a big favor if they can throw both of these pitches for a strike, in most any count to the batter, by the time they enter high school. This way they have a foundation of the two primary pitches needed to compete and win. During their four years in high school, they should implement a breaking pitch by learning to throw a curveball or a slider. It is critical that they also continue to polish their fastball and changeup by learning to command them in and out of the strike zone. When a high school pitcher attempts to throw more than three types of pitches, his primary pitches tend to lose effectiveness, and the pitches all start to look similar to the batter.

A curveball should not be thrown as a primary pitch until a pitcher is at least sixteen years old, and it is preferred that a slider not be thrown as a primary pitch until a player is at least seventeen years of age. However, by a high school player's junior or senior year, he should be physically strong enough and posses the correct mechanics to throw fastballs (two-seam and four-seam), changeups, and some type of breaking pitch. The key is that players must be able to command their pitches for a strike in the game; otherwise, they are generally useless.

Keep in mind: there is more than one way to grip a baseball when throwing a pitch. Therefore, players should first be introduced to the basic grips of each primary pitch. Once they have a good feel for the delivery and location of a particular pitch, they can be shown other possible grip options to create more movement on the ball. At that point, they can spend time tweaking their grips and finger placement to determine what works best for them.

For the sake of knowledge, various pitches will be revealed in this section. A word of caution: Some of these pitches should not be implemented because they place undue stress on a pitcher's elbow or shoulder, especially when they are thrown incorrectly. A few of these pitches are bad for a player no matter what age the player is or how the pitches are delivered. At the higher levels, some players turn to these types of pitches to help them extend their career when they are having more difficulty getting hitters out. In addition, they are much older (college and professional players), and their bodies are more mature and better able to handle the stress that these pitches place on them. Typically, pitchers at this level have the best care available to them, such as trainers and equipment to care for their arm, and they usually only pitch once every four or five games.

 Refer to "Advanced: Pitching Skills and Drills," then "Pitching Grips" on the DVD for detailed interactive instruction.

The following are the grips needed for middle school and high school baseball:

Four-Seam Fastball

The first pitch that must be mastered is the four-seam fastball. This is usually the easiest pitch to throw for a strike. If released properly, four laces of the ball rotate through the air, helping to keep the throw in line with the target. To properly execute a four-seam grip, pitchers should hold the baseball with their pointer and middle finger on the top laces or seams of the baseball. The pads of these two fingers rest across the seams. The thumb should be underneath the ball, approximately splitting the distance of the top two fingers. The ring finger and pinky finger rest on the side of the ball to give it balance (**Figures 5.42, 5.43**).

5.42

Front view of a four-seam fastball grip.

5.43

Side view of a four-seam fastball grip.

Two-Seam Fastball

Once a pitcher can command the four-seam fastball for a strike, it is time to introduce him to a two-seam fastball. This will create some movement to help deceive the hitter. The main variation from the four-seam fastball is how the laces or seams of the ball are positioned in the fingers. When a two-seam fastball is properly released, the ball cuts through the air, moving naturally from right to left or left to right. Some pitchers have trouble controlling this for a strike because the ball can start off in the strike zone and drift out by the time it reaches the plate. Additional movement can be created with a two-seam fastball by holding the ball slightly off center, adjusting thumb placement, or holding the ball next to the seams instead of placing the pads of the fingers directly on the seams (**Figures 5.44, 5.45**).

5.44
Front view of a two-seam fastball grip.

5.45
Side view of a two-seam fastball grip.

Sinker: Variation of a Two-Seam Fastball —H.S. Varsity Only 🎓

The sinker is a two-seam fastball with "late sink" or downward action. The "sink" is typically created by early pronation of the pitcher's wrist. Most pitchers who throw a sinker have this natural wrist action upon their release of the ball. However, other players learn to effectively deliver this pitch by intentionally pronating their wrists early on the release of their fastballs, or they use their index fingers to create pressure points on the ball that can sometimes cause a similar effect (**Figures 5.46, 5.47**).

5.46
Front view of a sinker grip.

5.47
Side view of a sinker grip.

Cut Fastball: Variation of a Four-Seam Fastball —H.S. Varsity Only 🎓

A pitcher should avoid implementing a cut fastball unless he can first command his four-seam fastball and two-seam fastball for strikes. Because this advanced pitch is meant to be thrown very hard (4 to 5 miles per hour slower than the fastball), the cut fastball or "cutter," as it is referred to by players and coaches, is classified as a variation of the traditional four-seam fastball. The goal of the cutter is to move just enough to miss the sweet spot of the bat barrel. The action of this pitch involves late, mostly horizontal movement generally opposite the break of a two-seam fastball (i.e., a right-handed pitcher's cut fastball would move away from a right-handed hitter). When first learning a cutter, a pitcher should slightly rotate the ball from the four-seam fastball grip, hold it

5.48

Front view of a cut fastball grip.

5.49

Side view of a cut fastball grip.

slightly off center, significantly increase pressure with his middle finger, and throw the pitch hard. Once a player becomes comfortable with the release and feel of the pitch, he can tweak parts of his grip in an effort to increase movement and deception. This can be accomplished by increasing pressure of the middle finger on the ball, varying the thumb placement beneath the ball, holding the ball increasingly off center, and altering the angle of the wrist upon release of the pitch. No matter which adjustment is made to the cutter grip, the key is to maintain near-fastball velocity while achieving late horizontal movement as the pitch nears the plate (**Figures 5.48, 5.49**).

Circle Changeup

A changeup is meant to deceive the hitter by appearing to be a fastball on release. However, it is really just 8 to 12 miles per hour slower. The fastball action of the pitcher's delivery will convince the hitter he is seeing a fastball; however, by the time he realizes it is a changeup, he will either swing early and miss, or the batter will hit the ball softly to the defense.

For a circle changeup grip, the ball is held deeper in the hand or the palm than a fastball. The index finger slides off to the thumb side of the ball, and the pinky raises up on the opposite side of the ball. This grip is referred to as a "circle change" or "O.K. change" because of the position of the hand. The changeup is a feel (touch) pitch, and it can be difficult for some players to throw a consistent strike using this grip. Some pitchers choose to overexaggerate the pronation of their wrist upon the release of their changeup in an attempt to get the ball to move to the right or the left as it travels to the plate (**Figures 5.50, 5.51**).

"C" Changeup: Variation of a Circle Changeup

The "C" changeup can be a good option for players who have smaller hands or have trouble with their feel for the circle changeup. To create the grip for a "C" change, a pitcher should attempt to hold the baseball like a football, where all four fingers line up opposite the thumb to make the letter "C". To add movement, the ball can be gripped off-center (where a portion of the ball protrudes out of the side of the hand between the thumb and index finger). This pitch is simply delivered with a four-seam or two-seam grip just like the pitcher would throw his fastball. As the player's hands grow or he gains more comfort with the feel of the pitch, he can gradually slide his index finger off the ball to the thumb side, and lift the pinky up to create his circle change (**Figures 5.52, 5.53**).

Palm Ball: Variation of a Changeup

A pitcher may choose to throw a changeup by using a palm ball grip. However, this is not typically the changeup grip of choice for most high-level pitchers. To correctly grip a palm ball, the pitcher should move the ball deeper into the flat part of his hand while bringing his thumb and pinky up to the middle of the side of the ball. It will appear as if all five appendages are on top of the ball. The pitch is thrown like a fastball with either a four- or two-seam grip **(Figures 5.54, 5.55)**.

Split-Finger: Variation of a Changeup—Danger! Don't Throw

We recommend that players do not implement the split-finger pitch, no matter their age. We are including it so coaches can identify this pitch when they see it. This pitch puts a lot of stress on the tendons of the forearm that tie into the elbow and wrist. A split-finger pitch is created by spreading the index finger and middle finger apart until there is slight tension in the forearm. The player rests his fingers in this position on top of the ball. The pitcher should throw this pitch like he would his fastball with two seams or four seams. Typically, the ball will have a slight tumbling action as it travels to the plate **(Figures 5.56, 5.57)**.

5.50
Front view of a circle or O.K. changeup grip.

5.51
Side view of a circle or O.K. changeup grip.

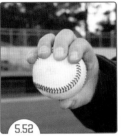

5.52
Front view of a "C" changeup grip.

5.53
Side view of a "C" changeup grip.

5.54
Front view of a palm ball grip.

5.55
Side view of a palm ball grip.

5.56
Front view of a split-finger grip.

5.57
Side view of a split-finger grip.

Curveball: Caution—High School Only

If the curveball is thrown incorrectly, it can put a lot of stress on the elbow and shoulder. Therefore, this pitch should not be thrown until a player is sixteen years old. The curveball is an off-speed pitch that breaks more from top to bottom (i.e., from 12 o'clock to 6 o'clock); thus, it changes visual planes (from high to low) to the batter. The pitch is gripped by holding the ball off-center with the index finger and middle finger side by side. The fingers rest beside the seam that creates the horseshoe, and the thumb rests on the opposite seam on the bottom of the ball. The curveball is initially thrown like a fastball until the hand gripping the ball gets beside the pitcher's head, where his fingers will move to the outside of the ball. At that point, the pitcher will attempt to slice the batter in half with his pointer and middle fingers, and then continue down in front of his body and finish by simulating stabbing himself in the thigh of his landing leg (or pulling down the cord of a window shade). This creates the top spin that will pull the ball down as it travels to the plate (**Figures 5.58, 5.59**).

5.58
Front view of a curveball grip.

5.59
Side view of a curveball grip.

Slider: Caution—H.S. Varsity Only

The slider puts extra stress on the pitcher's elbow and should not be thrown until a pitcher is a junior or senior in high school. The slider is thrown with fastball velocity but has late-breaking diagonal tilt (i.e., from 2 o'clock to 7 o'clock or 3 o'clock to 8 o'clock); thus, it fools the hitter by possessing fastball speed but also changing visual planes. The slider is gripped similarly to the curveball but held against the seams where the horseshoe comes back close together, and is released in a manner that will create tight spin (many rotations in a short period of time). The slider is thrown like a fastball until the ball gets close to the release point. To create the tight spin of a slider, the pitcher will replace his thumb with the big knuckles of his index finger and middle finger. This wrist action maintains most of the pitch velocity and gives it the desired late-breaking tilting action to make hitters swing and miss (**Figures 5.60, 5.61**).

5.60
Front view of a slider grip.

5.61
Side view of a slider grip.

Knuckleball—High School Only

The knuckleball is an off-speed pitch that is thrown to create deception due to the slow and uncertain path it takes to the plate. The pitcher attempts to throw the ball without rotation so the seams of the ball catch wind pockets and cause the ball to dance. The pitch is usually thrown with a four-seam grip, where the index finger and pointer finger are turned inward and down so the pads of each finger almost touch the top of the palm of the hand. Sometimes the knuckleball is thrown with three or four fingers in the same position. The pitcher delivers the ball with a pushing action at release point. This prevents the player from snapping his wrist, which creates undesirable backspin **(Figures 5.62, 5.63)**.

Front view of a knuckleball grip.

Side view of a knuckleball grip.

Implement the following drills to reinforce proper pitching grips.

Specific Ideas to Reinforce Pitching Grips

A. Throwing drills—Encourage pitchers to alternate a four-seam grip, two-seam grip, and changeup grip when executing throwing drills or playing catch.

B. Pitching drills—Suggest that pitchers implement a four-seam grip, two-seam grip, changeup grip, and curveball grip when executing specific pitching drills.

C. Throwing long—Encourage pitchers to alternate using a changeup grip with fastball grips when throwing long. This helps players maintain good arm speed with the grip, which is essential to throwing a good changeup.

D. Guessing game—Pitchers should vary their grips when throwing with a coach, teammate, or catcher. The receiver of the pitch should try to correctly identify the grip used for every throw. The goal of the pitcher is to make it difficult for the person to identify the grip based on the release of the ball. The difference in ball speed and/or movement should be how the partner determines the grip or type of pitch.

E. Kneeling curveball practice—Pitchers should get into a kneeling position with their front knee up and their back knee on the ground. The front foot should be pointed to their partner but slightly closed (ten degrees or less). The player's front shoulder should be pointed at their partner with his hands together at the position they separate in their delivery (by the navel). The goal of the pitcher is to create consistent upper body positioning and arm action to allow for proper rotation of the ball. This includes fastball action of the throwing hand until the ball gets beside the pitcher's head. The pitcher should then attempt to slice the batter in half with his pointer and middle fingers, continuing down to simulate stabbing himself in the thigh of his landing leg. However, since he is in a kneeling position, the hand will finish beside his glove-side ankle. This same drill can be done standing. However, it is best performed from a "post-stride" position. Therefore, the pitcher must take his stride prior to completing the action of the upper body, as he did from the kneeling position.

CHAPTER 6

ADVANCED CATCHER PLAY

Myth #1: THE MOST IMPORTANT SKILL A CATCHER CAN POSSESS IS A GOOD "POP TIME" TO SECOND BASE IN ORDER TO PREVENT OPPONENTS FROM STEALING BASES.

Secret: It certainly helps to have a quick release and strong arm when throwing to bases. However, this is just one part of becoming a complete catcher. The best catchers can receive the ball under control, consistently block pitches in the dirt, field bunts, and catch pop-ups behind the plate. In addition, they must be mentally tough leaders who set the tone for their entire ball club.

Myth #2: A GOOD CATCHER SIMPLY NEEDS TO BE BIG AND STRONG SO HE CAN BE A GOOD TARGET FOR THE PITCHER'S THROWS.

Secret: A catcher should be big and in good shape, but it takes more than a muscular body to perform the many skills needed to be an advanced catcher. Good catchers are very athletic individuals who have composure to lead their team, as well as a fierce desire to win!

Myth #3: A CATCHER PREPARES TO PERFORM IN THE GAME BY CATCHING BULL PENS FOR HIS PITCHERS.

Secret: It takes so much more than catching bull pens to become a prepared catcher. Time should be set aside in practice for catchers to specifically drill the finer points of their position. The coach's goal is to train a player so many of the skills needed to play this important position (i.e., blocking and receiving) become instinctive.

CATCHER DEVELOPMENT

At the middle school and high school levels, the position of catcher is critically important to a team's success. Catchers are considered the anchor on the field, and besides the pitcher, they are the next most important player on defense. For instance, a great team without a skilled catcher suddenly becomes very average. Great catchers are athletic, physically and mentally tough, smart, and focused. They inherit a certain amount of leadership from wearing the gear and getting behind the plate. Therefore, most catchers embrace their leadership role and set the winning tone for their ball club by playing the game hard. This is why great catchers have earned the right to receive the nickname "block head."

A catcher contributes leadership by maintaining the pace of the game. He keeps his pitcher and defense focused regardless of the score or situation. He constantly reminds his teammates of potential scenarios, including the outs, number of runners on base, possible team bunt defenses, possible first and third defenses, and he hustles to back up every infield throw to first base when there is no base runner in scoring position.

A fundamentally skilled catcher who can receive pitches with body control and precision can actually improve his pitcher's odds of umpires calling borderline pitches as strikes. In addition, if the catcher is efficient at blocking, he indirectly boosts the confidence of his pitcher, who will feel comfortable baiting the hitter to swing at a changeup or breaking pitch in the dirt with a runner on third base.

Other important attributes for catchers to possess are an above-average arm, quick feet, quick release, and an accurate delivery of their throws to bases. These help shut down the aggressive base running of opponents who may try to steal second or third base on the pitcher.

CATCHER STANCES

Catchers must implement a variety of stances to effectively do their job behind the plate. Each delivery of a pitch must first start with a sign, which is given from the catcher in his "giving signs stance." This lets the pitcher know which pitch to throw and where it should be located. When there are no runners on base, a catcher does not have to be quite as concerned about blocking pitches, so he can create his "primary stance," which is more relaxed. However, when base runners are aboard or there is a full count on the batter, he implements his "secondary stance." In this position, he is more prepared to quickly react to a pitch in the dirt or to move his feet in preparation to throw out a base runner attempting to steal a base. No matter what the game situation is, a catcher will be in one of three specific stances where he must create the proper distance from the hitter. To establish that distance, the catcher theoretically should be able to reach out and almost touch the back knee of the batter. If the batter moves to the front of the batter's box, the catcher should scoot up to maintain this relationship. The same is true if the batter moves to the back of the batter's box **(Figure 6.1)**.

 Refer to "Advanced: Catcher Skills and Drills" and then "Stances" on the DVD for detailed interactive instruction.

The following is the advanced skill progression needed for middle school and high school catchers to create appropriate stances.

Giving Signs Stance

Catchers should know the correct stance for giving the pitcher their signals. Signals tell the pitcher what kind of pitch to throw and where it should be delivered. The catcher should center his body behind home plate, and narrow the distance between his knees so only the pitcher and middle infielders can see his signals. The catcher's upper body should be tall or erect (not slouched over), and his body language should exude confidence. His right forearm should be on top of his right thigh, and the right hand should be deep between his legs to give the signals. The catcher's fingers should not extend where they can be seen from behind or possibly from the side. His mitt should be open and resting next to the left shin (between the left knee and left foot) to prevent the third base coach from peering in and stealing the pitch signs **(Figure 6.2)**.

6.1

This photo shows the approximate distance a catcher should be from the batter. The catcher should adjust to the hitter's placement in the batter's box.

6.2

The catcher's hand signal should be given deep between the legs to prevent it from being seen by the offensive team.

Flaw: A catcher should not continue to use a simple sign system when a base runner is on second base. This allows the offensive player to see the catcher's signal and the location he wants the pitch to be thrown, and now the runner can tip off the batter via his own signal as to what pitch he should expect.

Secret: When playing night games, a catcher may have to use body signals or touches so the pitcher and middle infielders know which pitch is going to be thrown.

Secret: The catcher must periodically watch the hitter to make sure he is not peeking back to steal the signal for the pitch.

6.3

This catcher has assumed a primary receiving stance.

6.4

A side view of the catcher's primary receiving stance.

6.5

A catcher should protect his throwing hand by hiding it behind his right ankle.

Secret: When there are runners on first base, a catcher should bring his knees closer together when giving signs so the base runner cannot steal the sign and relay it to his batter or use that information to attempt a steal on an off-speed pitch.

Primary Receiving Stance

This stance is used by catchers when there are no base runners aboard and less than two strikes on the batter because it is not critical that they perfectly block the ball or throw out any base-stealers. The catcher should create his primary receiving stance with his knees bent, feet outside the knees, toes pointed slightly out, and weight on the inside of the feet. He will be able to sink deep into his crouch with his glove-side elbow just beyond his knees to give the pitcher a good target. The fingertips of his glove should be close to a forty-five degree angle towards his pitcher. This also allows the catcher to receive the ball in front of his body with a relaxed arm and wrist. It is critical that every catcher learns to protect his throwing hand from being hit by a stray baseball by hiding it behind his right ankle (Figures 6.3, 6.4, 6.5).

Flaw: If a catcher does not pay attention to how far he is setting up from the batter, he may end up too far away. This gives borderline pitches a chance to appear to creep out of the strike zone, and they may cost his team a few close calls.

Flaw: If the catcher does not set up his target far enough out front, his glove-side elbow may get trapped between his knees when he tries to receive a pitch to his right or his left.

Secondary Receiving Stance

When there are two strikes on a batter, or runners on base, the catcher should assume his secondary receiving stance. This will give him the greatest mobility, quickness, and range while blocking a pitch in the dirt, transitioning to throw to a base when a runner is stealing, or attempting a pick-off. The catcher should slightly stagger his feet so his right foot is a little bit behind the glove-side foot (the toes on his right feet will be lined up with his left instep). His legs should be spread wider apart than shoulder-width, with his weight slightly forward, but not far enough to bring the heel of his cleats off the clay. He should slightly raise his buttocks to bring his thighs close to parallel to the ground, and his upper body should stay tall and not slouch. To be in a better position to make a quick transition to throw the ball, the catcher should place his hand a safe distance directly behind his glove. This will also help protect it from a foul tip (**Figures 6.6, 6.7**).

Flaw: If the catcher rests his exposed throwing hand beside his right knee when receiving the ball, it will be vulnerable to be hit by a foul ball.

Secret: Catchers should anticipate a ball in the dirt or a runner stealing a base so they will react with precision to execute the play.

6.6

Catchers should use their secondary receiving stance if base runners are allowed to steal bases and if there are runners on base.

RECEIVING SKILLS

Whether a catcher is using a primary or secondary receiving stance, he should implement correct receiving mechanics to give the umpire the best look at the pitch. Receiving is considered an art that can be learned and polished by catchers at the middle school and high school level. The overall goal of a catcher is to receive the pitch in the strike zone as cleanly and with as little body movement as possible.

6.7

 Refer to "Advanced: Catcher Skills and Drills" and then "Receiving" on the DVD for detailed interactive instruction.

The following is the advanced skill progression needed for middle school and high school catchers to receive pitches efficiently.

In a secondary stance, a catcher should protect his throwing hand by placing it behind his mitt. He is now in a better position to block balls in the dirt or throw to bases to cut down would-be base stealers.

Pitch Down the Middle

When the catcher is set up on the center of the plate and receives a pitch down the middle, he should simply catch it cleanly. This is an obvious strike so he can either "stick" the ball by keeping his wrist firm, or he can choose to slightly give with the ball in towards his chest, whichever is more comfortable (**Figure 6.8**).

6.8

This catcher is in his primary stance setup to receive a pitch down the center of home plate.

6.9

This catcher is in his primary stance, receiving a pitch on the inside corner to a right-handed batter.

6.10

This catcher is in his primary stance, receiving a pitch on the outside corner to a right-handed batter.

Secret: A catcher should set up quietly and late (just before the pitcher starts his delivery) for the pitch he called for. This keeps the batter from being able to determine the suspected location of the pitch. Catchers can also pat their glove inside and then move outside every once in a while to deceive the batter.

Secret: A catcher can create softer hands by wearing his glove more loosely. Ideally his glove should fit in a relaxed, semi-loose manner with the palm of the hand slightly exposed. His hand and fingers should form a "U" shape in the glove.

Secret: A catcher should learn the home plate umpire's first and last name, and ask if he prefers to be called by his first or last name. The catcher should use his name in a polite manner at appropriate times throughout the game.

Inside or Outside Strike

When the catcher is set up on the corner of the plate or just off the corner, and the pitch is thrown close to target, the catcher should attempt to catch the outer half of the baseball as close to the plate as possible. He should not let the ball pull his glove backwards or out of the strike zone (**Figures 6.9, 6.10**).

Flaw: When a catcher "sticks" (moves his glove forward to meet the ball and catch it firmly) a borderline pitch, he should not overexaggerate the "hold" (freezing the glove motionless for the umpire to get an extended look at where the ball was caught) if the umpire calls it a ball. This can frustrate an umpire who may feel that the catcher is trying to show him up. Therefore, just give the umpire a good look at the pitch when it is caught and then throw the ball back to the pitcher.

Up or Down Strike

When the catcher receives a pitch that is up in the strike zone, he should try to arrive early at the spot where he will catch the ball so he can attempt to receive the top half of it. He does not want the momentum of his mitt moving upwards to take the pitch out of the strike zone. In addition, when he catches a pitch delivered in the bottom part of the strike zone, he should attempt to receive the ball with his glove fingers above the ball instead of turning the fingers towards the ground **(Figure 6.11, 6.12)**.

Adjusting to a Pitch

When the catcher sets up to receive a pitch in a specific location of the strike zone and it is delivered to a different location, he should recognize this difference while the ball is in flight to the plate. Thus, he

6.11
This catcher is in his primary stance, receiving a pitch on the top part of the strike zone.

6.12
This catcher, in his primary stance, is receiving a pitch on the bottom part of the strike zone.

should gently "sway" or "rock" in the direction of the pitch to get his eyes and body behind the ball when receiving it instead of lazily reaching for the catch **(Figure 6.13)**.

Flaw: If catcher knows a pitch is a definite ball, he should not try to pull the ball back into the strike zone area after catching it. This incorrect movement will be obvious to an umpire and insult his integrity. When a catcher receives an obvious ball, he should immediately remove it from his glove and throw it back to the pitcher.

Flaw: The catcher should never become frustrated with an umpire's strike zone and start to show negative body language and/or verbally react to his calls. This can cause the umpire to "squeeze" or tighten the strike zone.

6.13
This catcher is in his primary stance and adjusted his body by swaying to get behind the ball to catch it.

BLOCKING A PITCH IN THE DIRT

Part of a catcher's responsibility is to learn how to effectively handle pitches that are thrown in the dirt or bounce before they get to the plate. It takes mental and physical toughness combined with anticipation, quickness, and proper technique to be consistent with this critical catching skill. Catchers must be drilled on a regular basis to keep their instincts and techniques sharp. Remember, a player who can handle all reasonable pitches in the dirt is a tremendous asset to his team, and this skill alone can win games.

Refer to "Advanced: Catcher Skills and Drills" and then "Blocking" on the DVD for detailed interactive instruction.

6.14

This catcher is in his secondary stance, ready to receive a pitch down the center of the plate.

6.15

This catcher recognizes the pitch is thrown in the dirt, and he has prepared his body to effectively block it.

The following is the advanced skill progression needed for middle school and high school catchers to block pitches efficiently.

Center Block

Catchers should be taught how to react correctly to a baseball pitched in the dirt directly in front of them. The catcher should instinctively fall forward to his knees and tuck his chin into his chest protector while watching the ball bounce into his chest. In essence, the catcher is following his glove to the ground. This decreases the relative angle of the ball that he is trying to stop with his body, and prevents the ball from getting by him, which could result in a passed ball or wild pitch. The catcher should quickly fill the 5-hole (the empty space created between his legs when he falls to his knees) with a wide-opened glove, while protecting his bare hand from being hit by the baseball by placing it completely behind the glove. He should simultaneously round his shoulders and relax to soften the impact and reduce the rebounding effect. The goal is to let the chest protector cushion the impact of the ball so that it falls in front of the catcher. Once the baseball is blocked, he should quickly get to his feet and retrieve the ball with his throwing hand. This is especially true if base runners are aboard **(Figures 6.14, 6.15)**.

Flaw: Some catchers have the tendency to jump into the air slightly before dropping to their knees. This should be avoided because it creates space for the ball to pass underneath the player.

Left and Right Side Block

This technique requires more coordination, confidence, and body control than the center block. As soon as the catcher determines that the ball will bounce in the dirt to his side, he must drive down the knee closest to the ball at an angle, while simultaneously pushing with the opposite foot. This action swings the catcher's body around the ball while reducing the angle of the block. He should lean forward, tuck his chin into his chest protector, and curl his shoulders in to form a soft pillow that will absorb the impact of the ball and keep it in front of him **(Figures 6.16, 6.17, 6.18, 6.19, 6.20)**.

Flaw: If the catcher recognizes that the pitch will be in the dirt, he should not try to scoop the ball or reach out to catch it with his glove, instead of blocking it with his body. This will result in many passed balls and wild pitches.

Secret: When pitchers throw breaking pitches, the baseballs typically have spin that causes them to kick in one direction or the other, unlike a fastball that tends to take a true hop. Therefore, a catcher must take this spin into account when he calls for a curveball or slider to be delivered.

Secret: Some catchers choose to use separate footwork to block curveballs or changeups. Because it takes more time for the ball to get to the plate, they can implement a "reach and grab" or "step and grab" technique, which can improve their blocking range if the pitch ends up in the dirt off to their side. However, it may be too advanced for some catchers to implement two separate styles of blocking. In this instance, they should choose one or the other to use in all scenarios. Keep in mind that when pitchers start to throw with superior velocity (89 MPH or greater), there may not be sufficient time to effectively use the "reach and grab" blocking style on wide fastballs in the dirt.

6.16

This catcher is in his secondary stance, ready to receive a pitch down the center of the plate.

6.18

The catcher is in good blocking position, ready to receive the ball with his body.

6.17

This catcher recognizes that the pitch is thrown in the dirt inside to a right-handed batter, and he drives his left knee on a diagonal to start the blocking process.

6.19

This catcher recognizes that the pitch is thrown in the dirt outside to a right-handed batter, and he drives his right knee on a diagonal to start blocking.

6.20

The catcher is in good blocking position, ready to receive an outside throw with his body.

THROWING OUT BASE RUNNERS

At the middle school and high school levels, base runners are free to attempt to steal bases. The average high school base runner can run to second from their lead at first base in 3.5 to 3.7 seconds. This means that in order to throw out players attempting to steal, a pitcher and catcher must work together to give each other a mathematical chance for success. For instance, if a catcher has a pop time (from the pop of their glove to the pop at the base of the fielder's glove) of 2.2 seconds, the pitcher should deliver the ball to the plate from his set position in less that 1.3 seconds for any chance of throwing out the fastest base runners.

Catchers choose to implement various types of footwork that can assist their ability to get the ball out of their possession and on the way to the intended base as quickly as possible. Regardless of what footwork he chooses to implement, the keys to a catcher's upper body will be consistent. These priorities include staying low, bringing the glove thumb to the right shoulder as the catcher makes a quick transition to a four-seam grip, getting the upper body into a power position with the throwing hand near the right ear, and taking his chin to the target. The player should simulate throwing down a narrow hallway to his intended target.

 Refer to "Advanced: Catcher Skills and Drills" and then "Throwing" on the DVD for detailed interactive instruction.

The following is the advanced skill progression needed for middle school and high school catchers to develop the proper technique for throwing to bases.

Throws to Second Base

When a runner is attempting to steal second base, the catcher can choose between a couple of different options for his footwork. Regardless of the choice, it is critical that he transitions his body to a power position as quickly and efficiently as possible.

REPLACE FOOTWORK

When a pitch is received somewhere between the catcher's shoulders or slightly off to his left side, he will typically implement throwing footwork similar to a shortstop who is quickly trying to deliver the ball to first base. When the base runner is stealing, the catcher should lean forward to gain some momentum into his throw. Just as the ball is about to impact the catcher's glove, he will begin to move his body into a power position by "clicking his heels" or replacing his feet. In this case, that means the right foot moves towards the left foot as the left foot simultaneously directs towards second base. Once the throw is released, the catcher should continue his momentum towards the base for a step or two **(Figures 6.21, 6.22, 6.23, 6.24, 6.25)**.

Flaw: If a catcher rises up while catching the ball to make his throw to a base, he wastes valuable time and takes energy away from the direction of the throw.

Flaw: Upon receiving the ball, the catcher should avoid flipping it out of his glove into his hand in an attempt to make a quicker transition. This usually results in a mishandled ball.

6.21

This catcher is in his secondary stance, ready to receive a pitch down the center of the plate and throw a base runner out if he attempts to steal second base.

6.22

The catcher receives the pitch and starts to rotate his glove to his right shoulder or ear. His feet begin to simultaneously replace each other as they prepare to bring the body into a power position.

6.23

The catcher is staying low in a full power position, ready to throw the ball to second base.

6.24

The catcher gets extension to his target and throws the ball on a line to his middle infielder just below belt height.

Flaw: If a catcher does not have the arm strength to throw the ball to second base, he should not compensate by throwing the ball in an arc in order for it to reach the base. This takes too much time and is rarely effective.

Flaw: It is a fact that the baseball travels faster than any human being. Therefore, a catcher should never run a few steps before throwing the ball in an attempt to throw it harder. The same principle applies to players who try to wind up in order to throw the ball as hard as possible to the base. This is all a waste of time. The key is to get the ball out of the throwing hand and on its way to its destination as quickly as possible.

Secret: Catchers who possess the quickest feet, transition, and release will typically have the best pop times. However, when you have those characteristics mixed with an above-average arm, you have a special combination that often results in superior pop times.

Secret: To give the fielder the best chance of handling the throw, it is acceptable for the catcher to throw a long hop to second base.

Secret: When a catcher has the arm strength to throw all the way to second base, he should attempt to throw the ball in a straight line in the air (without taking a bounce) so his teammate can catch it somewhere between knee high and belt high. This gives the ball extra carry and provides a margin for error if the throw is a little too high or low.

6.25

The catcher completes his throw by allowing his arm to finish outside his opposite knee.

T-STEP (ALTERNATE FOOTWORK)

The T-step is another footwork option for catchers throwing to second base. This can be used on any pitch location within reason. When the catcher is about to receive the pitch, he will gain some momentum to second base by taking a short, quick step with his right foot straight to that base while turning this same foot perpendicular to the pitcher's rubber or parallel to the front of the plate. This will rotate his body into a power position directly in line to second base. Once the throw is released, the catcher should continue his momentum towards the base for a step or two.

Throws to Third Base

It has been said, and most good base runners agree, that stealing third base is easier than stealing second base. This is true for a couple of reasons. First, the base runner can take a bigger lead and often can get movement towards third base prior to actually starting to run. Second, most pitchers and middle infielders do a poor job holding the runner close at second base. Therefore, catchers must be extremely efficient and accurate when throwing out a base runner attempting to steal third. The good news is that the catcher's throw has less distance to travel than a throw to second base.

CLEAR BEHIND

When a runner is attempting to steal third base, catchers typically choose to implement their "clear behind" footwork to give them the space needed to throw behind a right-handed batter. If a left-handed batter is hitting, the catcher can simply implement his "replace" footwork (as detailed previously in "Throws to Second Base"). To effectively clear behind the batter, the catcher will drop his right foot back behind him as he receives the pitch. His left foot will follow to move him into a power position to throw to third. Once the throw is released, the catcher should continue his momentum towards the base for a step or two (**Figures 6.26, 6.27, 6.28, 6.29, 6.30**).

Flaw: A catcher should not attempt to throw a runner out at third base by moving straight through the batter in the batter's box. In fact, the batter has a right to stand there as long as he intentionally does not attempt to get in the catcher's way. The catcher must implement proper footwork to work around the batter as he makes his throw.

Flaw: If it is apparent that the base is already stolen, the catcher should not throw for any reason, especially not to show off his arm. When there is no chance of getting an out on a play, only bad things can happen from an unnecessary throw.

JAB STEP

If a runner is attempting to steal third base, and the pitch takes the catcher to the right side of the plate or towards the left-handed batter's box, the catcher

6.26

This catcher is in his secondary stance, ready to receive a pitch inside to a right-handed batter when the runner at second base attempts to steal third.

6.27

As the catcher receives the pitch, he stays low and takes a drop step with his right foot to begin to clear the right-handed batter.

6.28

The catcher quickly brings his left foot in line with his right to create a power position to third base.

6.29

The catcher gets extension to his target, throwing the ball on a line to his third baseman, who will catch it between his knee and belt.

6.30

The catcher completes his throw by allowing his arm to finish outside his opposite knee.

likely will choose to use his jab-step footwork. The catcher will take a step with his left foot to meet the pitch, and then bring his right foot in line to create a power position to third base. This produces distance to the front side of the right-handed batter so that the catcher has a clear path to throw to third. Once the throw is released, the catcher should continue his momentum towards the base for a step or two. Some catchers choose to implement alternate footwork to clear the batter. They may feel more comfortable stepping towards a pitch on the outer half of the plate with their right foot first, and then bringing their left foot into a power position to throw to third base. Either way is acceptable (Figures 6.31, 6.32, 6.33, 6.34).

6.31
This catcher is in his secondary stance, ready to receive a pitch up and away to a right-handed batter when the runner at second base attempts to steal third.

6.32
As he receives the pitch, the catcher stays low and takes a jab step with his left foot towards the ball to begin to clear his body to the right-handed batter.

6.33
The catcher quickly brings his left foot in line with his right to create a power position to third base.

PASSED BALL OR WILD PITCH RETRIEVAL

Catchers must learn how to efficiently retrieve a passed ball (a ball that gets past the catcher) or a wild pitch. This is especially the case if a runner at third base may attempt to score. Learning to quickly locate the ball and track it down can make the difference between an out at the plate or a run for the opponents.

6.34
The catcher completes his throw by allowing his arm to finish outside his opposite knee.

 Refer to "Advanced: Catcher Skills and Drills" and then "Passed Ball" on the DVD for detailed interactive instruction.

The following is the advanced skill progression needed for middle school and high school catchers to develop proper technique retrieving a passed ball and a wild pitch.

Attack the Ball and Slide Glove-Side

Once the catcher recognizes that the ball has gotten past him, he should quickly spring to his feet, remove his mask, and run full speed after it. The pitcher should help the catcher locate the ball by pointing in its general direction as he is running to cover the plate. He should also shout "third" or "first" to indicate the direction of the ball at the backstop. The catcher should toss his mask away from the play and slide feet-first on his shin guards to the right

6.35

The catcher attempts to block a wild pitch in the dirt. However, it scoots by him to the backstop.

6.36

The catcher quickly pops up from his knees to his feet and hustles after the ball. The pitcher will point in the direction of the ball.

6.37

The catcher should slide feet-first beside the ball, bringing his chest over the ball and corralling it with his throwing hand and mitt.

side of the ball, field the ball, and throw, all in one motion, to the pitcher for the tag. If the ball is still rolling or moving, the catcher should use his glove to corral the ball into his throwing hand. If the ball has come to a complete stop, he should pick it up with his bare hand (Figures 6.35, 6.36, 6.37, 6.38, 6.39).

6.38

The catcher should rise up on his knees to put his body in a better position to make the throw.

6.39

The catcher should quickly make an accurate snap-throw to the pitcher covering home plate.

Flaw: If a catcher runs after the ball and picks it up with his back to the plate, he will waste significant time and probably lose the opportunity of getting the base runner out at the plate.

Flaw: If a ball gets past the catcher with a base runner on first, it is dangerous if he chooses to lazily trot after the ball in frustration. Often an aggressive base runner with some speed can go from first to third base if there is a large amount of foul territory or space from the plate to the backstop.

Secret: The catcher should attempt to throw the ball belt-high to the pitcher to allow for margin of error. If he tries to throw the ball exactly where the tag should be, he may throw the ball into the ground just before it reaches the pitcher's glove, making it very difficult to catch.

Secret: If there are runners aboard other than the one at third base, and the catcher retrieves a passed ball, he must make a split-second decision whether to throw to the plate or limit the damage by holding onto the ball. If he has a legitimate shot at the runner at the plate, he should release a snap throw to his pitcher covering the plate. If he senses that the runner heading home will be safe, he should hold the ball to prevent an unnecessary throw that could end up being mishandled.

POP-UPS

At the middle and high school levels, catchers must become more comfortable and increase their confidence executing the catch of a pop-up around home plate. This simply may be the most difficult play in baseball. This is especially true when the ball goes up and down directly over home plate or a few feet out in front of the plate.

 Refer to "Advanced: Catcher Skills and Drills" and then "Pop-ups" on the DVD for detailed interactive instruction.

The following is the advanced skill progression needed for middle school and high school catchers to develop proper technique for catching a pop-up behind the plate.

Find the Ball

Understanding the concept of how the ball spins off a hitter's bat can be helpful when attempting to make this very challenging play. In addition, understanding the flight of the ball when it is popped up directly behind the plate, or even in front of the plate, will allow the catcher to develop a game plan to track the ball for the catch. A right-handed batter typically fouls the ball towards the first-base side of the field (from a spot directly behind home plate all the way down the right field line). A left-handed batter is exactly the opposite. Therefore, a catcher should immediately remove his mask and look in the proper direction when the ball is hit upwards. However, a ball that is popped up directly behind or over the plate will have tremendous backspin. This will cause the ball to fly in the general direction of the stands (behind home plate), and then it will circle back towards the plate. If the ball literally goes straight up off the bat, it has the potential to end up at the pitcher's mound. A catcher must first accurately locate the ball in the air to eventually make the play **(Figures 6.40, 6.41, 6.42)**.

Flaw: The catcher should never give up on a pop-up around the plate, thinking someone else will take it from him.

Secret: Catchers must be aware of the wind direction because it will play tricks with the ball while it is in flight.

6.40

The catcher is in his secondary stance, ready to receive the pitch.

6.41

The catcher should react to the pop-up in foul territory by turning in the correct direction and removing his mask.

6.42

The catcher should read the spin on the ball and determine his path to the ball.

Make the Catch

Once the ball is located, the catcher must strategically track it down for the catch. Typically, a catcher will turn his back to the fair territory to make the play. When the pop-up has reached its peak and has started to descend, the catcher should call for the ball to let others know he is

6.43

The catcher should discard his mask and move forward to meet the ball as it spins back towards him.

6.44

The catcher should catch the ball in front of his face with two hands to secure it in his mitt.

going to make the play. When the catcher is certain he has a correct path to the ball, he should discard his mask by tossing it out of the way, off to his side. If possible, the player should catch the fly ball directly in front of his face. However, if he misreads the ball and is facing the field of play, he should attempt to catch this ball about belt-high with the palm of his mitt to the sky **(Figures 6.43, 6.44)**.

Flaw: If a catcher runs too hard after a pop fly directly behind the plate, he may actually overrun the catch, if he is not careful.

Secret: The pitcher should point at the pop-up in the air to help the catcher find the ball.

Secret: When the pop-up is going to land right beside a backstop or dugout, and the catcher is on the run to get to the play, he should slide feet-first while making the catch. This protects him from colliding face-first with any objects.

FIELDING BUNTS

At the middle school and high school levels, catchers must be more skilled at fielding bunts than younger players. When winning becomes the primary focus of playing, coaches will ask their players to sacrifice bunt or bunt for a hit to move base runners into scoring position. There is a specific technique used to field a bunt and throw to third, second, or first base. When the batter makes a movement to indicate that he is going to bunt, the catcher should shout "bunt, bunt, bunt" to alert his teammates of their defensive responsibilities. No matter where the ball is headed on the ground, the catcher should aggressively attack it, never assuming another infielder will make the play. However, if the catcher is called off by a teammate from making the play, he should peel off and get out of the fielder's way so he does not impede the attempt to make the out.

6.45

The catcher is in his secondary receiving stance and recognizes the batter is showing a sacrifice bunt.

6.46

The catcher should remove his mask and start to track down the ball. In this case, the bunt went to the third-base side of the infield.

Bunts Towards the Mound or First Base

When the ball is bunted towards the first-base side, the catcher should quickly move to the ball. He should approach it from the left side and get his body over the ball. If the ball is still rolling, he should field it by bringing his glove and throwing hand together to secure it. However, if it is stopped, he should retrieve it with his bare hand. Once the ball is secured, he should take a quick shuffle to get his momentum and direction towards the base of his choice, and then throw the ball. If it ends up near the first base line, the catcher must field the ball and then clear himself by taking a step towards the mound or the first base dugout to avoid hitting the base runner with the ball.

Bunts Towards Third Base

When the ball is bunted in the general direction of third base, the catcher should quickly move to the ball, approaching it on the right side of the ball. This will put his back towards first base. If the ball is still moving, the catcher must place his left foot beside the ball to give his body room to secure it with his glove and throwing hand. If the ball has come to a stop, he can place his right foot beside it, quickly secure it, pivot, and throw to first base **(Figures 6.45, 6.46, 6.47, 6.48, 6.49)**.

6.47

The catcher should turn his back to the infield as he brings his chest over the ball to retrieve it. If the ball has stopped rolling, he should pick it up with his bare hand.

6.48

The catcher swings his left foot towards first base to bring his body into a power position to throw.

6.49

The catcher makes a strong throw to first base for the forced out.

Work through the following drills and practice ideas to reinforce good catcher mechanics.

Specific Catcher Drills

 Refer to "Advanced: Catcher Skills and Drills" and then "Catcher Drills" on the DVD for the following drills.

Tennis ball—Improves the mechanics and confidence of catching a pitch with control behind the plate **(Figure 6.50)**.

Receiving variations—A catcher should use every opportunity to improve his receiving skills, such as when a pitcher is getting his side work (bull pen work) or he is simply playing catch **(Figure 6.51)**.

Block and recover—Improves a catcher's mechanics and confidence blocking balls in the dirt and then transitioning to quickly track down the ball to prevent the runner from taking extra bases **(Figure 6.52)**.

Blocking variety—Improves the mechanics of blocking baseballs that are off to the catcher's side **(Figure 6.53)**.

Passed ball—Improves a catcher's mechanics of retrieving passed balls or wild pitches, and then throwing to the pitcher covering home plate for the tag **(Figure 6.54)**.

6.50

See "Tennis ball drill" on the DVD.

6.51

See "Receiving variations drill" on the DVD.

6.52

See "Block and recover drill" on the DVD.

6.53

See "Blocking variety drill" on the DVD.

6.54

See "Passed ball drill" on the DVD.

6.55

See "Transition drill" on the DVD.

6.56

See "Pop-up drill" on the DVD.

Transition **(Figure 6.55)**:

> **Phase I:** Improves the catcher's ability to quickly transition the pitch from his glove to his throwing hand and get the upper body into a power position.
>
> **Phase II:** Improves the catcher's ability to transition the ball from his glove towards his right ear, upper body turn, and release the throw to second base.

Pop-up—Improves a catcher's ability to catch pop-ups around home plate **(Figure 6.56)**.

Additional Catcher Practice

A. Coaches can use a pitching machine (if one is available) to give catchers many repetitions to work on secondary receiving stances in which they must catch the ball and throw to second or third base.

B. Ask catchers to put on full gear and get behind the plate during batting practice to become accustomed to catching and blocking the ball when a batter swings and misses, takes a pitch, or the ball is thrown in the dirt. This can also give catchers experience throwing the ball back to the mound.

C. Coaches should encourage catchers to practice their receiving skills by controlling or "sticking" (moving the glove towards the pitch to meet it, and holding it firmly in place for a split second when the ball is caught) the baseball when they are performing their throwing drills or playing catch.

D. Catchers should participate in practice games or modified scrimmages to learn how to receive the baseball and block the ball with actual hitters in the batter's box.

CHAPTER 7

ADVANCED OFFENSE

Myth #1: THE MORE SWINGS A PLAYER TAKES, THE BETTER HITTER HE WILL BECOME.

Secret: *This is partially true. If a player has good swing mechanics, he will likely improve, assuming he has good pitch recognition skills and mental toughness. However, a player with poor fundamentals will likely reinforce his bad habits.*

Myth #2: THE BEST HITTERS ON THE TEAM DON'T NEED TO LEARN TO SACRIFICE BUNT.

Secret: *Every player in the game of baseball should learn to sacrifice bunt. It is selfish to think a particular player is too good at swinging the bat to help his team win a game in a critical situation by moving a key runner into scoring position.*

Myth #3: A PLAYER SHOULD ONLY LEARN TO BUNT FOR A HIT IF HE IS REALLY FAST AND BATS LEFT-HANDED.

Secret: *Bunting for a hit is another bullet in a player's offensive arsenal. Of course it helps to have speed; however, a well-executed bunt for a hit can be an asset to any player who is willing to put in the time to learn the proper technique.*

OFFENSIVE DEVELOPMENT

At the middle school level, winning games becomes more important. At the high school level and above, it is the main reason the game is played. Therefore, to become a complete offensive threat by the time a player reaches the high school varsity level, he should eventually be able to implement the three main aspects of hitting: pitch recognition, mechanics, and game plan. He should also be able to perform critical execution skills, such as the sacrifice bunt, bunt for hit, hit and run, base running, and team plays.

Throughout middle school and high school, pitchers continue to gain velocity, improve their command of pitches, and increase their ability to deceive hitters. A pitcher who throws 90 miles per hour can bring the ball to the plate in approximately four-tenths of a second. Therefore, a hitter who still has obvious offensive flaws, in spite of the success he may have had at the beginning and intermediate levels, will likely begin to struggle. It is imperative that these obvious swing weaknesses are properly addressed and eliminated as quickly as possible; it will become increasingly difficult for players to make changes to their muscle memory as each year passes. In other words, if coaches, parents, or the athletes themselves fail to address swing flaws, they are allowing a player's brain and nervous system to be falsely programmed. Once the obvious problems have been conquered, coaches and players must begin to concentrate on the finer aspects of swinging the bat or performing execution skills. Remember, in baseball, all the little things add up to big things.

ADVANCED HITTING MECHANICS

Good hitters come in all shapes and sizes. However, because the skill of hitting a baseball is so difficult, many coaches fall into the trap of thinking there is only one correct way for a player to swing the bat. They have a "one size fits all" mentality and try to force all hitters into their specific mold. The mechanics they teach may have worked for them personally, but they may not work for everyone who plays this game. If they did, all high school, college, and professional players would hit exactly the same way.

It is critical to start the phases of the swing correctly because an early flaw will often manifest itself into more serious problems as the player's mechanics progress to contact with the ball and finishing the swing. Once a player has established efficient swing mechanics that will enable him to handle various pitch types on the inside, middle, and outside of the plate, his confidence will soar. A swing that allows for a short path of the bat barrel to the ball and good extension will increase a hitter's odds for success, even against the best pitchers in his age group.

 Refer to "Advanced: Offense Skills and Drills" and then "Hitting Mechanics" on the DVD for detailed interactive instruction.

This player demonstrates the recommended "square" stance

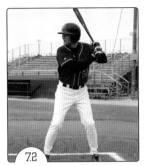

A side view of the recommended "square " stance.

This batter demonstrates an "open" stance.

The following is the advanced skill progression needed for middle school and high school players to swing the bat with fundamental mechanics.

Phase I: Stance

Players must strive to achieve an athletic stance to create the balance they need to efficiently swing the bat. As they step to the plate, they should place their feet slightly wider than shoulder-width apart, knees and hips slightly flexed, weight slightly forward, and head just over the toes. The player's head should be held straight up and down, with both eyes focused on the pitcher. The batter should raise his hands to a starting position somewhere near the top of the shoulder farthest away from the

This hitter demonstrates a "closed" stance.

pitcher or slightly higher. Both elbows should be relaxed. The angle of the bat should not be extreme; for instance, it should not be pointed straight up, parallel to the ground, or wrapped behind the hitter's head. The goal is to take a short, compact swing to the ball, and extreme bat angles can lengthen a swing and decrease a player's odds for consistent contact with the ball. Most batters create a stance with the toes of their feet parallel to the side of home plate. This is called a squared stance (Figures 7.1, 7.2, 7.3, 7.4).

Flaw: If a player sets up his stance too far from—or too close to—the plate, this poor plate coverage may induce flaws in the swing. The hitter will eventually have to adjust his swing mechanics to get the bat barrel to the baseball in the strike zone.

Flaw: When a batter consciously or unconsciously tightens his muscles, the muscles become slow. He may feel stronger, but good hitters know that ridged muscles are slow muscles, and relaxed muscles are fast muscles.

Flaw: When a batter improperly sets up his stance, he may close off his front shoulder, which turns his head away from the pitcher. This can block his more distant eye from seeing the pitch, which can significantly affect his depth perception and his ability to hit the ball.

Flaw: A hitter should not attempt to match his stance to that of his favorite professional player just to look good. Remember, professional baseball players are just that—professionals. If a middle school or high school player makes a significant adjustment to his stance, such as using an open and closed stance, very high or low hands, or standing erect or squatting down, the movement should have a purpose and increase the player's odds for success.

Secret: A player should choose a bat that he can control, feel comfortable swinging, and use to generate good barrel speed.

Secret: Great players establish a routine when getting into the batter's box to hit. Routines provide an element of comfort and familiarity, and this increases a player's confidence.

Secret: Most great hitters hold the bat in their hands where the fingers meet the palms. This is where they are strongest, and this grip generates the most quickness, power, and control when they swing. Players should learn to instinctively grip the bat close to where the knuckles of the four fingers of each hand (minus the thumbs) are lined up. The knuckles don't have to be perfectly aligned, just close.

Secret: Players should create a gentle rhythm or add slight movement to their batting stance. It is easier for a player to start his swing if his body is already in motion instead of frozen in a static stance.

Secret: Players should visually track the ball as it is released from the pitcher's hand. Quickly identifying spin, speed, and pitch location will significantly increase the decision-making skills of the batter.

Secret: Standing in the back of the batter's box allows a player more time for pitch recognition.

Phase II: Load (and Stride)

When the pitcher is about to deliver the ball to the plate, the batter should create his load and stride to be in a strong position to attack the ball. Some players load and stride at the same time, and others choose to load the upper body before they stride with their front foot. A player must implement what feels most comfortable to him. Some methods of loading include a distinct weight shift against his back side, a slight inward turn of the front knee, a very slight inward turn of the front shoulder, slightly pushing his hands back or back and up, or a combination of these. The key is that a player should feel the energy gather against his back leg. When the stride foot lands, the batter's hands should be at the "knockout slot" or in the position they would deliver a punch (4 to 6 inches off the back shoulder, or directly over the back foot). There are various ways for the batter to stride as well, including the traditional short movement of the front foot forward, a toe tap, a leg lift, or no stride at all. Regardless of the type of stride, it is critical that the batter puts his stride foot down in the clay in enough time for him to execute his

7.5

Players should be taught how to load and stride to create a strong position to attack the ball.

7.6

A front view of a player who has executed his load and stride.

swing. In addition, the player should gently land on his stride foot near the big toe or the ball of his foot. A batter's weight will usually shift slightly (a few inches) forward on the stride. However, his head should not move past the center point between his two feet **(Figures 7.5, 7.6)**.

Flaw: A player should never push his hands so far back towards the catcher that he effectively eliminates the elbow joint in his front arm. In this position, his arm appears as a "bar," hence the terminology "barring out." This action creates a very long and slow sweeping swing.

Flaw: If a batter unintentionally strides open or closed as he prepares to hit, he is changing the direction of his body with the step of his front foot. This can make it difficult for the player to get the bat barrel to the ball. Ideally a batter wants to stride directly to the pitcher, unless he strategically starts with an open or closed stance. If this is the case, the batter should stride to bring his body into a position where he is close to square, with the tops of both of his cleats parallel to the side of home plate.

Flaw: If a batter strides and simultaneously turns his front foot to point at the pitcher, he will prematurely open his front knee, front hip, and front shoulder. Each of these movements is detrimental to the hitter's effectiveness. Generally, a stride angle of forty-five degrees with the front foot is the maximum permitted until after the hitter makes contact with the ball.

Secret: The loading process gets a player "ready to hit." The batter should not load and stride to automatically swing at the ball. Pitch recognition skills will determine whether the batter actually swings at the pitch or not.

Secret: A player's load has the effect of stretching his core muscles. This is the result of the upper body moving slightly backward while the stride foot moves slightly forward. Some coaches use a verbal cue of "walking away from the hands" to help players visualize the stretching of the player's core that occurs during the loading process.

Secret: The harder a pitcher throws, the earlier a batter should load (and stride) to be ready to hit. The slower a pitcher throws, the later a batter can load (and stride) to be ready to hit. However, the loading process usually occurs close to the time a pitcher's hands separate in his delivery.

Secret: It is critical that a player keeps his head and eyes as still as possible when creating his load and stride to effectively see the ball and be ready to hit.

Secret: A batter's stride is typically short, soft, straight, and slow.

Phase III: Rotation

Hitters must allow the ball to travel from the pitcher's hand to the plate before they swing the bat. When a hitter decides to attack a pitch, he will instinctively drop his front heel straight down into "foot plant" to initiate a short weight shift from the back side into his front side. Simultaneously, his back heel will begin to lift off the ground as he engages his hips into the swing. During rotation, the batter's head should stay as still as possible. His back elbow, back hip, and back knee "stay connected" or work together to bring the hands down and along an inside path to the baseball. The knob on the small end of the bat essentially controls the barrel of the bat. This means the barrel initially follows where the knob goes in the swing. Thus, in order for the barrel to take a short path to connect with the pitch, the batter should initiate the knob of his bat to the inside half of the baseball. He should attempt to keep his bat barrel back and up as long as possible. This action, often referred to as "barrel delay," allows the gathered energy created through rotation to transfer and release into the bat barrel at the last possible instant before contact. The whipping action of the barrel through the ball at contact results in increased bat speed, ball speed, and power **(Figures 7.7, 7.8, 7.9, 7.10)**.

Flaw: During the rotation phase, the hitter should take care that his bat barrel does not prematurely move away from his body towards the opposite batter's box. This incorrect action is called "casting" and creates a long, slow swing.

Flaw: During the rotation phase, the hitter should not allow his bat barrel to drop lazily towards the ground, which creates a scoping effect to the swing. This flaw causes the hitter to have a long swing and hit many weak fly balls.

Flaw: When the hitter is in his rotational phase, he should not try to generate bat speed by pulling his front shoulder away from contact or "off the ball." This prematurely takes the bat barrel away from contact and out of the hitting zone.

Flaw: Because there is no time to waste when facing dominant pitching, every movement that takes excess time will eventually hurt a player's consistency. One such wasted action is excessively spinning the front heel towards the back foot on the way down into foot plant. In essence, the player's body has to wait for his heel to intersect the clay before he can implement the swing. In addition, the excessive spinning action of the front heel on the way to the ground can prematurely pull the front knee, front hip, and front shoulder off the swing, resulting in poor contact with the ball.

Secret: It is acceptable for hitters to initiate the rotation phase of their swing by either accelerating their hips slightly before starting their hands, or they can work at the same time. Some hitters have exceptional hip flexi-

7.7
The hitter begins his swing by initiating the hips into rotation.

7.8
A front view of the beginning of the batter's swing.

7.9
The batter's hips rotate his body; the back elbow stays close to the back hip to create a short, powerful swing path.

7.10
A front view of the batter's hip rotation and swing path.

bility and rotate by releasing their hips a split second before their hands. This is fine as long as the hitter's front shoulder can stay closed to the pitcher when his hips fire. This creates a whipping action of the hitter's body that brings his hands down and through contact with the baseball with increased barrel speed.

Secret: Due to rotation during the swing, a player cannot literally take the knob of his bat directly to the baseball. However, when a player initiates his swing with this intent, it results in a desired short swing path to the pitch. Many great hitters and hitting coaches say that the knob of the bat initially controls the direction of the barrel of the bat to the ball.

Phase IV: Contact

At contact, the hitter's head and body should be behind the baseball in order to create maximum leverage. His hands should be in a palm up/palm down position (one hand palm facing up, the other hand opposite) to allow for maximum extension through the hitting zone. The batter's head should be as still as possible and his eyes should be focused on the ball. The hitter's back elbow should be near the side of his hip, and the back arm should be bent close to an "L" position. His front arm should be slightly bent but firm. The batter's front knee should also be slightly bent, but it can straighten out at contact with the ball. His bat barrel will be below the height of his hands. The stride foot should remain mostly closed until after contact, and the hitter should be balanced with good posture. The back heel should raise off the ground to release the hips into full rotation, and the back leg should also be close to a power "L" position **(Figures 7.11, 7.12, 7.13, 7.14, 7.15)**.

7.11

The batter should use his body posture and rotation to create leverage when he makes contact with the pitch.

Flaw: When the player has a long swing, he will tend to swing around the ball, making contact with the outside of it. Coaches refer to this as a "hook and pull" hitter. This type of hitter must commit his swing to a pitch earlier than a player who has a short swing path otherwise he has more chance of failure.

7.12

A batter's position at contact—he should be behind the ball, back arm and leg near a power "L" position, and his hands held palm-up/palm-down.

7.13

Inside strike: The batter should attempt to make contact with a pitch on the inside part of the plate, out in front of his body in a strong posture position.

7.14

Middle strike: The batter should attempt to make contact with a pitch down the center of the plate deeper in the hitting zone.

Flaw: When a hitter has the incorrect perception that he must swing down on the ball all the way to contact, he ends up chopping at the ball. This does not create the best opportunity for consistent contact. Another problem is created when the player swings up at the ball or "upper cuts," trying to lift the ball in the air. Some players have the incorrect perception that this is how they should hit home runs.

Flaw: If a batter is fooled by the speed of the pitch, or he is impatient and attempts to take his chest and head to the ball in order to hit it before it get to the plate, his balance and posture will suffer. In addition, his back elbow will move to a weak position away from his back hip (disconnected), which usually causes the ball to be hit softly to the defense.

7.15

Outer strike: The batter should attempt to hit the pitch on the outside part of the plate slightly deeper than a pitch down the middle of the plate.

Flaw: A batter should not try to adjust the placement of his stride based on the specific pitch location. For instance, he may incorrectly attempt to stride towards the plate on an outside pitch, and step away from the plate on an inside pitch. A batter's stride foot should be down on the ground well before he knows the exact pitch location; otherwise, he will likely be late executing his swing.

Secret: Every hitter has "body eyes," which are his navel and the front of his back knee. At contact with the baseball, a player's body eyes should directly face the ball.

Secret: Each pitch location has an ideal contact point in the batter's hitting zone (see photos). The inside strike should ideally be hit to the pull side of the field. The middle strike should ideally be hit to the middle of the field. The away strike should ideally be hit to the opposite field. Typically, the hardest pitch location for batters to master is the outer third strike.

Phase V: Extension

Hitters get very good extension with the barrel of the bat through the "hitting zone," which gives the player more room for error when timing the pitch. For example, a batter should visualize hitting five baseballs in a line back to back, maintaining his hands in a palm up/palm down relationship. This keeps the bat barrel on the same plane as the ball for a longer period of time. The goal of the hitter's swing is to be short and quick to the ball, and then to get extension in order to stay through the ball. This desired action of the swing is referred to as "short to and long through." A hitter who prematurely removes the bat barrel from the hitting zone before achieving full extension of the barrel dramatically decreases the chances of consistently hitting the ball hard **(Figures 7.16, 7.17)**.

To increase his odds of hitting the ball hard, a player should achieve full extension (with the barrel of his bat) through the hitting zone.

Flaw: When a hitter prematurely turns his top hand over or "rolls" his wrist, it changes the path of the barrel to contact and prematurely removes the bat head from the hitting zone.

Secret: It is beneficial for the batter to keep his head as still as possible through contact and extension of the swing. The more a hitter's eyes move, the harder it is to track the baseball, recognize the pitch type, and make solid contact with the ball.

Secret: Ideally, a batter should try to hit the ball where it is pitched. This means he pulls an inside pitch, hits a middle pitch up the middle of the field, and hits an outside pitch to the opposite field.

A front view of the fully extended batting position.

Phase VI: Finish

The hitter should finish his swing the way he started it, with balance and good posture. The hitter's head should be close to perpendicular with his shoulders and his eyes focused on where contact was made with the ball. He should finish his swing near the height of his front shoulder (which is now facing away from the pitcher). However, the actual height of the finish will vary based on the pitch location. For example, pitches at the top of the strike zone will create a swing finish that will typically be lower than when a pitch comes in at the bottom of the strike zone. It is ideal to keep both hands on the bat (instead of removing the top hand); however, this is a personal preference (**Figures 7.18, 7.19**).

The hitter should finish his swing balanced, with his head and eyes in the direction of contact with the ball.

A front view of the hitter finishing his swing.

Flaw: The batter should avoid rotating too much on his back foot, thereby finishing his swing with poor posture and balance. This is called "over-rotation."

Secret: Some players finish their swing up on the tip of their back toe, but others feel more comfortable finishing on the ball of the back foot, and still others actually lift their back foot completely off the ground when they hit the ball (bringing it back down to the ground after contact). It is a matter of personal preference.

Swing from start to finish: From side and top views **(Figures 7.20, 7.21, 7.22, 7.23, 7.24, 7.25, 7.26, 7.27, 7.28, 7.29, 7.30, 7.31, 7.32).**

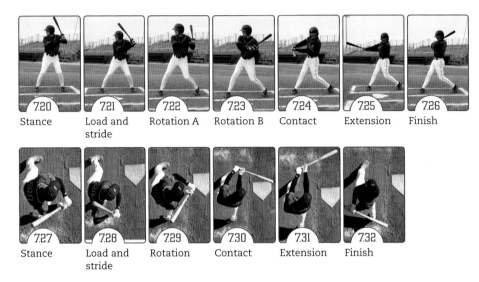

7.20	7.21	7.22	7.23	7.24	7.25	7.26
Stance	Load and stride	Rotation A	Rotation B	Contact	Extension	Finish

7.27	7.28	7.29	7.30	7.31	7.32
Stance	Load and stride	Rotation	Contact	Extension	Finish

Work through the following drills and practice ideas to reinforce good swing mechanics.

Specific Hitting Drills

 Refer to "Advanced: Offense Skills and Drills" and then "Hitting Drills" on the DVD for the following drills:

Tee work—Improves the fundamental swing mechanics of a hitter **(Figure 7.33).**

Basketball tee—Helps hitters create good extension through the ball **(Figure 7.34).**

One arm bat—This drill can be executed with the top or bottom hand to link the body parts together to create a good swing plane, extension, and finish **(Figure 7.35).**

Double tee—Creates a good swing plane or bat path to the baseball with an emphasis on extension **(Figure 7.36).**

Double tee command—Helps a hitter get into a position so he is ready to hit before either attacking an inside or outside pitch (off the tee) **(Figure 7.37).**

Noodle tee—Helps hitters create a short swing path to the ball **(Figure 7.38).**

Bat inside stride foot—Helps a hitter avoid excessive rotation of his front heel into foot plant **(Figure 7.39)**.

Front foot platform—Prevents hitters from lunging or jumping at the ball **(Figure 7.40)**.

High tee—Helps hitters create a correct swing path to the baseball **(Figure 7.41)**.

7.33

See "Tee work drill" on the DVD.

7.34

See "Basketball tee drill" on the DVD.

7.35

See "One arm bat drill" on the DVD.

7.36

See "Double tee drill" on the DVD.

7.37

See "Double tee command drill" on the DVD.

7.38

See "Noodle tee drill" on the DVD.

7.39

See "Bat inside stride foot drill" on the DVD.

7.40

See "Front foot platform drill" on the DVD.

7.41

See "High tee drill" on the DVD.

Additional Hitting Practice

A. Side toss—Adults can set up a station where they kneel off to the side of a hitter in up to a forty-five degree angle. They can toss the ball underhand to the player, who hits the ball into a net. If it is a bad feed, the hitter should "take" (not swing at) the simulated pitch. It is critical that adults make good feeds so they are not creating flaws when the child is trying to hit the ball. The goal is to enforce proper swing mechanics; therefore, the feeder must not hurry and rapid-fire one feed right after the next. Caution: if an errant feed is made and the hitter mistakenly decides to swing, it can put the feeder at risk of being hit with the ball. This can cause serious injury or even death.

B. Front toss—Adults can set up a protective screen, such as an L-screen, directly in front of and a short distance away from the hitter to ensure accuracy. Feed a firm underhand toss to the hitter from the side of the screen (making sure to keep your hand and body behind the screen to avoid being hit with a batted ball). This allows the batter to swing at strikes from an angle similar to one they would see in the game. It is a great way to elicit many swings in a short time and to build confidence.

C. Batting practice from the coach and/or a batting machine—Simply throw batting practice to hitters or use a pitching machine to provide extra opportunities for athletes to hit the ball.

D. Hitting peas with a dowel—This helps hitters improve their hand/eye coordination. A player either delivers the peas underhand or overhand from the side or front. Caution: The person throwing the peas should wear protective eye gear to prevent eye injury.

E. Film hitters—Adults can set up a video camera to tape each player taking three to five swings. Play back the video frame by frame to help expose flaws that cannot be discerned with the naked eye.

EXECUTION SKILLS

Execution skills are offensive weapons that a player can possess to help his team win games. Sticking with the weapon analogy, execution skills are the number of "bullets in a player's gun," and the more a batter possesses, the better. A one-dimensional offensive player has limitations. The time will come when a certain pitcher will have his number. If he has no chance of putting the ball in the field of play, he is worthless to his team and becomes nothing more than a free out for the defense. Thus, possessing the threat of being able to sacrifice bunt, bunt for a hit, hit and run, slash, or squeeze bunt provides valuable options for a player to help his team win games. Note that sacrifice bunt mechanics are the only specific execution skill taught in this chapter and on the DVD.

 Refer to "Advanced: Offense Skills and Drills" and then "Sacrifice Bunt" on the DVD for detailed interactive instruction.

Sacrifice Bunt

A sacrifice bunt is a method used by batters to put the ball in the field of play so the base runner(s) can be advanced into scoring position or from second base to third base. A properly executed sacrifice bunt does not impact the batting average of the hitter in a negative way. Typically, a batter will attempt to sacrifice bunt the ball to the first-base side of the field when a runner is on first base. When runners are on second base or first and second bases, the batter will attempt to sacrifice to the third-base side of the field to provide the best opportunity to successfully advance his teammates. When sacrifice bunting, it is critical that the player only attempt to bunt strikes. If the pitch is a ball, the player should simply pull the bat barrel out of the strike zone before the ball arrives. Sometimes a player will be asked by his coach to attempt to sacrifice bunt with two strikes when a foul ball will constitute an out. In addition, the batter is not concerned about fooling the defense. Thus, he must square around early enough to give himself the time he needs to get into a good bunting position. If the defense wants to overly commit to charging, then the coach may decide to counteract by implementing a slash bunt.

When a player is asked to sacrifice bunt, he should move to the front of the batter's box to create more fair territory. There are various ways a batter can turn his body to get into a bunting position, such as squaring his feet or pivoting. The key is that the athlete must establish balance and square his chest to face the pitcher, distributing his weight slightly more to his front side. He must then establish the proper distance from the plate where the barrel will cover the strike zone. This is called "plate coverage." The batter should establish a proper bunting grip by sliding his top hand up to the balance point of the bat. He should pinch the back of the bat so his fingers are protected from getting hit with the ball. The player's bottom hand should slide up a few inches off of the knob to provide more bat control. It is this hand that will create the angle with the bat to first or third base. He will then position the bat out in front of his body where his arms are extended but remain slightly flexed. This will help cushion the ball as it impacts the barrel. The batter will flex his knees and hips to lower himself behind the bat to line up his eyes

7.42

The batter should move up to the front of the batter's box to give himself more fair territory to get his sacrifice bunt down in the field of play.

with the barrel and the pitch. This is referred to as "eye-bat ratio." The player will then make sure his bat starts at the top of the strike zone, with the bat's barrel slightly higher than its knob. The hitter will attempt to maintain this upper body alignment by simply bending his knees to lower to any pitches at the bottom of the strike zone (Figures 7.42, 7.43, 7.44, 7.45).

Flaw: If a player attempts to bunt a pitch by lowering or dropping the barrel of his bat to a low strike, he will put the bat in a bad position. Typically, when the barrel goes down, the ball gets popped up.

Flaw: When a batter slides his bottom hand (knob hand) too high on the bat and positions it next to his top hand, he will destroy the integrity of the bunting grip. A pitch thrown with above-average velocity can then knock the bat barrel backwards due to the lack of stability.

7.43
The hitter should square his body to create good balance and make sure his hips and shoulders are facing the pitcher.

7.44
The batter should create good plate coverage, eye-bat ratio, and keep the barrel slightly higher than the knob of his bat.

7.45
The batter should create good plate coverage, eye-bat ratio, and keep the barrel slightly higher than the knob of his bat.

Flaw: A batter should never turn his head diagonally to the ground when setting up or executing his sacrifice bunt. His eyes should remain parallel to the ground through his bunting mechanics.

Flaw: A batter should not attempt to sacrifice bunt by stabbing or jabbing the bat barrel at the pitch. The goal is to soften the ball as it impacts the barrel by maintaining flexion in the elbows and wrists. This acts to naturally deaden the ball on contact.

Secret: The batter should focus on the top half of the pitch as it travels to the plate. This will help him hit the bunt down on the ground.

Secret: If the pitch enters the strike zone above the barrel of the bat, it is a ball, and the hitter should not attempt to bunt.

Secret: Some advanced bunters choose to start their sacrifice mechanics at the bottom of the strike zone and rise up to bunt a high strike. They do this because they feel it is easier to adjust in this manner than to start at the top of the strike zone and lower to a position to bunt a low strike. Either way is acceptable.

PART TWO

Outside the Lines

his section offers valuable insight to baseball coaches and players who desire to take their game to the highest level. It is important that serious baseball enthusiasts seek wisdom about the much-overlooked and underappreciated mental side of the game. Unfortunately, many individuals involved with coaching or playing baseball choose not to take the mental aspects of baseball seriously. They may feel the information is far-fetched or not practical to actual game performance.

It is true that all players are not ready to grasp and apply this cutting-edge information. However, coaches must use their best judgment to determine when a player is serious enough about his game and mature enough as a person to benefit from principles revealed in the "The Mental Edge" chapter. Keep in mind there comes a time when only the mentally and physically strongest survive to play baseball at the game's highest levels.

In addition, this final section of the book reveals critical information about the much-misunderstood topics of the college recruiting process and the Major League Draft.

Many high school players who are blessed with comparatively superior physical talent may desire to one day continue their game at the collegiate or professional levels. However, playing college or professional baseball is far from automatic, and raw talent alone is not always enough to make it happen for a student-athlete. Chapter nine "The College Recruiting Process" and chapter ten "The High School Player and the Major League Draft" reveal critical information and insight that can help players and their families set realistic guidelines that can help make these lofty dreams a reality!

CHAPTER 8

THE MENTAL EDGE

Myth #1: IT IS NOT WORTH A PLAYER'S EFFORT TO SPEND TIME LEARNING ABOUT THE MENTAL SIDE OF THE GAME OF BASEBALL. ALL OF HIS TIME SHOULD BE DEVOTED TO LEARNING BASIC FUNDAMENTALS IF HE WANTS TO REACH HIS FULL POTENTIAL AND PLAY AT HIGHER LEVELS OF THE GAME.

Secret: *Players who want to reach their full potential must tap into every advantage available to them. Practical application of mental principles can produce great dividends for a relatively small investment. In addition, it takes superior mental toughness to play the game of baseball at the highest levels.*

Myth #2: BASEBALL IS A GAME OF REACTION. THINKING TOO MUCH KILLS A PLAYER'S GAME. THUS, IMPLEMENTING A MENTAL GAME WILL ONLY REDUCE A PLAYER'S PERFORMANCE, NOT MAKE HIM BETTER, BECAUSE HE WILL THINK TOO MUCH!

Secret: *Baseball is 80 percent mental and 20 percent physical. The best players perform with a high degree of confidence. Effective application of mental skills is one way to improve confidence. Mental skills are executed in between pitches so a player can react correctly without interfering with performance.*

Myth #3: SEEKING WISDOM ABOUT THE MENTAL GAME IS HELPFUL; HOWEVER, THERE ARE SO MANY PRINCIPLES THAT THEY ALL GET JUMBLED TOGETHER. MOST PLAYERS WILL NEVER FIGURE OUT WHICH CONCEPTS WORK BEST FOR THEM.

Secret: *Every person has strengths and weaknesses. Players should continually review practical application of mental skills and determine which areas need the most attention. If a player implements one mental skill at a time and learns to effectively use it, he will be ready for more advanced concepts that can help him reach his potential.*

THE POWER OF THOUGHT

Whole courses of study are taught on the science of the mind and its impact on sports performance. Sports science experts spend years researching how the mind controls the body and learning new techniques to improve our mental capabilities. However, the eventual challenge is to make this critical information digestible and functional by making it practical. A player or coach should focus on a short list of important mental principles that can be implemented in the average to above-average player's game. If an athlete is fortunate to play at the college or professional level, practical mental skill application becomes more specific and essential.

Physical baseball tools can take a player a long way in this game, but, sooner or later, only the mentally strong survive the daily grind of professional baseball. Clyde King, former manager of the New York Yankees, states, "Mental toughness is so important! You must prepare yourself mentally and physically for every game." Often the greatest challenges a player will face in the game of baseball are not his opponents but himself. However, if a player has not shown interest in advancing his physical tools, then trying to get him to implement a "power" mind game will be futile. On the other hand, a player who buys into the benefits of mental training should begin by focusing on practical mental aspects that give him the greatest reward for the smallest investment of time.

Baseball players at all levels rarely tap into their full mental potential. The power of the human mind is so much greater than most players understand. For instance, the mind is capable of creating real or imagined images that can help a player succeed or cause him to fail. The power of the mind is also demonstrated in our dreams, which can seem so real and intense that we think we have actually experienced what were mere thoughts. Memories can cause people to cry, laugh, become angry, excited, or anxious. Familiar smells can invoke distant memories of childhood, as well as positive or negative experiences from someone's past. Hearing old songs takes a person back to another place and time. The mind can play tricks on a person as it registers images with the subconscious that are not recognized by the conscious mind.

For the Skeptics

Using the brain can give a player an edge on his opponents. In addition, a strong mental game is necessary if a player wants to fully enjoy baseball and maximize his full potential at the high school level and beyond. Unlike other baseball skills, improving a player's mental game does not require physically swinging a bat or throwing a ball. It is a skill that should be refined and perfected over time though consistent practice and application.

If a player is skeptical about the benefits of the mind's role in the game then his brain's power to improve his performance will be significantly limited.

For instance, most dedicated baseball players don't think twice about spending countless hours perfecting their swing, fielding ground balls, throwing bull pens, or lifting weights. Yet they snicker at the thought of dedicating any time to improving their mental performance.

To witness the power of mental training, the skeptic should look no further than his own kitchen for proof. Close your eyes and picture a bright yellow lemon in a fruit bowl on your kitchen counter. Reach into the bowl and remove the lemon. Using the sharpest knife in the drawer, slice the lemon into equal parts. Droplets of fresh lemon juice run down the peel of the lemon and start to form a small pool on the counter. Reach for the most luscious segment of lemon and take a big bite, releasing bursts of juice all over your mouth and tongue. Is your mouth filling with saliva in anticipation of the sour taste? This is happening over an object that does not exist except in your mind. It is just a small example of the mind's power over the body. Therefore, it should be evident that we can train our minds in a way that our bodies will react to what we think. For instance, we can apply this information in baseball to cause our bodies to react correctly to training.

If that does not convince the skeptic, then possibly he should study world-class or Olympic athletes who regularly tap into the power of their minds to perform at the world's highest levels. For example, a high diver closes his eyes while envisioning successfully completing each move of his descent before ever climbing the ladder to the platform above. The athlete visualizes a successful dive repeatedly in his mind until the body replicates to perfection what the mind has already perceived. Those athletes know that a person can only achieve what he will allow his mind to perceive! The more times a player successfully completes a skill, both in the physical realm and in the mind, the more confident and consistent he becomes.

PRACTICAL MIND GAMES

The hard-working player will enjoy the mental challenge that the game of baseball provides. He is the player who will try all positive things that can give him the winning edge. Ultimately, if a person plays this game long enough, he will realize that everyone can hit, field, and throw. Therefore, the factor that separates one player from the next is finding and capitalizing on the mental edge!

For a player or team to fully benefit from the mental side of baseball, it is helpful for their coach to additionally grasp fundamental concepts of the mental game and continually reinforce them throughout the season. The key is for them to simplify mental principles so they can be successfully applied to the game. The second option is for players to learn these principles on their own. Here is a list of ten concepts that can give any player the mental edge over his opponents.

Principle #1: Mental Movies

Flight schools have million-dollar simulators that effectively train their pilots by giving them a realistic experience of what it is like to fly an airplane while they are simply looking at a computer screen or sitting in a hydraulic capsule. Baseball players have their own training simulator, which is just as effective as the pilot's million-dollar machines but cost nothing more than a player's time. This game simulator is the player's mind! The first mental skill that baseball players should learn and master is successfully executing physical skills in their minds. Coaches often refer to this as the skill of visualization. Players should locate a quiet place to sit, relax, close their eyes, and begin the practice of seeing themselves successfully performing baseball skills in their mind's eye.

PRACTICAL APPLICATION: FIRST-PERSON VS. THIRD-PERSON IMAGERY

The first way to implement visualization skills is to practice completing the process in first person. This is nothing more than imagining looking at things through your own eyes, using a visual perspective. The second way is to see yourself in the third person. This is imagining yourself from the perspective of others looking at you as if you are the star in a movie. Generally first-person visualization is more effective than third person for actual game performance, but a player who can practice using both perspectives in combination will realize the greatest benefit.

A parent or coach can begin to introduce simple visualization skills to their team or child at the beginning levels of baseball. Like the physical skills needed to play the game at a high level, it takes time before a player will see the direct benefits of visualization. For example, players can visualize themselves performing the various phases of a basic fundamental swing. Players can imagine five swings in first person and five swings in third person before going to sleep at night, and repeat the process again first thing in the morning when they awake. Over time, a player will find that his muscles learn the actual skill of hitting at an increased rate.

Through effective mental rehearsal, players can actually improve their muscle neuron patterns (muscle memory) without physically performing a skill. In simple terms, muscle memory can be defined as how a player's body performs a baseball skill. Coaches often refer to a player's muscle memory as "a habit." They can have good or bad physical habits. Because baseball is a game of repetition, a player's main objective is to learn and train the body to react correctly in a game situation. No matter when or how a player decides to practice visualization, be sure he focuses on generating the adrenaline rush associated with game success. His goal is to heighten his senses and nervous system to feel like he would in the actual game.

A word of caution: Make sure the player has been taught correct fundamental baseball skills, or has an accurate understanding of how the specific skill should be performed before he begins implementing visualization or mental rehearsal skills. That is one of the reasons why we have created the skills and drills videos on the accompanying DVD. It is healthy for someone to watch the videos over and over again to reinforce proper technique. Remember, a player is reinforcing his muscle memory or habits when he visualizes himself performing a skill with his brain. Thus, he does not want to reinforce or possibly even create bad habits through the process of visualization.

Once the basic skills of visualization have been learned and effectively applied, players can use this in many other scenarios to improve game performance. For example, players can spend time visualizing before the competition, in pre-game preparation, or even while competing during the game. No matter where a player is implementing visualization, it is vital to see his visualized performance using the first- and third-person perspectives. In addition, he should attempt to make his mental movies as real as possible. He can accomplish this by incorporating as many of the five senses as he can—hearing, taste, smell, feel, and sight.

For example, a player can use visualization before he goes to sleep, when he wakes up, or any other time of the day when he wants to close his eyes to reinforce excellence. He may start his mental movie in which he watches his third-base coach giving him signs as he imagines the distinct fragrance of fresh-cut grass. He then steps into the batter's box to hit, digging his leather cleats into the damp red clay beneath his feet as he takes his practice swings. He hears the rumbling of the crowd in the background and a bead of sweat runs down the back of his neck. He glances up to see his teammates standing on the edge of the dugout cheering him on. He glances to the pitcher with his fielders behind him, and brings his attention to the logo on the pitcher's cap to bring his eyes into the correct depth perception to track the pitch. He watches the pitcher go through his windup, and he tracks the release of the ball as it travels towards his hitting zone. He sees himself attacking a fastball as he gets full extension through the ball, and watches and hears the sound of the ball exploding off the bat. He peeks up as he is running to first base to see the ball fly into the left-centerfield gap for a stand-up double.

Another effective use of visualization is when a player is at practice, hitting off a batting tee. Physically hitting the ball is certainly beneficial to skill development; however, the addition of the imagination can provide a simulated pitch for a player to hit, even though the ball is actually stationary. To replace the boredom of continually looking at a ball on the tee, the player can visualize hitting off of the best left-handed pitcher in his league. He can imagine the pitcher completing his delivery, and track his breaking pitch from release point to the hitting zone. He can see the spin of the laces on the ball, and hit the pitch to the area on the field based on the tee placement.

Taking this principle one step further, a player can transfer his visual imaging skills to the actual game. The most logical time to apply visual imaging is when a hitter is getting ready to bat in the on-deck circle. This player can imagine himself in the current batter's shoes as he watches a series of pitches from off to the side. As he observes each individual pitch to the plate, he can choose to either take the pitch (not swing) or simulate hitting the pitch as he actually would in the batter's box. Once it is his turn to bat, he is ready and confident to succeed. The truth is that the human mind cannot always distinguish between what is imagined and what is real. In essence you've "been there and done that," so just relax and let it happen again in real life!

Principle #2: Positive Reinforcement

A player will gain confidence performing a skill when he receives positive reinforcement or feedback as a result of fundamental execution of that skill in a game or practice. It can result from verbal or non-verbal cues from a coach, teammate, parent, or member of the community. Positive feedback increases players' confidence by reducing negative clatter from their brains and encouraging them to believe they are capable of success.

PRACTICAL APPLICATION: USE VIDEO

Most people are aware of the benefits of using video analysis to break down a player's swing and diagnose mechanical flaws. However, video can also serve a greater purpose: to build confidence. Most individual players and teams have streaks when they are playing well and streaks when they struggle. Coaches and players call bad streaks "slumps." In order to create a confidence, video should be archived of a player or team when they are performing their best. Store these highlights away and let the player or team watch the DVD when they begin to struggle or slump. For example, games at the high-school level can be filmed, and clips from each game can be "tagged" and stored in hard drives where team or individual highlights can be gathered and burned onto a DVD for continued positive reinforcement and to build confidence.

Very often the reinforcement of watching one's self perform positive actions from the past can trigger positive results in the present. In addition, the player or team can compare video of the present to video of the past, and identify aspects of their game that have changed or need to be adjusted to get back on track. Some players prefer to watch successful video even when they are doing well as a form of "pre-habilitation" or "prehab." Prehab is the opposite of rehabilitation or "rehab." It is a form of preventive maintenance that helps players maintain their skills at the highest level and reduces the likelihood that they will digress.

Principle #3: Setting Goals

Goal setting is an essential skill to apply to all areas of one's life. Successful people engage in it regularly, for they understand the benefits of creating a road map for their lives. Setting expectations for ourselves, writing them down, and working to make them actually happen is a form of self-efficacy. This is a person's belief in his ability to achieve what he desires for his future.

For these same reasons, setting goals is a valuable process for both baseball players and teams. Like all other skills, goal setting must be practiced, refined, and often adjusted over time. It is more than just making a statement about what you hope to achieve, but rather it is devising a plan to reach an intended result in a specified period of time. Setting goals can be detrimental or ineffective if the goals are unattainable or unrealistic. The ultimate objective is to build a player's or team's confidence in their ability to achieve higher levels of performance by proving to themselves and others that they are capable of accomplishing what they set out to do. In addition, this process serves as motivation to work hard every day at practice in order to perform at peak levels during games.

PRACTICAL APPLICATION:
KEEPING A BASEBALL GOAL JOURNAL

Baseball players of all ages should begin writing in a baseball goal journal before the start of their next season. The power of the written word can help keep a player positive when facing adversity; it can improve his focus in the face of distraction; and help him persevere in the face of temporary setbacks. Words imprint a desired outcome on a player's brain. It has been said that a dull pencil is better than a sharp mind. Therefore, a player is more likely to remember what he writes down than what he tries to commit to memory. The intent of goal setting is to provide a player with daily purpose, direction, focus, motivation, and, ultimately, success.

If possible, goals should be specific, measurable, meaningful, and attainable. Each goal should include three to five strategies that will assist the player to accomplish each written objective. If a player cannot determine how he is going to achieve his written objectives, then the goal is more accurately defined as a "dream." In addition to writing specific achievement objectives in his journal, it can be helpful to place an abbreviated copy of the player's goals on his bathroom mirror somewhere visible each morning, in his wallet, or on the ceiling above his bed. It is futile for a player to attempt to set so many goals that he can't possibly reach them all or set a goal that he has no control over reaching. That would likely be setting one's self up for failure.

Players should refer back to their goal journals regularly, and read their goals aloud to themselves to reinforce what they are striving to accomplish. In addition, they should visualize themselves (in vivid detail) accomplishing each goal, and very specifically imagine what it will feel like to succeed. Players should write the date next to each goal as they accomplish it, as well as noting the location and circumstances surrounding the moment. The next phase is to construct new goals that will continue to push the player and challenge him to improve. A player should never be satisfied with his current standing in the game of baseball. He must humble himself and realize that there is always room to improve. Ideally a player's goal journal should be divided into five sections: off-season goals, pre-season goals, in-season goals, long-term goals, and reflection.

The player's first objective is to begin setting short-term goals for the off-season. For example, if one of the player's goals is to improve his arm strength, he could write:

Goal #1: *Improve my arm strength so I can throw the ball 250 feet in the air with proper throwing mechanics.*

Strategies:
  A. Implement a comprehensive throwing program three days a week.
  B. Complete a video analysis of throwing mechanics and address my weaknesses using specific throwing drills.
  C. Participate in a rigorous strength and conditioning program that emphasizes full-body power, hip explosiveness, and arm care.
  D. Incorporate crow hop into my long-toss program to work on a hip loading.

The second objective is to implement goals for the pre-season and then work towards in-season goals. When setting goals for the long term, players should create a road map for the next year, the next two years, the next five years, and so on. In the reflection section, a player can write down anything that is on his mind, or something that provides insight for future goal setting; for example, his thoughts about the keys to accomplishing a goal, what delayed the accomplishment of a goal, or what prevented the goal from being met.

Players can also use their goal reflection section to make notes on certain pitchers or teams, providing insight that may help at a later date. Their notes may include answers to questions such as: What was the opposing pitcher's "out pitch" (the pitch that was thrown when he needed a strike out)? Which pitch did he throw to start most batters? Did he do anything noticeable to tip which pitches he was going to throw? The player should also note any particulars about the pitcher's pick-off move (to various bases) or other keys that may give the player an advantage at a later time. Chances are this player will see that pitcher again in the future and he will already know something about his strengths and weaknesses. He should try to state negative emotions in a positive way because we believe the messages we send to ourselves. If we want to become positive, we must use positive self-talk by thinking, talking, and writing in an affirmative way. Ideally a player should keep a separate journal for each new season. Over time, players will create a personal library of past goals and experiences.

Principle #4: Surround Yourself with Positive People

Most positive people prepare for success wisely. They avoid negative people, poor choices, and vulnerable situations. A baseball player with goals to play at the highest level his abilities will allow should strive to become accountability partners with a positive teammate who can help him stay focused on his goals and dreams. In other words, if you fly with eagles, you soar, and if you run with dogs you get fleas.

We are all going to experience hard times, disappointments, and failures in baseball. We must look deep into a negative experience and discover what went wrong and why. Positive people do not let negative situations get them down for long. We will experience situations such as striking out three times in one game, making four errors, or giving up the winning home run in the championship. These are all situations that can depress us and cause us to spiral downward if we are not careful. Positive players will encourage teammates who are experiencing disappointment or failure. An encouraging word or positive body language at the right time from a teammate or coach can lift a player's spirits and get him back in a positive frame of mind.

PRACTICAL APPLICATION:
CHOOSE FRIENDS WISELY

One poor choice, or negative thought or behavior, can separate a player from the game of baseball forever. A player's choice to associate with or become friends with negative thinkers can start a gradual downward cycle of negative influence and behavior. Friends who lack direction and purpose in their own lives tend to inadvertently distract their focused friends from their goals. They become jealous of the success of others because it brings to light their own lack of direction, poor work ethic, failures, and disappointments. In addition, people who are caught in the cycle of negative thinking, trouble, and despair do not like to suffer alone. In other words, misery loves company. Don't be surprised when a good person goes down largely because of the influence of negative thinkers.

On the other hand, positive friends are probably more "like-minded" to a player who has set goals for himself; thus, they influence each other the right way. They tend to encourage, lift up, support, and respect one another. Positive people are usually goal setters, and goal setters are usually motivated people who improve those around them. For example, a team of positive players and coaches can achieve great things because they are not going to wallow in self-pity, make excuses for their mistakes, or place blame on others. They learn from their mistakes, negative experiences, and disappointments by quickly putting the past behind them and focusing on the future and their next opportunity to achieve success.

Positive players should be aware of the one exception to putting the past in the rear-view mirror. If the negative experience can serve as motivation for the future, the player should write down the event as vividly as possible in his baseball goal journal and store it in the back of his mind so he never forgets it. When the player does not feel like working towards his goal, he should quickly reflect back on that stored memory or read that part of his goal journal, and it should be all the motivation he needs to refocus and get to work. Examples may include the sick feeling a player had when he lost a big game, struck out four times in a row, made three errors on defense, or what it felt like to be cut from a team. If these types of thoughts get a player motivated to give his best every day, then it is the type of "fuel" that he never wants to run out of.

Principle #5: Consistent Mental Preparation

Baseball players are often guilty of coming to the park mentally unprepared to practice or play a game. They may be tired, distracted, or take for granted the focus required to play the game of baseball at a consistently high level. Each player should learn what is needed to sharpen his focus to the highest level each and every time he arrives at the ballpark. Of course this is much easier said than done. For example, at the start of each season, every player is hyped up and excited to get the season underway. However, by the middle of the season, the reality of the team's performance or the daily grind of practice and games makes it harder to maintain that original level of excitement. Another example includes players who get excited and improve their focus for certain opponents but take other teams for granted. Their focus is like the waves in the ocean with peaks and valleys, and as a result, so is their performance.

PRACTICAL APPLICATION:
ESTABLISH ROUTINES

Baseball may be a game of adversity and change, but that is exactly opposite of the way a player prepares to perform. Therefore, a player who knows how to consistently focus and prepare is more likely to have success because pre-established routines breed familiarity, comfort, and confidence. This includes those days when a player does not mentally and/or physically feel well.

Once a player finds a routine that gives him results, he sticks to it. For example, a routine may include listening to certain music on the way to the field and arriving at the ballpark early to hit off of the batting tee. On a really "bad day" when the player does not feel like practicing, he might close his eyes and reach back into his memory for a positive or negative past experience that will get his adrenaline flowing and improve his focus. In addition, he could reference his baseball goal journal to review the goals he has set for himself. This should be enough to reignite his competitive flame and get him ready and focused for that day's practice or game.

Every player must seek and find what works best for him individually within the team routine that his coach establishes. Due to a variety of variables, it is impossible to have the exact same routine, day in and day out, especially at the youth or high school level. However, it is possible to establish a basic routine that can be replicated consistently to prepare the mind to focus on giving the best every day, regardless of how the player feels.

To accomplish this, a player must be able to detach himself from emotions such as feeling good or bad, pumped up or down, and prepare himself to execute skills at a high level of success. The fact is: He is not going to "feel good" 100 percent of the time he steps on the field. However, he must still find ways to focus and perform at a very high level. Therefore, the ability to focus on excellence and accept personal responsibility is an essential character trait for advanced baseball players.

Principle #6: Prolonged Mental Focus

It is a unique challenge for middle school, high school, or college baseball players to perform at peak levels for extended periods of time. Ideally, players arrive at the ballpark ready to practice or compete in a game. Their veins fill with adrenaline and their minds race with anticipation of the challenge that lies ahead. They are pumped up! However, because of a lack of understanding, poor preparation, or not taking themselves seriously, they are vulnerable to forfeiting their mental edge before a practice or game is complete due to physical and mental fatigue. For example, physically demanding practices, games played in extreme heat or cold, or intense games against heated rivals are all scenarios in which players can lose their focus, intensity, productivity, and consistency as time goes on. This is especially true if players were mentally or physically fatigued to start with.

PRACTICAL APPLICATION:
PROPER REST AND NUTRITION

The mind's ability to focus and concentrate for extended periods of time, and the body's ability to perform at peak levels, both require adequate rest and sufficient fuel. If a player starves his mind and body of rest and healthy food, he will be unable to perform at a maximum intensity level for a sustained period of time. Just like a high-performance race car cannot operate to its full potential on inferior fuel, the same holds true for the human brain and body. It can race, but it won't win! A player can perform for short periods of time without the proper nutrition or rest, but he cannot sustain the 100 percent focus and execution needed for seven or nine innings combined with practice, day in and day out. In fact a player's mind and body will often fail him just when he needs them the most

Players who are serious about their performance and want to give themselves the greatest opportunity to consistently operate at peak levels, as well as reach their long-term goals, should consciously eat the right foods and get adequate rest every night. This does not mean they should become fanatical about nutrition and sleep, but seeking balance is the key.

Principle #7: Positive Self-talk

If players believe the words of their coaches, parents, and teammates, why would they not believe the words they speak to themselves? The answer is . . . they do believe their own words. And most baseball players are in a continuous state of self-talk. They do it before they hit, between pitches, on the field, and running the bases. Once a player becomes conscious of this fact, not only will he see how often he speaks internally, but how negative he can be to himself if he is not careful. The goal is to replace the negative messages with positive ones. If not, a player is defeating himself before he even has the chance to suc-ceed. For example, when a player makes an error during the game he thinks, "I stink, I could not field a ball if it were rolled to me" or when he strikes out he says to himself, "I could not hit water if I fell out of a boat."

In fact, players are often much harder on themselves than those exam-ples. The sad part is that players can become so negative, they internally cuss themselves out in pure frustration. Over time, a player who has poor self-control may let his internal thoughts become spoken words. If the coach does not deal appropriately with this player, his words will eventually manifest themselves into negative body language. Therefore, the player is bombarding himself with three sources of negative reinforcement. This must be stopped, and that entire negative mentality must be replaced with a more powerful and effective positive mentality for the player to have any hopes of excellence on and off the ball field.

It is easier if a player never allows himself to get to this point. Players must be made aware of the benefits of positive self-talk, and they must learn to send themselves positive messages every chance they get to combat the nature of this sport, which has so much failure inherent in the fabric of its design.

PRACTICAL APPLICATION:
SCREEN YOUR INTERNAL CALLS
The good news is that if a player believes his negative self-talk then he will conversely believe his positive self-talk! Therefore, the more positive mes-sages a player tells himself, the more he will believe them, and he will feel better about himself and his ability to overcome obstacles. Positive self-talk is a skill that is hard for some players to understand and even harder for others to successfully implement on a daily basis. Just like all other skills in base-ball, positive self-talk takes practice and should be introduced at the begin-ning age levels. An example of a positive self-talk statement would be, "I am going to hit this pitch because I'm skilled, I have prepared for this moment, and I enjoy the challenge."

Principle #8: Emotional Control

Emotions certainly have their place at all levels of baseball. However, displaying or internalizing too much negative emotion can eventually destroy an individual baseball player or an entire team. A display of negative emotion redirects the focus of teammates and coaches from the game and spotlights it on the player acting up every time something goes wrong. Over time, this type of behavior will aggravate and embarrass teammates and coaches who feel that this person's foolish actions are a reflection on them.

Baseball, by its very nature, creates a unique emotional landscape for everyone involved including players, coaches, umpires, and parents. For example, in baseball all eyes in the ballpark are on one particular player at a time. The pitcher stands alone on the mound. The batter stands alone in the batter's box. When the ball is hit, there will be one fielder who receives the ball, and he will throw it to another teammate. Unlike most other team sports, when a player makes a mistake in baseball, everyone knows it.

In addition, a baseball player must often wait for long periods of time to redeem himself after a poor at-bat or a mistake on the field. For example, three innings may pass before a player gets another chance to hit because eight teammates have to bat before him. A fielder who makes an error may not get another chance to redeem himself until the next game. In the meantime, he will likely mull over his mistake for a few days, mentally replaying what he could have done to prevent the error and what he will do differently next time. This is unlike most team sports, where there is so much action at one time that mistakes by an individual are often unnoticed by those in attendance, and usually the player will quickly have another chance to redeem himself.

PRACTICAL APPLICATION:
DON'T BASE SELF-WORTH ON PERSONAL PERFORMANCE

In order to play baseball at the highest levels, a player cannot live and die with every at-bat or each play on the field. Players cannot relate self-worth to daily performance on the baseball diamond. Even the best players are going to have below-par games; it is just the way baseball is designed. Therefore, emotional stability is a huge asset for an aspiring player. Players must avoid the emotional mountaintops and valleys, and establish an emotional "even keel" about their demeanor. Coaches call this a businesslike approach to the game. Don't be mistaken . . . there will be plenty of times when an individual or team will get fired up and show excitement. But it should not be an emotional roller coaster about every little thing that happens in the game.

I will admit, this approach to the game is much easier said than done. People generally become irrational when they are emotionally tied to something. Most baseball players prepare themselves to succeed and they are disappointed when, in spite of all their efforts, they play poorly. They may even get very angry with themselves and become irrational. For instance, watch a parent whose child does not get the playing time they feel he deserves. When this parent gets angry, there is very little anyone can say, including the coach, that will make rational sense and calm his or her spirit. The emotions resulting from poor personal performance have a similar effect on individual players. If they get frustrated with their performance, they try even harder to succeed the next time; if they happen to fail again, they press harder to succeed until their whole skill set comes crashing in around them. This usually results in a slump, and consistent poor performance lands a player on the bench. Negative emotions can be so powerful that some players or coaches carry the game home with them and take out their frustrations on family and friends.

It can also be damaging for players to measure themselves by the standards of other people. Many players strive for "success" and end up frustrated because they are never sure if they achieve it or not. Whose definition of success are they striving to reach? Trying to live up to the standards of others can often leave a player feeling emotionally frustrated and inadequate.

Baseball puts a large amount of stress on young men who are trying their best to be perfect in a game that resists perfection. Players who show a lack of emotional control by verbally lashing out, crying, or using negative body language demonstrate to everyone, including their opponents, that they are emotionally weak. It is common for opponents to take advantage of an emotionally fragile player by mentally "breaking" him. They will continually attempt to "get into his head," which will decrease the player's attention on his actual performance and increase the opponent's chances of winning.

In addition, most players and teams suffer a significant drop in performance when they lose emotional control and become angry or frustrated. Players must be taught and begin to accept that the game of baseball is inherent with failure. George Whitfield, North Carolina Baseball Coaches Hall of Fame inductee states, "Baseball is a game of failure. Round bat, round ball, and you have to hit it square. Nine against one, the pitcher has the ball, and you're on offense. Baseball is a very difficult game. You can fail seven out of ten times in your career and be in the Hall of Fame. You have to be able to make adjustments from pitch to pitch. If you can't, this game will kill you."

A player who demonstrates emotional control in the heat of the game will often become the emotional leader of his team because others can count on him to keep his cool and perform under pressure. On the other hand, a player who continually demonstrates emotional ups and downs, based on his team or personal performance, can become irritating and even cause disharmony among his fellow teammates.

So, how do most professional baseball players calmly walk away from the plate and avoid showing negative emotion after striking out in a critical point in the game? It is a skill that they have perfected over time. They have learned to control their emotions. Players at all levels who develop mental toughness by successfully applying the principles in this chapter have the greatest chance for consistent excellence.

Principle #9: Capture Momentum

Momentum is confidence gained from positive results. In baseball, when a teammate successfully performs a skill against the opponent, it shows other teammates that they, too, can succeed when it is their turn to perform. It is a contagious process. Therefore, momentum provides a team or an individual player with increased mental confidence. It is an invisible force that can literally be captured by an individual or team. It can make a player better than he really is, and without it, he can actually perform below the levels of his actual ability.

PRACTICAL APPLICATION:
CAPTURE "BIG MOE"
Momentum or "Big Moe," as my junior college coach called "him," was the tenth player that we wanted sitting on our bench for the whole game. In order to help our team understand the importance of momentum to victory, my coach personified momentum and taught us that Big Moe was a "fair weather" teammate. In other words, Big Moe does not usually stay with one team throughout an entire game. He shifts from one dugout to another based on who is playing the best baseball. The goal was to keep him on our bench as long as possible, and, in order to accomplish that, we had to continue to do something positive on offense and defense.

Good baseball players and teams understand the mental advantage that capturing momentum provides to each player or an entire team, and it is something they all try their best to control. A big play, a key hit, good base running, or striking a batter out with the bases loaded can swing momentum in one team's favor and get them back in the ball game. A successful "squeeze" play or a pick-off at second base can give a team a mental boost while emotionally deflating their opponents. If they are an emotionally inferior ball club, this swing of Big Moe can mean the difference between winning and losing the ball game.

Big Moe has a direct impact upon individual players as well. Good players strive for consistent mental and physical performance and eventual success. Big Moe spends the day watching all the little things that players do to either make them better or detract from their performance. For instance, he arrives early to the field and makes note of the way the player is dressed for practice or games. Does he wear his uniform correctly? He studies the body language of players and watches the way they carry themselves, how they warm up and throw, and how they approach pre-game practice. He analyzes their attitude towards the game and how they handle failure and disappointments. Finally, Big Moe determines who he thinks is most prepared to win that game or perform at the highest levels in practice, and he joins them. When Big Moe becomes your companion, the breaks seem to go your way. That is because preparation creates opportunities, and opportunities create possibilities for success.

Principle #10: Confident Thinking

Confidence is the greatest mental asset that any baseball player can possess, and it cannot be measured by a mathematical equation, device, or test. Most good coaches have an instinct for identifying confident players. These are the players who want the ball in tight situations. They love to hit with the game on the line, face the opponent's best hitter when it matters most, or they want the ball hit to them when the pressure is at its maximum. Confident players have an internal swagger. It is nothing the player says or does, but rather a glow that radiates from his performance.

However, the inherent level of failure that is interwoven into the fabric of baseball tears away at the confidence of players who try to conquer it. In addition, players must continually battle the self-destructive, negative thinking that attempts to seep into their brains, overtake their confidence, and cripple their ability to succeed. This is why coaches say it takes a "mental giant" to play baseball at the highest levels.

Unfortunately, confidence cannot be purchased off a shelf in a sporting goods store or given as a gift in a time of need. Rather, it is a belief in one's ability to successfully perform that must be slowly grown one experience at a time, while continually being bombarded by failure and disappointment. A player who can successfully develop his self-confidence in this difficult environment now has a mental edge that will reduce his odds of being paralyzed by the ups and downs of the game. In addition, a player who can maintain his confidence is a player who will likely be most consistent and handle pressure more effectively as he progresses to higher levels of the game. Because of this, confident thinkers are prevalent in collegiate or professional baseball.

The fact is: In baseball, players usually achieve what they think they can achieve! It is a form of self-fulfilling prophecy. If a player thinks positive thoughts, he will usually respond positively. On the contrary, if he thinks negatively, he will often generate a negative result. It all goes back to the tremendous power of thought. For example, great players know they can perform skills under heavy pressure, average players think they might be able to perform skills under pressure, and below average players are pretty sure they cannot perform skills under pressure. All three players may have the same fundamental skill sets; however, the player who knows he will get the job done is the one who will succeed the majority of the time.

PRACTICAL APPLICATION:
TAKE SMALL STEPS TO IMPROVE CONFIDENCE

A player's confidence is significantly impacted by his daily preparation, his past performances, and effective goal setting. A player seeking to improve his confidence should create game-like stress on himself whenever possible, including individual or team practice. For example, a player can implement his visualization skills to simulate game experiences that will heighten his senses and increase his adrenaline rush while performing hitting drills. He can secretly compete with teammates to be the best at each skill, drill, or practice activity, and he can challenge himself to give his best mental and physical effort in everything he does. Therefore, when a player commits himself to practicing the game with enthusiasm, focus, and superior effort, he will gradually become more consistent, efficient, and prepared to perform in game situations. In other words, he has taken small continuous steps to build his confidence.

Accumulating successful experiences in game play will also have a significant impact on a player's confidence level. These small "personal victories," whether getting a hit in a big situation, fielding the ball with more regularity, or striking out a batter with bases loaded, begin to add up to improved confidence to perform in the present. They have the effect of a snowball rolling downhill. It starts small, however, with more confidence there is more success, until it becomes easier to succeed and handle the pressure the next time. With accumulated positive experiences, a player will soon find himself in a comfort zone where his confidence is so high he feels no one can stop him from succeeding. Even when things are going poorly, a confident player deletes his temporary failures from his short-term memory. He is well aware that it may be his next swing that brings home the winning run, and he looks forward to being at the plate with the game on the line.

Lastly, confidence is developed in part by setting small attainable goals and reaching them (see principle 3). Once the player's goals are met, he must establish new goals, and the process keeps repeating. For example, a child crawls before he walks. In other words, building confidence through goal setting is a gradual process that does not happen overnight. Each goal that is met provides a small dose of confidence that wipes away a portion of a player's fear, doubt, and anxiety, which increases the player's odds for success.

CHAPTER 9

COLLEGE RECRUITING PHILOSOPHY

Myth #1: A PLAYER'S GAME STATISTICS ARE THE MOST CONSISTENT WAY TO DETERMINE HIS POTENTIAL TO PLAY COLLEGE BASEBALL.

Secret: *A player's statistics may often be inaccurate and misleading. A team's statistics, if recorded and compiled by the same person, may serve the purpose of comparing players who compete against the same teams game in and game out. However, there is not much value comparing the statistics of players from different teams due to many variables that can skew the results.*

Myth #2: IF I START FOR MY VARSITY BASEBALL TEAM THEN I AM GOOD ENOUGH TO PLAY COLLEGE BASEBALL.

Secret: *College baseball is far from guaranteed. For instance, a high school player does not automatically graduate from high school to a college baseball team. In fact, approximately half a million student-athletes play high school baseball, with less than forty thousand of those moving on to play at the college level!*

Myth #3: IF MY SON WORKS HARD ENOUGH ON THE FIELD AND IN THE CLASSROOM, HE CAN EARN A FULL DIVISION I BASEBALL SCHOLARSHIP.

Secret: *It is very important to set goals and work hard to achieve them. However, less than 1 percent of all high school athletes receive a full scholarship at the Division I level. The truth is: There is often significantly more money awarded by college admissions departments for superior academic skills than for superior baseball skills.*

RECRUITING LANDSCAPE

College baseball programs each develop their own recruiting philosophy, which they implement in hopes of signing the top players in the nation, their state, or local area over their competition. The National Collegiate Athletic Association (NCAA) establishes recruiting guidelines for its member colleges and universities, which make up the majority of secondary learning institutions in the country. These member schools compete at the Division I, Division II, or Division III levels, and include junior college programs, which are subdivided in the same fashion. The NCAA "College Bound Student-Athlete Manual" can be found at www.NCAA.org.

It is important to realize that all colleges and universities across the country are not bound by the NCAA. Some secondary institutions are governed by the National Association of Intercollegiate Athletics (NAIA). The NAIA has established its own standards and guidelines for recruiting college-bound athletes. If a player has interest in a school governed by the NAIA, it will be important for him to learn the specific rules regulating those institutions. Information on the NAIA can be found at www.naia.org.

In spite of the efforts of both collegiate baseball programs and their respective governing bodies, the recruiting procedure of individual baseball players remains one of the most misunderstood processes in high school athletics by players and their parents. Families who want the best for their child can gather partial truths from Internet chatter, ballpark hearsay, and recruiting services about how college baseball recruiting works. These random facts, half truths, and myths, combined with the often-unrealistic perception of the child's playing abilities, can lead to confusion, disappointment, frustration, anticipation, anxiety, and anger.

Therefore, for most players and parents, recruiting is a learn-as-you-go adventure that is usually figured out once the journey is completed . . . when it is too late to do anything about it. This can leave a family reflecting on what they could have or should have done differently to bring about a different outcome or better overall experience for all involved.

Desired Qualities of a College Baseball Prospect

College baseball recruiters have the responsibility of locating and identifying superior baseball prospects at the high school level. They attend high school games, summer games, showcases, and college camps, as well as receiving information from professional scouts, recruiting services, and others who know how to identify potential college baseball talent. Often, the first thing that catches someone's eye will be a player's superior physical tools, such as how he throws, hits, fields, or runs. However, in most cases, it takes more than just superior physical skills at the high school level to become a successful college baseball player. Thus, once the desired physical tools are identified, superior college recruiters do their homework by talking to the player's high school coach, summer coach, school counselors, etc., to ensure they attract a player who can produce in the classroom, contribute on the ball field, and stay out of trouble once he arrives on campus.

Most college recruiters project the future baseball potential of a prospect by factoring specific variables into a general recruiting formula. This equation looks something like the following: Physical tools (strengths and weaknesses) + Body type (genetics) + Makeup (mental toughness and character) = "Project-ability" (potential to play college baseball). These factors give coaches clues into a player's future value to a college baseball program. For instance, coaches often seek a favorable body type to complement a player's defensive position. They may even go as far as to evaluate the player's parents to form a judgment on this prospect's future growth and body composition.

Another characteristic that is highly sought after, but more difficult to accurately measure, is a player's psychological makeup. This includes a player's character, mental toughness, competitiveness, intensity, desire to improve, "coach-ability," and willingness to be a team player. Therefore, a high school prospect who possesses superior physical skills, makeup, mental toughness, and a positive academic record is highly sought after and usually equates to a winner on the field!

1. PHYSICAL TOOLS

A baseball player's physical tools are categorized into five distinct areas, which include hitting, hitting for power, fielding ability, arm strength, and running speed. Generally, recruiters will not find many players who grade high in all five areas. The rare "5-tool" player is highly sought after by professional baseball scouts and the top Division I baseball programs in the country.

Most college baseball programs are attracted to "athletes." These are youths who can perform the difficult skills required to play the game of baseball and make it look easy. Joe Sottolano, Head Coach at USMA at West Point states, "Baseball athleticism, the ability to perform a variety of baseball-related skills well with at least one of those skills being done exceptionally well, is the number one thing we look for in a recruit." However, in reality, most players who have above-average tools in some areas usually have weakness or deficits in others. Generally, to be considered a college baseball recruit at some level, a player who has a deficit with one tool should make up for it by excelling in another area. Compared to Division I recruiters or professional baseball scouts, Division II and Division III coaches are often more forgiving when it comes to recruiting prospects who may lack superior physical tools. Please reference "The Five Tools of a Professional Prospect" in chapter ten, "The High School Player and the Major League Draft." These same tools are evaluated and desired by college recruiters when seeking potential college prospects for their program.

2. ACADEMICS

A player's academic record is often a strong indicator of the overall type of a person a college is potentially recruiting. In other words, student-athletes who make good grades in high school demonstrate that they grasp the importance of their education. They likely possess good study habits, punctuality, pay attention to detail, and score well on entrance exams such as the SAT (Scholastic Aptitude Test) or the ACT (American College Testing). In addition, college and university admissions departments tend to extend academic grants that can significantly offset the cost of attending their institution to student-athletes who have proven themselves academically. Very often these financial grants significantly outweigh any money extended for baseball alone. College baseball coaches typically don't want to have to babysit players in their program to make sure they attend class in order to stay academically and athletically eligible.

3. BODY TYPE

A player's body type (how he is physically built) and how it relates to his skill set and potential defensive position(s) is another factor that college baseball recruiters take heavily into consideration. For example, an 18-year-old catcher who is 5'6" and whose mother and father are 5'5" and 5'7" respectively has most likely grown to his maximum height. This player's physical limitations will probably prevent him from moving to the next level of baseball unless he possesses above-average tools as a catcher and hitter. Another example of body type is a six-foot, two-inch, senior shortstop who weighs 160 pounds. He has an athletic frame and his parents are 6'5" and 5'10". He possesses above-average arm strength, hits the ball with gap power (the ball flies through the outfield gaps), and has average to below-average foot speed for a college middle infielder. This player will likely still be recruited based on his skill set and body type. He has the frame to put on muscle over his next four years in college. In addition, if his foot speed does not improve, he can transition to a corner infield position (first or third base) or possibly even play a corner outfield position.

4. MAKEUP

Once a player has demonstrated that he has at least the minimum desired tools for the recruiter who has watched him play or practice, the college will then begin to evaluate the player's makeup, or mental toughness, to see if this prospect has what it takes to play in their program. Makeup is hard to measure and even harder to project. However, it is a quality that is heavily sought after by college baseball recruiters who are increasingly seeking quality people for their programs. Some aspects of playing college baseball that require mental toughness include practicing daily, attending weight training, being punctual to required team functions, studying, and not making decisions off the field that will reflect poorly on the team.

Players must also be mentally tough with the failed experiences that are so inherent in baseball. If a player cannot mentally handle failure, he will prematurely eliminate himself from the game. As explained in the previous chapter, an emotionally fragile player has the potential to act out negatively or inappropriately, and to become a source of distraction, and ultimately, an embarrassment for a program. Too many athletes want the title and perks that come with being a college player, but they don't want to make the daily physical and mental commitment that go along with them.

Pressure in the college game can be very intense. At the Major Division I level (top 25 programs in the country), a player's job is on the line every time he arrives at the ballpark. A bad practice or game can land him on the bench where there may be two or three very capable players ready to take his place. College recruiters want to know if a player can produce when the game is on the line. Will he thrive in big game situations, or will the game be "too big" for the player? The higher the level of college baseball, the more intense the pressure will be to produce consistently. There is pressure for head coaches to win conference championships, to host a regional or super-regional, and to play for the national championship. In fact, the livelihood of some college coaches depends on winning titles. Therefore, it is critical for a perspective student-athlete to have the mental toughness to withstand these demands.

5. CHARACTER

Other intangibles that are highly sought after by college baseball recruiters include character and integrity, clean living, responsibility, desire, intensity, focus, preparation, coachability, and loyalty. These qualities are also very hard to measure and are becoming increasingly hard to find. Most college coaches agree that players who possess these qualities often make up for any deficit they may have in raw ability. Great college coaches know the value of scattering players with these intangibles throughout their lineup (the more of these players the better). They also know that players with strong character do not take days off, and they do work hard in the classroom and stay out of trouble! Jerry Meyers, pitching coach and recruiter at The University of South Carolina concurs: "The most important quality any prospect can possess is character. Desire and work ethic are also included in this. Our recruits must have the necessary physical ability, but it is their makeup that will ultimately give them the opportunity to succeed."

Most college baseball recruiters are turned off by players with questionable character. They prefer recruiting men who demonstrate responsibility and accountability for their actions. College baseball programs cannot afford the negative publicity that comes with student/athletes who make poor choices on or off the field. Recruiters are well aware of the fact that players who can avoid the temptation of drugs and alcohol can make all the difference with wins on the field and consistent behavior off the field.

6. PHYSICAL APPEARANCE

Physical appearance, fairly or unfairly, plays a role in the college recruiting process. It is an indication of a player's priorities and personal focus. Some college programs place more emphasis on this particular attribute than others. In general, baseball is a sport in which coaches expect their athletes to look and act like baseball players. For example, being "clean cut" (short hair and clean shaven) demonstrates to others that this player operates within a team concept and is not trying to draw attention to himself by being different from his teammates.

Players should avoid the temptation to become "accessorized." This may mean the player owns two sets of batting gloves and four wristbands, wears sunglasses on his hat and eye black all over his face, and embroiders his uniform number on everything he wears. Before long, the player looks more like a model out of a recent baseball catalog than a hard-nosed ball player. This behavior can set off a red flag that says this player is more concerned with the name on the back of the shirt than the one on the front. A player's goal should be to let his ability, not his attire, draw the attention of others. Most recruiters would prefer to see more dirt on the uniform from playing the game hard than to see an overly accessorized player. This same principle applies to practices where players should dress appropriately to prepare for hard work. Most importantly, a college baseball recruit should look like a ballplayer, act like a ballplayer, and play like a ballplayer!

When Can Recruiting Officially Begin?

In recent years, the fierce competition to land the nation's best college baseball prospects has forced many college baseball programs to initiate the recruiting process earlier than ever in a high school player's career. For instance, it is becoming more common to hear of major universities receiving verbal commitments from players as early as their freshmen or sophomore year of high school. However, there are still plenty of prospects who fall into the more traditional recruiting timeline that usually begins in a player's junior year or even as late as his senior year of high school. Therefore, the college baseball recruiting process may begin in different years of high school and may look nothing alike for two different players who both have the goal to play college baseball.

For example, the first player may be a dominant high school pitcher at a tradition-rich program in a large city of his state. Because of his superior talent, favorable body type, and good psychological makeup, he has become well known across the nation by college recruiters and professional baseball scouts. In his freshmen year, he plays his high school baseball schedule and moves on to play on an elite showcase team that travels the country during the summer months. Besides performing in his games, he does nothing extra to gain exposure to college recruiters. By the fall of his sophomore year, he has several scholarship offers and will need to make a difficult choice between a handful of top tier Division I programs. He officially signs his letter of intent during the "early signing period" in the fall of his senior year.

The second player is an above-average second baseman from an average high school program in a remote part of his state. He spends the summer playing in tournaments for his high school coach, the fall participating in a few select showcase events, and the winter attending a couple of college hitting camps at schools he would love to attend. By the fall of his senior year, he is still not actively recruited by college baseball programs. However, he continues to focus on his academics and to prepare with his teammates for the upcoming spring season. In the middle of his spring schedule, a junior college coach, who noticed this second baseman at a showcase he attended the previous fall, decides to check on the player's progress by calling his high school coach. He gets a good report. The college coach decides to go watch this scrappy, hard-nosed player perform against game competition and loves the way he prepares, focuses, and performs. As a result, the coach starts actively recruiting this player, who eventually signs a letter of intent to play junior college baseball the summer after his high school graduation. As you can see, both players mentioned above ended up playing college baseball, but their paths to that goal looked nothing alike.

Increased Exposure

A student-athlete who has the goal of playing college baseball may choose to attend individual or team showcases at some point in his high school career to increase his exposure to college recruiters. He may also choose to employ a recruiting service to increase his odds of being noticed. For most players and their families, the primary goal of attending showcases, college baseball camps, or using recruiting services is to get themselves "on the radar." This means that someone important watches them perform and may see present or future athletic potential, or a recruiter is informed by a trusted source that he should take the time to learn more about a particular student-athlete.

Well-selected baseball showcases (team or individual) can be a strategic choice for a student-athlete with college baseball potential because recruiters must invest their time wisely. As a result, college coaches logically focus on showcase venues where many talented players will be on hand at one time. Some coaches also choose to follow the leads provided by recruiting services that they trust.

It is important that a player is mentally and physically ready for the showcase experience so that he has the best chance of performing well. Generally, upper-tier prospects start attending showcases the summer after their freshman year of high school. Other players who attend these events usually do so between the summer of their sophomore year and the fall of their senior year. Be sure to choose showcases and recruiting services with care because some of these can cost $500 or more, and can make impressive promises to help a player find the college of his choice. But when it's said and done, they fail to deliver.

NCAA Clearinghouse

The NCAA Clearinghouse is a branch of the NCAA that determines athletic eligibility. It combines a student-athlete's core academic grades with his Scholastic Aptitude Test (SAT) score and/or American College Testing (ACT) score, and uses a sliding scale to determine whether the athlete is eligible for play. If the NCAA Clearinghouse determines a student-athlete has not met the academic and testing standards then he is not eligible to compete for his freshman season (visit ncaa.org. for specifics). A student-athlete will have to meet NCAA standards at some point in the future to regain athletic eligibility. Generally speaking, once a student-athlete enrolls in college for his first semester of school, the clock starts ticking. He now has a total of four years of eligible play to be performed in a five-year time span. In essence, this provides the student-athlete a one-year cushion in the event he has to "red shirt" (sit out) due to academic ineligibility or injury.

Communication with College Programs

NCAA and NAIA rules distinctly influence what a college or university may or may not do to communicate with a potential prospect during his high school years. Here is a brief timeline outlining NCAA written, phone, and electronic communication guidelines. At any time during this process, a prospective student-athlete can verbally commit to a college but that typically does not happen until sometime between a player's freshman and senior years. Keep in mind these guidelines can be modified by the NCAA from year to year.

Elementary and Middle School: A student-athlete can receive camp information and/or a general questionnaire as well as take an unofficial visit to any campus. A student-athlete can also call, email, or Facebook "friend" college baseball coaches, but if he does not reach the coach directly, the coach or his staff cannot call, email, or return Facebook messages. In addition, college coaches cannot text-message prospects.

Freshman Year: At this point, student-athletes are generally considered "prospective" student-athletes by the NCAA and may continue to receive camp information and/or a questionnaire as well as take unofficial visits to college campuses. The athlete can also call or email college baseball coaches, but if he does not reach the coach directly, the coaches or their staff cannot call or email back. This includes Facebook. In addition, college coaches cannot text-message prospective student-athletes.

Sophomore Year: The process is the same as the freshman year.

Junior Year: As of September 1 of a student's junior year, college coaches can send out specific recruiting mail as well as send email and return a prospect's emails. Otherwise, the process is the same as the previous two years of high school. However, on July 1 before a prospect's senior year, coaches can make phone calls and return phone calls as well as emails. College coaches still cannot text-message student-athletes.

Senior Year: Coaches can send specific recruiting mail, make and return calls, send and return e-mails and Facebook messages. Prospective student-athletes can make official and unofficial visits to college campuses. Some seniors will sign a national letter of intent to commit themselves to specific programs during the early signing period in the fall. Once a player signs his national letter of intent, his future coaches can now text-message this player. Other seniors will not sign a national letter of intent until the spring season or the summer after graduation.

CHOOSING THE RIGHT COLLEGE OR UNIVERSITY

Ultimately, college is about receiving an education. Therefore, prospects should not wait to start the application process until they are recruited by a college or university baseball program. It is recommended that a student-athlete apply to colleges that he would want to attend if baseball were not part of the equation. For instance, if a player suffered a career-ending injury; where would he want to get his degree? If a college baseball program begins to recruit a player, they will give him the opportunity to apply to their school even when the application deadline has passed for a traditional student.

Randy Hood, top college baseball recruiter and Associate Head Coach at the University of North Carolina, Wilmington, states, "You want to choose the right college because if baseball is taken away from you because of injuries, academic issues, etc., you want to be happy and comfortable at that school knowing that you don't have baseball in the picture any more. Athletic fit, academic fit, social, and 'comfortability' fit should all factor into the decision."

Create a Roadmap

Once it is determined that a player is a college baseball prospect (at some level) and he has the goal of playing college baseball, his family should create a plan or devise a roadmap to help him achieve his goal. This includes developing a general course of action for his years in high school while avoiding common pitfalls associated with the recruiting process (see the "Ten Traps to Avoid in Pursuit of Collegiate Baseball" later in this chapter).

Keep in mind that not all players show the athletic potential or the desire to play college baseball when they first enter high school. Most players change mentally and physically during their four years of high school, some for the better and some for the worse. In fact, some student-athletes may not blossom until their junior or senior year. In extreme cases, some players develop college potential after high school graduation. Therefore, if a player demonstrates average physical tools but possesses above-average desire, commitment, and work ethic, he may become a prospect later in his high school career.

A good approach is to treat the college baseball recruiting process like a marathon. It is a gradual process . . . a little here and a little there. If it is treated like a sprint, the player and his parents will physically and mentally burn out before it is complete and this can create significant stress. This is especially true when a player still needs to perform at high levels on the ball field.

Typically, players begin marketing themselves to colleges in an attempt to "get on the recruiting radar" as early as their sophomore year and no later than the start of their junior year. For those who are borderline prospects, there are recruiting services and showcases that can help create additional exposure to college coaches. Some recruiting services charge hefty fees and make big promises. Some recruiting services deliver, and others do not. They prey on the emotional vulnerability of parents who want the best for their son and want to give him every chance to achieve his goal. Some services subtly make parents feel guilty by insinuating they must do everything in their power to "market" their son if he is going to get recruited by college baseball programs. Often, parents who cannot afford to spend large amounts of money will do so to give their child his "shot," and their child may not even be a potential college baseball prospect. It is important to remember that spending lots of money does not always equal receiving good exposure!

If a student-athlete does not take part in a fall sport for his high school, he can participate on a fall showcase team that will play games at colleges and in tournaments that may be scouted by college recruiters. This also gives him the opportunity to play for another coach who may have contacts with college coaches. There are also individual showcases available in which a player can display his skills to college and professional scouts in attendance.

Another way to increase a player's exposure is to attend fall and winter baseball camps at the college for which he has an interest in playing. If the prospective athlete is an upper classman in high school, he should contact a coach on the staff prior to arriving at the camp to let that coach know he has an interest in playing for that school. This gives the college coach an opportunity to meet the player and see him perform in a more personal setting over a two- to three-day period.

The best self-marketing any prospect can do is to perform at higher standards in the classroom and on the ball field because the best skilled student-athletes tend to sell themselves. First, student-athletes should just get out there and play baseball wherever and whenever they can, within reason. Secondly, they should be consummate team players. Thirdly, they should practice and play the game hard. Colleges have recruiting coordinators who scout high school games. Also, most college programs have high school coaches who they trust to help identify possible recruits. If the player is talented and a good person, there is a very good chance that his name will reach the right ears.

However, it never hurts for the player to get some extra exposure. If he participates in an exemplary high school program, he has better chances of being seen. If he is not in a creditable program, then it may become necessary for him to do more to get his name and face on the recruiting radar such as through camps, showcases, or searching out a reputable recruiting service. The best way to locate worthy showcase events or respected recruiting services is for parents to contact college baseball coaches over the phone or via email. Remember, college baseball coaches have contact restrictions with student-athletes so be politely persistent when seeking this advice.

Timing Is Critical

A college baseball team's specific need for talent changes from year to year. Before actual recruitment begins, the coaching staff will evaluate their depth chart for returning players at each defensive position (a depth chart details the number of returning players for a specific position). The staff will then determine how many players are graduating and from which positions, and how many of their players may get drafted into professional baseball. This gives them a feel for what positions they must fill and how much money they have to offer prospects.

A high school player should try to match himself up with a program that will value his services. He should research which schools may have needs for his position in the next recruiting class or two. Nevertheless, a great player may not be recruited by the college of his choice because that program may have to fill other defensive positions first even though, in a perfect world, they would probably love to have this player.

For example, a player may be a top infield prospect in his state and would like to attend University "X" (which is an Associated Press top twenty-five college baseball program). However, the entire starting infield is returning to University "X" next year and the school has quality backup depth at this player's primary position—both of those players are college freshmen. In addition, there is a good chance none of their current upper-class infielders will be drafted in this year's Major League Draft. In this case, University "X" is probably not going to recruit this infielder this year even though he may be a great talent.

CREATING A BASEBALL PORTFOLIO

A well-organized recruiting packet mailed to college coaches can be an efficient way of creating a relationship with prospective recruiting coordinators. Packaging pertinent information with a short, well-constructed skill video can give colleges a chance to see a player's tools without making a costly recruiting trip. This can be particularly valuable to smaller college programs that may not have the time, resources, or manpower to travel to see a player perform. Coaches can also learn more about the player by viewing his resume and academic transcript. In addition, a player's high school coach can be valuable in the process. If he has credibility with various college coaches, he possibly can give them a "heads up" with a phone call, email, or text message that the recruiting packet and video is on the way.

Portfolio Contents

A recruiting packet (portfolio) should only be put together for a player who has proven that he is a college prospect at some level. It is very important to send the packet in its entirety. Sending it in parts can become confusing and irritating to a college coach. If the prospect or his high school coach do not have the time, credibility, or knowledge to put together a recruiting pack or skills video, then a reputable recruiting service can help get your name to the right coaches based on your ability.

A recruiting packet should include the following:

I. **Cover Letters:** Both the high school head coach and the player should write cover letters. Each letter should be short, to the point, and summarize the contents of the recruiting packet.

II. **Skills Video:** Put together a three- to five-minute skills video (DVD). The purpose of the video is to showcase a prospect's physical tools including most of the following: hitting, fielding, pitching, throwing, running, and working on drills. Most college coaches prefer watching players perform skills and drills instead of game highlights. This DVD gives recruiters the chance to see the player's skill mechanics without traveling to watch a game.

Recruiters desire to see the prospective student-athlete performing appropriate skills and drills for their position from various angles, including the front, back, and side. In addition, there should be no editing between repetitions. It is acceptable for the player's video to contain game highlights, but those should last no longer than two minutes and be included at the end of the DVD. Below are recommendations for what to include in the skills video. Note that every tape should begin with an introduction that contains the prospect's name, year in school, home address, email address, and phone number(s).

A. Offensive Focus

1. Hitting off the tee: side and back view (from umpire's view).
2. Bunts: a few sacrifice bunts and bunts for hits (if this is a strong part of your game).
3. Live swings: show the ability to hit to all fields (film from the side and from behind).
4. Game footage: one minute maximum (only include if it is good-quality offensive footage).

B. **Defensive Focus: Infielders**
1. Speed: 60-yard dash.
2. Speed: Home to first base with swing.
3. Infield drills.
4. Ground balls: show range, double play feeds and pivots, and body control fielding slow rollers.
5. Game footage: one minute maximum (only include if it is good-quality defensive footage).

C. **Defensive Focus: Outfielders**
1. Speed: 60-yard dash.
2. Speed: Home to first base with swing.
3. Outfield drills.
4. Fly balls and throw to base: show your range and arm strength.
5. Game footage: one minute maximum (only include if it is good-quality defensive footage).

D. **Defensive Focus: Catchers**
1. Speed: 60-yard dash and home to first base with swing.
2. Receiving: demonstrate ability to receive pitches from a pitcher or a machine.
3. Blocking: demonstrate ability to block pitches to sides and in front.
4. Throwing: Receiving and throwing to second base (pop time).
5. Ask the fielder to straddle second base and let the ball come to him.
6. Pop-ups: fielding pop-ups hit in foul territory behind home plate.
7. Game footage: one minute maximum (only include if it is good-quality defensive footage).

E. **Defensive Focus: Pitchers**
1. Delivery to a catcher: film from third-base view, behind center field, and from umpire's perspective.
   b. Windup mechanics
   c. Stretch mechanics
2. Note: Throw at least three repetitions of the same pitch before you change to another pitch (use your glove to tell the camera what pitch is coming).
3. Game footage: one minute maximum (only include if it is good-quality pitching footage).

III. High School Coach, Summer Coach, and Fall Coach's Evaluations

Include written evaluations from the player's high school coach, summer ball coach, and, if applicable, his fall ball coach. The evaluation should focus on the prospect's physical and mental tools and his makeup.

Each coach's evaluation should include:
1. Contact information for both the coach and the player.
2. Scout's names and contact information if they know and have seen the prospect perform.
3. Recent baseball honors.
4. General information about the prospect's high school (the conference they compete in, size and location of the school, level of competition they compete against).
5. Accurate varsity, summer, and fall team statistics.
6. Player's personal information: height, weight, bats, throws, GPA, SAT, graduation date, positions, 60-yard dash time, home to first base time, etc.
7. Offensive strengths and weaknesses.
8. Defensive strengths and weaknesses.
9. Character summary.
10. Rated skill evaluation.

IV. Unofficial Academic Transcript

Include a transcript printed from the high school's main office or guidance department that gives the coach an idea of the player's academic standing.

V. School and Sports Resume

Enclose a resume that highlights the player's school involvement, clubs, and activities in the community. Include sports and other relevant information.

VI. High School, Summer, and/or Fall Game Schedules

Enclose the player's most recent schedules. This will allow the colleges an opportunity to map out his games and to schedule seeing him play in person.

VII. Newspaper Articles and/or Scouting Reports

College coaches do not have time to read newspaper articles. However, if a player has a significant achievement that was covered in the news, it is appropriate to include it in the portfolio. In addition, in this section of the portfolio include written evaluations from showcases he attended.

RECRUITING TIMELINE

The recruiting timeline of a student-athlete begins at the start of his freshman year with the formation of a continual record of his academic and athletic performance. It is important for a player to prepare academically and athletically if he plans to one day play college baseball. Simply put, those who fail to plan, plan to fail! Remember, there is no need for a student-athlete to follow a timeline if he does not want to play college baseball. It will also not do him any good if he does not have the physical or mental skills to compete at the next level. However, if the player is not yet sure of his goals then he may want to put together a skeleton plan in the event he eventually decides he wants to play college baseball.

The student-athlete and his parents should sit down at the start of each semester and look at the following timeline to make sure he stays on track. Using the calendar and the player's baseball goal journal, they should map out and pencil in specific dates for which to prepare the student on his recruiting journey. Many of the focus elements on this timeline repeat each and every spring of the high school years. These items are list below under the title "Common Elements for Grades 9-12." Each item is listed according to category: Academics, Athletics, or Motivation. Additionally, there are a few "special items" to attend to each specific year as shown under the titles "Freshman Year," "Sophomore Year," "Junior Year," and "Senior Year." Again, each item is listed under one of three categories: Academics, Athletics, or Motivation. This checklist is specifically aimed at the student.

Student-Athlete's Recruiting Timeline
Common Elements for Grades 9-12

FALL SEMESTERS
Academics

1. Familiarize yourself with NCAA and eligibility requirements.
2. Create an academic plan with a school guidance counselor for all four years of high school to be NCAA-eligible at graduation.
3. Communicate to your guidance counselor, academic advisor, and teachers that you have goals of playing college baseball.
4. Try to take more challenging academic courses this semester.
5. Seek academic tutoring if you start to struggle with a class.
6. Join clubs that will reflect your community involvement on your resume.
7. Conduct yourself in a professional and courteous manner both inside and outside the classroom.
8. Always do your best work and hand it in on time.
9. Study for all tests and strive to make A's.

Athletics

1. Register for weight training and conditioning class for this semester if your school has qualified and certified coaches teaching the course.
2. If the preceding does not apply, hire a personal trainer who knows how to condition specifically for baseball. Start to research the effects of nutrition and rest on the human body.
3. Let strength coaches know your goals of playing college baseball.
4. Play fall baseball or focus on eliminating your weaknesses if you are not playing another sport in high school. *Note:* It is recommended that you play another sport to prevent burnout with baseball.
5. Purchase a blank, hardcover book to create this upcoming season's baseball goal journal.
6. Participate in "skill sessions" with your high school coach. If that is not available, take lessons from a qualified instructor. Focus on both offensive and defensive skill sets.
7. Attend baseball camps offered by respected college and university programs.
8. Try to take at least eight weeks off in the fall or winter from throwing so you can rest your arm.
9. Begin a comprehensive throwing program after Christmas break or eight weeks before the high school season begins.

Motivation

1. Read at least one book about baseball knowledge, the life of an inspirational player, or a true story about an inspirational team.
2. Watch non-fiction and fiction sports motivational movies.
3. Attend a leadership camp.

SPRING SEMESTERS

Academics

1. Balance academics with the baseball season and be sure your grades remain a top priority!
2. Seek academic tutoring if you start to struggle with a class.
3. Communicate with your coach if you begin to struggle academically in any class.
4. Conduct yourself in a professional and courteous manner both inside and outside the classroom.

Athletics

1. Register for weight training and conditioning class for spring semester if your school has qualified and certified coaches teaching the course.
2. Play baseball for your middle school, junior high, or high school team.

3. Be a team player by putting your team first in everything you do!
4. Be sure to eat nutritious meals and get a minimum of eight hours of sleep each night.

Motivation

1. Record your goals in your goal journal and make daily entries.
2. Attend college baseball games at all levels on the weekends. Be sure to arrive early to watch both teams take batting practice and perform infield/outfield routines.
3. Watch college baseball games on TV. Listen carefully to the announcers and specifically watch the players who compete at your position to see how they prepare and perform.
4. Watch motivational sports movies.
5. Read a motivational or educational book that can make you a better person.
6. Watch the College World Series on TV.

SUMMERS

1. Play with your high school teammates in the summer if a team is available. Otherwise, play on a team that will compete against the best competition you can find.
2. Review your goals and read through your goal journal to see if there are any adjustments that you need to make heading into the summer season. Repeat this process before beginning a fall season.

OFF-SEASONS

Spend time away from baseball. The body and mind require rest to heal, rejuvenate, and repair damaged muscle, tendons, etc.

Student-Athlete's Suggested Timeline Specific Elements for Grades 9-12

FRESHMAN YEAR (NINTH GRADE)
FALL SEMESTER

Academics

1. 1. Take the Preliminary Scholastic Aptitude Test (PSAT) if you have not already completed it in middle school.

SOPHOMORE YEAR (TENTH GRADE)
FALL SEMESTER

Academics

1. Take an SAT preparatory class.
2. Establish an email address that includes your first and last name to make it easy for people to remember.

Athletics

1. Create a "dream list" of twenty possible colleges where you would one day like to play college baseball.

2. If you feel physically and mentally ready to show others your physical tools, attend a showcase or two in an attempt to get your name on the recruiting radar.

SPRING SEMESTER

Athletics

1. If your team does not film games, ask your parents to film as many games as possible to use for self-evaluation. Work on exposed weaknesses and reinforce what you are doing well.

JUNIOR YEAR (ELEVENTH GRADE)
FALL SEMESTER

Academics

1. Take the SAT and/or ACT test until you are satisfied with your scores.
2. You and your parents should attend a financial aid seminar together to learn more about how financial assistance specifically works; however, actual financial aid forms usually will not be filled out until February of the prospect's senior year.
3. Register for the NCAA Clearinghouse (this can be done online at ncaa.org).
4. Seek leadership positions for the clubs in which you participate.
5. Create and distribute your baseball recruiting packet. (See the sections labeled "Create a Baseball Portfolio" and "Portfolio Contents" to learn how to properly assemble the packet.) Be sure to include your fall and spring baseball schedules.

Athletics

1. Begin to research the effects of nutrition and rest on the human body. Implement a nutrition plan as well as a speed improvement and agility plan.
2. Narrow down or modify your list of colleges to ten. Be realistic. Try to take unofficial visits with your family to your top three choices.
3. Attend showcases to draw the interest of coaches who may want to see you play in the spring.
4. Attend baseball camps where you have interest in attending college.

Motivation

1. Watch college baseball teams practice.

SPRING SEMESTER

Motivation

1. Attend college baseball games at all levels on the weekends.
2. Watch the college baseball regional or super-regional on television.
3. Try to see the College World Series in person.

SUMMER

Motivation

1. Attend professional baseball tryout camps in your area (if available).
2. Attend one or two quality showcases.

SENIOR YEAR (TWELFTH GRADE)

FALL SEMESTER

Academics

1. Take an SAT and/or ACT again if you need or want to improve your scores.
2. Apply to all colleges you would like to attend.
3. Disburse an updated version of your baseball recruiting packet to programs you have interest in or those interested in you. Be sure to include your fall and spring baseball schedules.
4. Re-familiarize yourself with NCAA eligibility requirements and make sure you are on track with your plan.
5. Double-check with a guidance counselor to be sure you are not missing any courses needed to obtain a diploma.
6. You and your parents should attend a financial aid seminar together if you did not attend one in your junior year.
7. Seek leadership positions for the school or community clubs in which you participate.

Athletics

1. Narrow down your prospective college "wish list" to five. Be realistic. Try to take unofficial visits to these campuses if you have not already done so. (If the college has interest in recruiting you as a prospect, they might invite you on an "official visit.")
2. Attend showcases to draw the interest of coaches who may want to see you play in the spring.
3. Attend baseball camps where you have interest in attending college.

Motivation

1. Watch college baseball teams practice in the fall.

SPRING SEMESTER

Motivation

1. Attend college baseball games at all levels on the weekends. Arrive early to watch batting practice and infield/outfield routines.
2. Try to see a college baseball regional or super-regional in person.
3. Try to see the College World Series in person.

FACTORS TO CONSIDER WHEN CHOOSING A COLLEGE OR UNIVERSITY

One of the most difficult choices a young person will have to make is deciding where he wants to attend college. This is especially true if choosing between baseball programs is part of the decision. A student-athlete should sit down with his family and weigh the pros and cons of each possible choice. Answering a series of questions can provide direction and help to reveal factors that may not seem obvious or significant, but which have the potential to greatly impact the decision. Carl Lafferty, Recruiting Coordinator for Ole Miss Baseball states, "When recruiting a prospective student-athlete, I want to find out the key factors that will influence his decision. It can range from scholarship, education, to the tradition of the baseball program, and it is different for every kid. I want to identify their concerns and answer any questions they have."

The student should feel free to use the following series of question to consider the areas of finance, the player's general interests, and the program's staff, baseball facilities, recruiting focus, and past accomplishments.

Finance

1. How much does it cost to get an education at this school? Is this affordable?
2. How much financial aid were you awarded to offset costs?
3. How much academic money were you awarded?
4. How much grant or scholarship money, if any, were you awarded?
5. Do you want to pay in-state or out-of-state tuition?

General Interests

1. Do you prefer to play baseball in warm or cool weather?
2. What class sizes are most conducive for your learning? Do you like personal attention or prefer to be more anonymous in class?
3. How far from home do you want to travel? Is the college or university in a city or country setting?
4. Does the college or university offer the degree you are interested in obtaining?
5. Do you need to live on campus or would you prefer to live off campus?
6. Are you allowed to drive a car on campus? Can you keep a vehicle at school your freshmen year?
7. What are the graduation percentages of baseball players on the team?

Coaching Staff

1. Who are the coaches?
2. What kind of experience do they have?
3. Do you respond to their style of coaching?
4. How many assistant coaches does the program have, and what coach is responsible for the position you play?
5. How long has the staff been at this college?
6. Who is the strength and condition coach, what is his background, and what are his certifications?
7. Is the strength coach primarily hired for football but just happens to handle other sports as well?
8. Does the program train the baseball team specifically for baseball?

Baseball Facilities

1. What is the playing surface like?
2. What are the dressing facilities like?
3. What types of baseball training facilities are available, such as indoor batting cages, weight room, training room, etc.?
4. How nice are the weight training facilities?
5. When does the baseball team have access to the best facilities on campus?
6. Is there more than one weight room for athletes to use?

The Program's Recruiting Focus

1. Does this college have a chance, year in and year out, to play in the College World Series in Omaha?
2. Who else is being recruited for that year's recruiting class?
3. If you end up a pro-prospect, how many players have been drafted from that program in the past?
4. In what conference does this college play?
5. Where is the conference ranked in baseball compared to other conferences?
6. Which teams does this college play out of conference? Are you playing power baseball programs or relatively unknown schools?
7. Who is currently in the program at your position? Which year are they in school? If you attend this college, how many players will you be competing against to win a starting position?

Past Accomplishments

1. Is this traditionally a winning program? Does the college have high expectations for winning?
2. How many players at this school are on scholarships?
3. Does the school tend to spread its money around, or does it offer full scholarships to their top recruits?
4. Do they "red-shirt" players (sit out a year of competition), and, if so, how many?
5. Have red-shirts in this program ended up on the official roster the next year?
6. How many players are carried on the active roster?
7. What is your chance of playing as a freshman, sophomore, etc.?
8. Does this college have "walk-on" tryouts?
9. How many players are recruited from junior college vs. high school?
10. How do you compare athletically to the current players?

Questions for Players and Coaches to Ask

Whether a prospective student-athlete is on an official visit or talking to a college baseball coach on the phone, it is important to ask questions. This is how a family learns specifics about a program and how it does business. However, the same holds true for the coaching staff when considering recruiting a player. Here is a series of questions that a prospect can ask, and what a player can expect to be asked by a college recruiter.

Sample Questions to Ask College Baseball Coaches

1. What is a typical day like in this program, both in-season and out of season?
2. How do you see me contributing to your program?
3. How many other players are you recruiting for this position?
4. What is your policy for red-shirting players?
5. What positions are the assistant coaches responsible for managing?
6. What is the program's philosophy about strength and conditioning?
7. When and where does the baseball team lift weights?
8. Is there a mandatory or voluntary study hall, and are there tutors available to baseball players?
9. Where would I live?
10. How are a player's roommates determined?
11. How much is tuition and all other fees for this school?

12. What happens if I get hurt?

13. Where do we go from here? What is the next step?

Sample Questions College Baseball Coaches Might Ask

1. What are the key factors that will impact your decision to choose a school?

2. Why do you want to play for our program?

3. Which school is your first choice? (*Note:* It always helps for a college to know that they are your first choice.)

4. Who else is recruiting you?

5. Have you been officially offered a scholarship of any kind by anyone else?

6. Have you been promised playing time by other programs?

7. What factors are you seeking in a college baseball program?

8. Do you have any questions for us?

COMMITTING TO A COLLEGE PROGRAM

Once a player has verbally committed to a college baseball program, he should write a short thank-you note to all the schools that showed interest in recruiting him and follow up later with a phone call. This demonstrates that this student-athlete is considerate and understands that he was not the only player recruited for a particular position. Once a college coach knows that a player has committed elsewhere, he can refocus his efforts on another prospect. In addition, the coaches will appreciate the player's honesty and demonstration of his character even if they are disappointed the prospect did not choose their program.

A player should never burn bridges with a college coach or a college program. One day, circumstances could cause a player to transfer schools, and he may need to approach these same coaches again. In addition, baseball coaches frequently change jobs and theoretically could end up as the player's head coach or assistant coach in the future.

Ten Traps to Avoid in Pursuit of Collegiate Baseball

College baseball prospects and their parents can fall victim to many traps that can destroy the possibility of getting to the next level, steal the joy of the recruiting process, or make a player's life miserable once he steps foot on campus. Take time to review these common snares or potholes. They will help keep the student on the straight path to his goals, and will also help to reduce potential future disappointments and frustrations along the way.

TRAP #1: GRADES DO NOT MATTER

The myth still exists that great baseball talent will somehow overshadow and overcome college academic entry standards if that program wants a student badly enough. The sad truth is that many parents also believe this myth. The fact is: If your son wants to play in an NCAA- or NAIA-accredited baseball program, he must meet the standards set by both the NCAA or NAIA and that individual college. Therefore, if a high school athlete will commit himself to the same rigorous standards in the classroom that he sets on the ball field, he will likely be accepted to the school of his choosing on academic merit alone. Secondly, at most schools, he will become eligible to earn additional financial assistance through potential academic scholarships. It is not uncommon that these awards outshine the financial assistance garnered through baseball! It is really nice when a university can tie the two figures together as an award to a player who has prepared in the classroom and on the ball diamond.

TRAP #2: BEING UNREALISTIC

For some odd reason, many parents do not realistically evaluate their son's baseball skills and abilities. They often look at their child through rose-colored glasses. Then they falsely convince themselves, and their child as well, that he is better than he really is. Of course, most children believe what their parents tell them. It is not a bad thing to love and praise your child's efforts, however, to mislead him into thinking he is much better than he is only sets him up for failure and disappointment.

Players and parents need to digest the fact that, on average, less than one player per high school program per year goes on to play college baseball at any level. It is far from automatic. It takes superior physical and mental talent, as graded against a large talent pool, to make the jump to college baseball. Parents should educate themselves on what a college baseball player looks and plays like early in their son's high school career. For instance, a player and his family can attend college baseball games as a measuring stick. Attend Division I games along with Division III and junior college games. Arrive early and take time to watch both teams go through batting practice, field pre-game ground balls, and throw in the bull pen. Evaluate each player's size, speed, arm strength, accuracy, athleticism, and consistency when performing skills. In addition, try to watch all of this from field level. If possible, move close or stand next to these players to get a good feel for their size and strength. Often, this alone can be a sobering experience. Size is much more apparent up close than from the stands.

A comforting thought is that if a player possesses the physical and mental skills needed to play college baseball, it is likely that colleges will eventually find out and take notice. Unquestionably, someone watching a high school game will have the right contacts. It can be someone as obvious as the player's head coach, opposing coach, umpires, fans, or a college baseball scout in attendance to see a player on the other team. Thereafter, that player will be contacted by mail, phone and/or email. Very rarely does real talent fall through the cracks and get passed over. The harsh reality is that the vast majority of high school baseball players end their official baseball career upon completion of their last game of their senior season . . . and that is okay. Not everyone is meant to be a college or professional baseball player.

A small percentage of families with sons who have the talent to play college baseball can fall victim to misconceiving their child as a prospect at the highest college baseball level (Division I) when they are actually legitimate recruits for the lowest level (Division III). This misjudgment can really hurt a family's pocketbook. Parents often spend large sums of money and time trying to market their son to top Division I colleges when that money would be much better spent targeting schools at the athlete's true ability level. The challenge is to seek a balance between goals, dreams, and reality. It is always good to set your goals high and strive to meet them, however, it can be harmful to put all your eggs in one basket and not have a backup plan in place.

TRAP #3: WHOSE GOAL IS IT?

Is it the student's goal to play college baseball or is it his parents? Once this can be honestly answered, you can put things into perspective. A parent should never falsely assume that their goal for their child matches the child's actual goals! This false assumption can be very dangerous and cause heartache, frustration, and wasted time. Many baseball players feel pressured by their parents to act like college baseball is what they really want for their future, and most kids do not want to disappoint their parents. College baseball is not for everyone. Even if a player is very talented, it does not mean he wants to take his game to the next level.

College baseball is usually an all-consuming sport. When a student is not in class, he is lifting weights, going to practice (on his own or with the team), attending study hall, or sleeping. That does not leave much time for socialization and other associated college pastimes. A high school student-athlete who wants to play college baseball should love the game itself, have a passion to compete against the best, and be willing to make serious sacrifices to achieve that outcome. If he is also blessed with the necessary skill sets and body type needed to play college baseball, then the chances are good that his goal will end up a rewarding one.

TRAP #4: THE FALLACY OF STATISTICS

Another misconception that must be dispelled is that a player's statistics or "stats" are the best way to measure and compare his ability to play college baseball compared to other student-athletes. If a player's stats are presented to a college recruiter from a trusted source, then they have validity and can make an impact on a coach. Even so, in most instances, stats alone usually do not guarantee recruitment.

However, it must be noted that stats can have the opposite effect by significantly reducing a player's chances of being recruited. This is because stats are not typically manipulated to be lower than they really are. Thus, bad stats usually correlate to low-ability levels whereas the opposite is not always true. The harsh reality is that high school baseball stats can often be misleading. Most agree that statistics are a form of measurement and that is certainly a positive. The problem is that statistical records are rarely completed consistently from person to person, team to team, or parent to parent.

Statistics can be skewed by factors as basic as the person recording the information. Is it a dad or mom of a player? Is it another teammate assigned by a coach to keep the book for that game, to be replaced by a different player the next game? Is it a coach keeping the stats or a reporter from the local newspaper? It is reasonable to question whether any of the aforementioned people would provide accurate team stats for an entire season.

Other variables that skew statistics include a limited data sample (repetitions or chances) and the level of a competing team. For example, a player may make four outs on the day but hit all line drives. Another player may hit two "floaters" off the end of the bat that fall in for hits just behind the infielders, and hit two "roll-over" ground balls that somehow find a hole, and finish the day four for four (four hits out of four at bats equals .1000). Limited statistics suggest the second player is the better hitter. However, anyone evaluating potential talent will be more impressed with the .0000 player who hits the ball hard (on the nose) all four times at bat.

Another example of misleading statistics can be seen from a player who competes at the 5A level in a very tough conference that has excellent pitching from top to bottom. He hits a legitimate .300 for the season. A second player competes in a weak 1A baseball conference with just a few good pitchers in the league and hits a legitimate .420 for the season. Who is the better hitter? On paper it looks like the player who hit .420, but that is probably not the case. You can begin to see why most college coaches put little emphasis on a player's stats, and some coaches pay them no mind at all. The sooner a player and his parents learn that stats can be misleading, the sooner they will begin to focus on factors that really make a difference in the recruiting process.

TRAP #5: SHOWCASE FEVER

Players and parents sometimes get a nervous or anxious feeling that they should attend every baseball showcase and college camp or register for every scouting service that is available. If they don't, they feel the student-athlete will miss his chance to play college baseball. However, exposing your child to showcases, camps, and recruiting services too soon has potential dangers. First, young players typically do not "show well" because they are not physically ready to perform at a high level compared to older, more mature players. The second danger is that a young player can become intimidated by the whole experience or develop future anxiety associated with showing others his skills. The third danger is that the parents will spend a lot of money unnecessarily. Parents, literally, can spend in excess of ten thousand dollars to get their son seen by recruiters in hopes of attaining a scholarship. Only then do they discover, if they attain a scholarship at all, that it does not add up to the money they spent on showcases, camps, and recruiting services.

TRAP #6: LOVE VERSUS COST

Sometimes a very difficult choice must be made by prospects and their parents regarding college baseball and the financial investment it may take to make playing at the next level a possibility. Your son may have the borderline ability to play college baseball, but it may be at a private university or a Division III college. If you are financially blessed, this probably will not become a factor or concern. However, if finances are an issue, then this question should be answered before a commitment is made: "Is playing college baseball worth years of likely financial debt that will result from four years of expensive tuition and fees?" Everything should go into the family's overall financial equation to determine whether the college baseball experience is affordable.

A private college education is relatively expensive when compared with state colleges and universities, and scholarships in baseball are usually small. It is not uncommon for a family to pay $100,000 for a four-year education just so their son can play baseball at a private college. How much tuition money is worth paying for your son to fulfill his goal to play college baseball? Division III colleges cannot offer athletic scholarships. Therefore, even after financial aid is awarded, playing at a Division III school may possibly end up an expensive proposition. Each family must make its own decision about how valuable playing collegiate baseball is to them.

TRAP #7: GET OUT OF YOURSELF AND INTO YOUR TEAM

Many of today's high school players are diving head-first into this trap: They are so wrapped up in their own dreams and goals that they lose focus of what the game of baseball is really about . . . the team. Parents can be just as guilty. For instance, it is not uncommon to hear parents say they would rather their son play on a losing team and start than play on a winning team and be a role player (someone who performs a small but important duty to his team, i.e., a pinch hitter).

It is important for a player to have personal goals, such as to be a starter on his team or to eventually play at the college level. However, personal goals should never be put in front of team goals. Undeniably, players who perform best within a team environment have the best chance of excelling at the college level because teams that are unselfish win, and college programs are all about winning. If you don't think so, just ask the next college coach you happen to speak with.

Players at any level who only worry about themselves eventually lose the respect of their teammates and gain the label of being an "I player" due to their disease of "me." The first symptom of this lethal illness can be witnessed when a player starts to judge success and failure based on his individual performance with no regard for how his team does. For example, his team wins and the player is upset because he did not get his three hits.

Players who exhibit selfish thinking have been more recently coined "a showcase mentality player" by college and high school coaches. This is due to the strong emphasis that is now placed on summer showcase teams and showcase events for high school prospects. Many athletes play all summer long on expensive teams in hopes of gaining a stage on which to shine in front of college and professional scouts. This includes continually focusing on who is behind the fence that day to see the prospect play.

Unfortunately the danger of playing in too many showcase events over the course of years can create a self-centered mindset if a player is not careful. Therefore, it is critical that the parents of prospects, their coaches, and teammates continue to combat this problem of selfishness by emphasizing the importance of team play to the student-athlete. Always stress: "BIG TEAM . . . little me."

TRAP #8: FOCUSING ON THE FUTURE

In their pursuit of college baseball, another common trap that players often fall into is looking to the future and not living in the moment. People play baseball because it is fun! They should enjoy their daily experience with their team competing on the diamond in practice and games. That is what high school baseball should be about. However, some players become so focused on getting to the next level of baseball that they write off their current experience and miss out on the fun of today. If not careful, this mindset can cause baseball to suddenly become a job in which players become consumed with personal results or how they perform. As stated earlier, it is important to set goals and strive to achieve them by preparing for the future, but it is equally important to avoid getting consumed by those goals.

TRAP #9: LOSING YOUR COMPETITIVE EDGE

There is a growing segment of the high school baseball community that forgets there is actually a winner and loser when they play a baseball game. When players participate in showcase games that usually do not have consequences for winning or losing, their mental approach towards performing under pressure can suffer.

For instance, most games in showcase tournaments are played on a time limit, and an actual overall champion is rarely declared. Usually, each team's schedule for the tournament is predetermined regardless of wins and losses. The primary goal of the games is for players to showcase their physical tools to scouts in attendance. It is standard for each player to get a few at-bats, pitch a few innings, make a few plays, go back to the hotel, and do it all over again the next day or the following weekend. It should be obvious that a player who regularly performs in this environment is not under the same game stress as a player on a team that is trying to win a conference, region, state, or a summer league championship.

College coaches like showcases because they can see many players in one location, however, they also like to see how players handle winning and losing, success and failure, and playing and performing under pressure. There is no better way to observe these characteristics than by observing a game where winning and losing matters to the team.

Over time, a player who is not under game stress can become immune to the true reason the game of baseball is played . . . to win! There is a winner and a loser in every college baseball game that is played, and it matters who wins.

TRAP #10: LACK OF ACCOUNTABILITY

A player who is blessed with superior physical skills at the high school level is subject to falling into the trap of thinking and acting as though he is superior to everyone else. His incredible ability as a player leads him to a false assumption that he is no longer accountable or held to anyone else's standards such as coaches, teammates, umpires, and fans. In the eyes of this highly talented player, nothing that goes wrong is ever his fault and he is even quicker to pass blame for his own below-par performance. Before long, the player begins to intentionally or unintentionally belittle his teammates, as well to treat high school baseball as recreation or like it really does not matter.

In addition, this unhealthy way of putting oneself on a pedestal can lead to eventual stagnation or even possible regression of the player's individual baseball skills. After all, this player thinks he is ready for the big leagues, so why does he need to get better? As a result, there is no real sense of urgency to improve his game and eliminate weaknesses on a daily basis, and his skills begin to suffer.

Any player who is blessed with superior skills should strive to avoid this nasty trap at all costs. On the contrary, his goal should be to improve his skills, his character (humility and likability), and to become a true team leader in the process.

It all comes back to a player and his coach holding the student-athlete accountable and the internal desire of the prospect to exceed the standards of others. In addition, the athlete should seek to make everyone on his team better by setting a strong example of work ethic and dedication to team goals. This type of player realizes that the world is a big place, and sooner or later he is going to regularly compete against players who are as physically talented as he is, if not better. Therefore, he prepares every day to be the best, and sets the tone for the rest of the team. For example, he takes pride in being the first to arrive at the ballpark and the last to leave.

A player with this healthy perspective of himself and his team is a joy for anyone to coach. Because of the prospect's level head, he will likely take his game to heights that his talent will allow. In addition, his teammates will be left with fond memories of this player, who was extremely talented but, more importantly, fun to be around and exciting to compete with every day back in high school.

RECRUITING FACTS AND GENERALIZATIONS

This section offers a list of sobering facts and generalizations about the college recruitment process. Contrary to popular belief, college baseball is not just the "next step" for a high school baseball player. If a high school player sets his goal to one day play college baseball, he should be realistic by being aware of the possible obstacles he must overcome in order to persevere. Some of these important concepts have been covered earlier in the chapter but are included as part of this list so players, parents, and coaches can see them in place.

On average, less than one player per high school program goes on to play college baseball each year.

Most college baseball programs are not fully funded (offering the maximum number of scholarships allowed for their division). Therefore, many college baseball players are "preferred walk-ons" and pay full tuition to their college, or they may receive some academic assistance to help pay for their education if they achieved very good grades in high school.

Most college baseball "scholarships" are small, partial grants that offset a few of the student-athlete's academic, housing, meal, or book costs.

College baseball programs choose very carefully the type of person and player they recruit. They do not have time to babysit their players or their players' parents.

Grades and the SAT/ACT scores are very important to college coaches and their admissions departments. Therefore, they should be important to the prospect as well.

A prospect's high school, summer, and fall baseball coach's credibility with the college recruiter is vitally important. A player and his parents should expect all his coaches to be "brutally honest" and never mislead a college coach on their behalf.

College baseball recruiters often seek information about a player's attitude, work ethic, desire to improve, family situation, commitment to baseball, and the intensity in the weight room, etc. They get personal because they cannot afford to make mistakes in the recruiting process. One bad apple (recruit) can significantly set back their program and steer them away from their goal of winning championships.

High school, summer, and fall baseball coaches do not get scholarships for their players! The athletes earn their own scholarships by performing at superior levels in the classroom and on the ball field. In addition, they must possess the physical tools, body type, and mental makeup desired by a college recruiter. The student-athlete's current or former coach's job is to assist in the process if he feels comfortable recommending the player.

Dominant high school pitchers have the greatest opportunity to receive larger baseball scholarships. Dominant pitching is the key to winning at any level, and college teams need many good pitchers to play approximately sixty games on their spring schedule.

A growing percentage of high school baseball players will verbally commit to a college baseball program in their freshman and sophomore years of high school, and later sign with that college baseball program in the fall of their senior year. This is especially true at the Division I level. However, many verbal commitments will be given during a student-athlete's junior and senior year of high school. Not to mention, a small portion of prospects won't have the opportunity to commit to college programs until the summer following their graduation.

Not every high school baseball player has the goal to play college baseball, even though a player may have the physical talent to do so or his parents may want him to.

There are many examples of baseball players from superior high school baseball programs that did not start for their high school team during their junior season. Yet they became starters and college prospects by the end of their senior year. A prospect and his parents should not panic if the student-athlete has a goal of playing in college, is on a very good team, but does not start his junior year. There is still time and opportunity for his goal to become a reality.

CHAPTER 10

THE HIGH SCHOOL PLAYER
AND THE MAJOR LEAGUE DRAFT

Myth #1: ALL HIGH SCHOOL PROSPECTS WHO ARE DRAFTED INTO PROFESSIONAL BASEBALL RECEIVE SIGNING BONUSES THAT WILL ENABLE THEM TO BE FINANCIALLY SECURE FOR LIFE!

Secret: *A select few high school players each year, who are top MLB draft choices and invest their signing bonus wisely, will likely be financially set for life. However, most draft choices will not receive signing bonuses that will provide that same luxury.*

Myth #2: IT IS IMPOSSIBLE TO MAKE A NICE LIVING PLAYING PROFESSIONAL BASEBALL IN THE MINOR LEAGUES.

Secret: *If a player possesses the desired physical and mental tools and can perform at a sustained high level in the minor leagues for a handful of years or more, he will likely make a modest to nice salary in professional baseball.*

Myth #3: IF A HIGH SCHOOL PITCHER CAN THROW THE BALL 90 MILES PER HOUR, HE WILL GET DRAFTED INTO PROFESSIONAL BASEBALL.

Secret: *Being able to throw a baseball 90 MPH or more is a great asset for a pitcher to possess, however, it far from assures him that he will be a major league draft pick. Other variables such as his ability to command two pitches for a strike, his throwing mechanics, mental makeup, and college plans will be factored into the equations for scouts to determine whether he has what it takes to one day face major league hitters.*

PLAYING THE ODDS

Upon high school graduation, most players will never be involved in organized baseball again. On average, less than one player per high school program will move on to play at the collegiate level each year. A startlingly smaller percentage, less than 1 percent of all high school seniors who play baseball, will be inducted in the Major League Amateur Draft. Therefore, high school players who are drafted by major league clubs will be faced with life-altering decisions that must be made before and during negotiations to determine the course of their future. These include ironing out specific details of their signing bonus and pro contract.

If a player possesses superior baseball talent in his junior or senior year, when compared to the top 5 percent of players in his state, he should thoroughly read this chapter to learn about the Major League Draft. It will be vital to know how professional baseball scouts and the draft process operate in the event the player is eventually chosen in the amateur draft after his senior year. Both the player and his parents should begin seeking wisdom that will allow them to make an informed decision about the prospect's future. Questions such as those below, and many others relating to the MLB draft and professional baseball in general, should be addressed well before the prospect graduates. The player should ask:

- How am I evaluated by pro-baseball scouts?
- If I get drafted, should I give up my college education to sign professionally?
- What kind of signing bonus is reasonable to expect based on various draft rounds?
- Is it considered acceptable protocol to contact and/or secure a family advisor or agent?
- What are my actual chances of making it to the big leagues?

Focus on the Game

A pro scout's job is to find talent. If a high school senior possesses superior physical baseball tools and potential professional makeup, he should notice professional scouts in attendance at his games. Furthermore, if he garners interest as a possible top-round draft pick, he can expect many scouts at his games, especially early and late in his high school season. These scouts will include "cross-checkers," "national cross-checkers," and possibly even major league scouting directors as they diligently seek to make their final determinations as to who the nation's best players are for the upcoming draft.

It can be a big challenge for a high school player who is a possible draft pick to keep his focus on what is happening inside the fence (on the game) instead of outside the fence (on the scouts). A significant indicator of a player's professional worth is how he handles the pressure of being a pro prospect and the attention that he naturally gets from teammates, coaches, fans, the media, and so on. This includes the player's ability to cope with below-par performances when he wants to play at his best every time he steps on the diamond.

In addition, the prospect should continue to be a team player, play the game hard, and help his team win games. The scouts have previously noted superior tools and mannerisms that they admire. If a prospect suddenly becomes selfish, outwardly cocky, arrogant, or lazy, it may indicate immaturity and will likely decrease his odds of being a high pick or possibly even being drafted at all.

A Pro Prospect Versus a College Prospect

Make no mistake about it: College recruiters and professional baseball scouts both desire players who possess superior baseball skills and mental makeup. However, there is a fundamental distinction between the few high school players who are top draft picks and those who go on to play collegiately. In general, pro baseball is more about developing a player's raw physical abilities to one day help the big league team win a World Series. Major League Baseball places a premium on drafting prospects with "impact tools" and "projectability." This means professional scouts are seeking the world's most elite players who possess such a high level of baseball skills that the scouts project these players can make a significant impact at the major league level. (See "The Five Tools of a Professional Prospect" later in this chapter.) In addition, a player with impact tools has better odds of fighting through and surviving the daily struggles of minor league baseball. Scouts refer to the process of a player's impact tool(s) helping them get to the top tier of professional baseball as "carry."

On the other hand, college baseball recruiters put greater emphasis on "winning now" with players who possess a blend of above-average talent and intangibles such as desire, work ethic, focus, game savvy, and the will to win. In other words, they seek players who may or may not possess the impact tool(s) of a pro prospect, but can still play the game at a high level and contribute to a collegiate championship right away. However, the best high school players in the nation are usually sought after by our nation's top college baseball programs and professional baseball scouts, each hoping to attract the services of "difference makers."

This does not mean that a prospect who plays in college will not have the chance to one day be drafted and play professional baseball. Many collegiate players develop or improve during their years in college, or they demonstrate that they can consistently produce against the very highest level of amateur competition in spite of not possessing a bona fide "impact tool." Note that a player who attends a four-year college will have to wait until his junior year before he regains his draft eligibility status. However, a player who attends junior college maintains his draft status every year. Therefore, college baseball does provide the opportunity for many college student-athletes to continue pursuing their dream of playing professional baseball.

Another way professional baseball differs from the college ranks is the number of years that players are allowed to participate. In college baseball, players use up their eligibility after four or five years. However, in pro ball there are both "rookies" (first year players) and seasoned veterans of more than ten years pursuing the same thing . . . a spot on the big league roster. In fact, in pro baseball, players never officially age out. They either become injured, lose interest in playing, or one day they are informed that their services are not needed anymore.

PLAYER EVALUATIONS

Each major league team hires scouting directors, associate scouts, area scouts, cross-checkers, and national cross-checkers who comb the nation's high schools, summer ball leagues, showcase events, fall leagues, and college campuses seeking the next major league star that can one day help that team win a World Series.

Each MLB team spends a great deal of time, effort, and money finding and evaluating high school prospects. The more data that is gathered by scouts about a particular player, the better the chance of getting an accurate estimate of this prospect's future worth to their ball club. Thus, the greater the potential a high school senior possesses to make an impact at the big league level, the higher the draft round in which he will be selected in that year's major league draft. As a result, there is pressure on scouts and the scouting director to identify and select the nation's actual "top picks."

When completing reports or evaluating players, MLB scouts use a standard 20-80 scale. A grade of 20 would be the furthest thing from a major league prospect, a grade of 50 would be an average player in the major leagues, and a grade of 80 would equal the future potential of a Hall of Fame player. This grading system provides a consistent method for all organizations to rank players that they are considering for the draft or for a trade.

However, many teams take the process a step further and expand upon the standard 20-80 scale to provide greater insight into a player's potential worth within their own system. This is due to the fact that raw numbers alone don't always give an accurate picture of a player's future or current major league potential. When a scout watches, evaluates, grades, and writes a report on a player, he is synthesizing many variables to determine the player's actual skill, mental makeup, and project-ability, or his future potential to be an impact player or difference-maker at the big league level.

Theoretically, it just takes one scout to like what he sees in a player's ability and character traits for that player to be drafted. However, to be a high draft pick, a player will need to impress a number of people within an organization with his ability, score well on his psychological evaluation, and be cleared on his athletic physical. Often scouts seek players whose tools and actions (mannerisms) remind them of a current or former big leaguer because what has been proven to work in the past will likely work again in the future.

The Five Tools of a Professional Prospect

Physically, a position player is graded on five tools to determine his potential major league impact. These include running speed, fielding ability, arm strength, hitting ability, and hitting power. (See "Tool #3" below to learn how pitchers are evaluated differently.) Most position players, even top draft picks, do not typically grade exceptionally high in all five tool categories. Thus, the goal of most scouts is to find players who grade well based on their projected defensive position. They then come up with an overall grade for each player by adding together the specific rating for all five tools and dividing by five. For example, an overall grade of 60 equals an "excellent" prospect. Sometimes this same grading process is completed with the player's top three tools that are most relevant to his defensive position.

The greatest asset for a possible draft pick is a superior or "carry" tool—the more the better. Once all the physical tools of a prospect are graded, the scout's job is to give the player an overall projection. In other words, how much "ceiling" or "upside" (potential improvement for the future) the scout feels this player possesses based upon his tools, makeup, and body type. Projection is considered by many in the business as the most difficult aspect of scouting. For example, unless a scout has a crystal ball, there is no sure way of telling how good a player will actually be in five or ten years. Therefore, a scout will use his experience and expertise to grade a prospect on his current ability, and project what he feels the player's future potential will be at the big league level.

TOOL #1: RUNNING SPEED

When grading a player's speed, a scout will clock a prospect's times in the 60-yard dash and his time from home to first base with a swing. A 60-yard dash time of 6.9 seconds is average major league speed so the player would receive a rating of 50 for speed. A player's time from home to first base will typically vary based on whether a batter is right-handed or left-handed. A time of 4.3 seconds from the right-hand side is considered average major league speed and would receive a grade of 50. A time of 4.1 from the left-hand side is considered above major league average speed and would receive a grade of 60.

TOOL #2: FIELDING ABILITY

When grading a player's ability to field the ball based on his position, the scout must rely heavily on his own professional opinion. Therefore, this grade is subjective. Pro scouts make note of a fielder's actions, such as whether he has quick feet to the ball, good range, soft hands on the catch, a quick transition from the glove to release, and whether the fielder handles a routine play as well as a difficult play consistently. In other words, does he make fielding and throwing the baseball seem easy or effortless?

TOOL #3: ARM STRENGTH

Professional baseball scouts use varying methods to evaluate the arm strength of position players and pitchers.

POSITION PLAYERS

When a scout evaluates a position player's arm strength, he looks primarily at the flight of the ball. He watches to see if the ball appears to explode out of the athlete's hand, if it carries a long distance, and if it stays on line to the intended target. Players who possess superior arm strength stand out in a crowd. Very often at the high school level, players with the best arms are also dominant pitchers for their teams. In some instances, a player's arm can be evaluated from his position with a radar gun. However, there is no standard to compare this data to others. It just provides more insight into his arm strength.

PITCHERS

When a scout evaluates a pitcher, he combines objective and subjective information to provide a grade. A radar gun provides data on the pitcher's top velocity, average velocity, and bottom speeds from the distance of 60 feet and 6 inches. It also provides data on pitch speed differential such as how much slower the player's changeup, curveball, slider, etc., are from his fastball. A right-handed pitcher who executes velocity of 89 to 91 MPH would be considered an "average prospect" for the major leagues. Thus, he would receive a rating of 50 for arm strength.

The scout will then use his professional eyes to rate the pitcher's command or ability to throw more than two pitches for a strike. Each pitch will receive a grade. He will make note of how many walks he feels this pitcher would surrender at the major league level in nine innings. He will then grade the player's mechanics, including his ability to repeat the delivery from the windup and the stretch. He will likely make note of the pitcher's ability to deceive hitters, compete on the mound, and win games. Lastly, the scout will write a report about each pitching prospect, describing the player's future potential in the major leagues, and provide it to his parent organization.

TOOL #4: HITTING ABILITY

Scouts put their experience and professional eyes to use when evaluating high school hitters and their future potential to swing the bat at the big league level. Scouts desire hitters who possess superior pitch recognition, swing mechanics, ability to make adjustments, handle pressure, and the knack to "barrel up the ball" (hit the ball off the barrel). This includes demonstrating superior balance, bat speed, hand-eye coordination, and the ability to consistently control the bat and hit the ball hard against the nation's top high school pitchers.

TOOL #5: HITTING FOR POWER

Professional baseball scouts are always looking for prospects who possess raw hitting power. This is a player who can change a game at the major league level with one swing of the bat. Players with exceptional power at the high school level may not get the chance to swing the bat very often because they are pitched around, in fear that they will change the game outcome every time they step to the plate. When a power hitter attacks a baseball, it makes a distinct sound that is much different than when hit by a non-power hitter. A player who is projected to hit fifteen to eighteen home runs at the big league level would receive a grade of 50, which is considered average major league power.

Psychological Testing

Because of the large financial investment that is put into top draft picks each year, professional teams cannot afford to make mistakes. Thus, most major league teams set up meetings with possible high draft choices prior to the MLB draft during which they usually administer some form of psychological aptitude and leadership skills tests. An example of such a test is called the "PF-16," which consists of approximately 180 multiple-choice questions. The answers to these questions help teams determine whether a young man possesses the makeup to become a professional ballplayer in their organization.

"Sign-ability"

Just because a player is a Major League Baseball prospect in high school does not mean he will always be drafted by a major league franchise. Factors such as a student-athlete desiring to play college baseball or asking for a hefty signing bonus can impact an organization's decision to draft (or not draft) him. Therefore, before an organization wastes a valuable draft pick on a player who may not sign a contract, area scouts and scouting directors attempt to pre-determine if the player is "sign-able." In other words, if they determine, after much research, that a player won't sign even if he is drafted, they pass over this prospect for a player they feel has a better chance of signing.

For instance, if a prospect and his family determine that he will not sign professionally for less than two million dollars, they have essentially restricted this player's potential status in the draft. If an interested organization determines his impact tools warrant him to be drafted in the first round, then this player will likely still be drafted. However, if the draft gets past the second round, and this young man still has not been selected, he probably will be passed over in future rounds as well. However, had this same family made it clear that the player would sign for $500,000, he likely still would have been drafted in the first few rounds.

Another example includes a potential high school draft choice who possesses one impact tool, is a very good student, and has a large scholarship offer at a top college program. If a MLB organization feels confident that this player's potential draft round will not offset the value of his college financial package, then he will probably be passed over in the draft. However, major league scouts will likely follow the yearly progress of this player in college to see if he continues to improve his overall performance and understanding of the game. If this is the case, his draft status may improve from where it was when he graduated high school.

Family Advisors and Agents

There are so many unknowns for a family whose child is being pursued by major league ball clubs. Deciding what to do with one's future can be frightening, and it is important to understand all of the possible options in order to make an informed decision. This is especially true when large sums of money are at stake in a signing bonus, including the option of possibly forgoing a college baseball scholarship to play professionally.

Therefore, many families of potentially high round draft choices choose to seek the guidance of a "family advisor." Advisors are essentially agents who take on a slightly different role prior to the draft to preserve the amateur status and collegiate eligibility of the player in the event he decides to forgo pro ball to play in college. Advisors can help provide direction to a player and his family about making the choice between signing professionally and pursuing college baseball. Beware, though! There are many advisors/agents who are only concerned about one thing—money! If you are a potential high draft choice, you will probably have to ward off these advisors like you would a hungry swarm of mosquitoes. Keep in mind that a family always has the choice to negotiate the player's contract and signing bonus themselves.

Therefore, choosing an advisor to represent the family for the amateur draft should not be a quick decision. Pre-qualify all interested family advisors and/or agents, and narrow down the list to about two or three exceptional choices. Follow up by getting to know the advisors. Build a relationship with each one by asking questions and watching how they go about their business. Over time it will become more evident which advisors match up closest with your family's personality, values, and goals. It is very important to feel confident with this person because he may eventually be the one responsible for negotiating the prospect's future. In addition, this person is going to reflect the family's thoughts and wishes at the negotiating table.

If a player decides to forgo college and turn professional, family advisors change roles and become agents. An agent can assist a player with future professional career decisions that the player will not want to handle by himself.

These include future contracts, endorsement negotiations, baseball card contracts, and the like. This allows the player to keep his attention and focus on performing at the highest level possible on the ball diamond, which will give him the best odds of reaching his goal of making it to the big leagues.

Factors to Consider Before Signing

Should a player sign professionally? This is a question that only a "draft pick" and his family can answer. It is the player who must eventually live with the consequences of this decision . . . whether positive or negative. As mentioned, the odds of signing and making it to the major leagues are very small. Only 42 percent of first-round draft picks ever put on a major league uniform. That is less than one out of every two! The odds drop significantly from there. Approximately only 4 to 7 percent of all draft picks ever make it to the big leagues. In addition, approximately 2 percent (or less) of all draft picks have sustained careers in the major leagues.

On the other hand, the odds of making it to the big leagues are zero if a player never tries. A player who possesses a number of tools is likely to have the "carry" he needs to make it to the big leagues and possibly be an impact player for years to come. It is helpful for a top prospect to secure a significant signing bonus that will help sustain him through tough times, injuries, or a few years of average performance. In other words, it is much more difficult for an organization to release a player with many carry tools and financial backing compared to a solid player with an average signing bonus. A few issues that should be considered by a prospect and his family before making a decision to sign are his age, academic capability, and social maturity level. The family must also consider where the prospect will receive the best baseball instruction.

If a player is a poor student academically, and his main goal is to play professional baseball, then signing might be his best option. Going to college, or a junior college, might end up an educational disaster. A student-athlete will be expected to study for tests, complete assignments, get to class, get to practice, and avoid the temptations available on college campuses. Signing professionally will also provide unique social challenges for the player such as living on his own, traveling from place to place, sleeping in hotels, and free time with possibly lots of money. However, he will not have to concern himself with the additional elements of an education—this will help him focus on baseball.

Every player wants to improve his abilities and therefore increase his odds of making it to the big leagues. Pro organizations will tell a prospect that the pro ranks will provide the best possible skill instruction he will receive to accomplish this goal. Most colleges will counter by telling a player that they will provide the most thorough skill instruction and development. In reality, you need to compare the quality of instruction offered by the specific major league organization with the particular college. For instance, The

Atlanta Braves organization does a great job teaching baseball fundamentals to their younger prospects. That is one reason they win year after year with homegrown talent or players within their farm system. At the college level, most of the top programs in the country are well versed in teaching the finer points of the game.

One fact is certain, baseball is a business, and the older a person gets, the more likely his skills will diminish, decreasing his value to a ball club. On average it takes a player five years once he signs to make it to the big leagues. Therefore, if a player signs a professional contract at the age of eighteen, he will be a rookie in the majors at twenty-three. On the other hand, if the player enters a four-year college at eighteen and plays three or four years before turning pro, then plays another five years in the minor leagues, this player will be twenty-six or twenty-seven when he steps foot in a major league ballpark. If a general manager of a major league franchise is choosing between two players of similar ability, and one is twenty-three and the other twenty-seven, who is he likely to pick? The younger player has four more years of service to provide at the major league level. It is the reality of business!

A player's maturity level upon high school graduation, including physical, mental, emotional, social, and spiritual maturity should be considered before a prospect makes a decision to sign professionally or go to college. Most high school stars have not had to deal with much failure or disappointment on the ball diamond up to this point. In addition, most players at the age of seventeen or eighteen are immature. Throw in the temptation that is afforded with a signing bonus, abundant freedom, and lifestyle, and you have a potential recipe for disaster. These young men barely have their driver's license, and they are being asked to pay bills, get themselves to places on time, and do laundry, as well as deal with the media, teammates, and coaches. What will be the result of their first prolonged slump, negative publicity, or booing from the fans? Sometimes it is hard for high draft picks to live up to all the expectations. A big factor to consider is whether the prospect will give up on himself in times of struggles or reach down deep and fight through difficulties. A player with a strong mental makeup has a much better chance of making it to the show.

Signing Bonus Negotiations

When a player gets a fair offer for the round in which he was drafted, he must remember that holding out for a larger offer can create a stalemate in the negotiation process. This can potentially delay the start of a prospect's professional career. If the process is significantly delayed, it may mean missing instructional ball, or possibly even spring training. Keep in mind, if a student-athlete's goal is to play Major League Baseball, then his objective should be to "ink" a fair contract as soon as possible and get to work.

Baseball is big business. If a player is given millions of dollars as a signing bonus, it reflects poorly on the organization if this player does not make it to the major leagues. It also reflects negatively on the scouts and cross-checkers who recommended this player if he does not live up to the expectations of his signing bonus and is released. Thus, this player is usually given ample opportunity to succeed. The signing bonus given by a club can be looked at as a financial investment in the future worth of this player to the organization. Financially, it is a much easier decision to give a low-round player his release than a top-round draft pick.

To help slow the rate at which large signing bonuses are being awarded, the commissioner's office of Major League Baseball has set parameters for what it "suggests" each draft round should bring from a dollar standpoint. Thus, the first round should get "X" amount of money, the second round should get "Y" and so on. This puts some control back with the organizations that are drafting players in an attempt to build their professional franchise, yet it does not handcuff organizations from smaller markets who cannot afford to award as much money to their draft picks.

Therefore, when making the decision whether to sign right out of high school, money should be heavily considered by the player and his family. Signing bonuses are taxed heavily and, if not invested wisely, can be used up in a few years. If a player is going to give up four years of his college experience and possibly a chance to play for the College World Series, you want to be confident that the organization is going to give that player a reasonable amount of time to mature and reach his potential, even if he has some less-than-par seasons. Many times money can help assure that the player will be looked after and is given a chance.

Life on the Farm

If a player decides to sign professionally, he must be ready physically, mentally, socially, and emotionally to play baseball every day during the season and prepare to improve in the off-season. He should love to play the game with a burning passion. He should be mentally tough and know how to cope with attention from strangers, handling the media, the pressure of performance, handling failure, and recovering from disappointment. He should be mentally ready to spend long periods of time away from his family and friends at home. He should have the ultimate goal of competing at the highest level and the confidence to make it happen. Professional baseball will likely challenge a person down to his very core, and once his pro contract is signed, he should fasten his seat belt and get ready for the ride of his life!

What people see on TV in association with Major League Baseball is not always an accurate depiction of life in the minor leagues. This is especially true at the lower tiers of pro ball. Major League Baseball, unlike the National Football League or National Basketball Association, has affiliate developmental teams that most players work their way through. Life in "the minors" is typically filled with long bus rides, fast food, and cheap hotels. It is a dog-eat-dog world where young men compete with players on their own team, within their own organization, and sometimes from other teams (trades) to eventually win a spot on a big league roster.

Most organizations have a five-tier pyramid system. The levels of professional baseball include Rookie ball, A-ball, AA-ball, AAA-ball, and the major leagues. Some organizations may have two teams at one level, such as two single-A teams (high A and low A). It is a daily challenge to persevere, stay strong, healthy, and competitive. David Toth, an eleven-year veteran of professional baseball in the minor leagues states, "Most of these kids are coming from programs where they were the best on their team. They enter a situation where everybody on the team was the best. Then they play in a league where every team is loaded with the best. It can be overwhelming and intimidating for many young kids." As mentioned, on average, it takes five years in the minors to get to the big leagues. That means years of living with teammates, making initial salaries below a thousand dollars to a few thousand dollars per month, playing games virtually every night, sometimes practicing on game days, and living in hotels, all in hopes of fulfilling a lifelong goal.

Talent, Proper Preparation, and Timing

What we find is that baseball parallels life in many ways. It takes lots of talent, proper preparation, and being in the right place at the right time to fulfill the dream of becoming a major league player. First, a player's impact tools, such as the ability to steal bases, hit home runs, or run a ball down in the gap, gives him "stay-ability" to sustain his minor league career. This will help keep him gradually or quickly moving up the ranks of the minor leagues until he gets his shot in the big leagues. A player's ability to consistently perform day in and day out, and year in and year out, is what keeps him in the big leagues as an "everyday player" or possibly even an all-star.

Secondly, in many instances, the most talented players seem to be the luckiest. This is because talent with proper preparation creates opportunities for success. For instance, prepared talent increases a player's chances of having a great day when the "right person" in an organization is in attendance. In addition, circumstances or timing can be just as critical to a player getting his first "cup of coffee" (day in the big leagues). For example, a big league player who gets injured, traded, or released can give a minor league player his first shot in the majors. Another example of timing is playing in an organization that is not "top-loaded" with talented veterans at the big league level. Sadly, there are numerous instances of talented individuals in the minor leagues who get stuck behind big league greats. The only option for these players is to consistently perform at high levels, hope to get traded, or to one day become a free agent.

INDEX

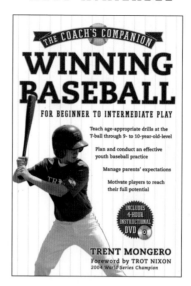